LIFE IN THE REAL WORLD

HOW TO MAKE MUSIC GRADUATES EMPLOYABLE

EDITED BY DAWN BENNETT

LIFE IN THE REAL WORLD

HOW TO MAKE MUSIC GRADUATES EMPLOYABLE

EDITED BY DAWN BENNETT

Common Ground

First published in Champaign, Illinois in 2012
by Common Ground Publishing LLC
as part of the Arts series

Copyright © Dawn Bennett 2012

All rights reserved. Apart from fair dealing for the purposes of study, research, criticism or review as permitted under the applicable copyright legislation, no part of this book may be reproduced by any process without written permission from the publisher.

Library of Congress Cataloging-in-Publication Data

Life in the real world : how to make music graduates employable / edited by Dawn Bennett.
    p. cm.
Includes bibliographical references and index.
ISBN 978-1-61229-078-2 (pbk : alk. paper) -- ISBN 978-1-61229-079-9 (pdf : alk. paper)
1. Music--Vocational guidance. I. Bennett, Dawn.

ML3795.L446 2012
780.23--dc23

2012033200

Table of Contents

Part I : How do we make Music Graduates Employable?

Chapter 1: Music, Musicians and Careers 3
Dawn Bennett, Angela Beeching, Rosie Perkins, Glen Carruthers and Janis Weller

Introduction 3
History repeating itself? 4
    Rethinking 'career' for music students: Identity and vision 6
    Musicians made in the USA: Training, opportunities and industry change .. 6
    Composed and improvised: The transition to professional life 6
    Staying afloat: Skills, attributes and passion 6
    Musicians in society: Making the connection 7
    Change and the challenges of lifelong learning 7
    Reflections on the protean music career 8
Concluding comments 8
References 9

Chapter 2: Rethinking 'Career' for Music Students 11
Identity and Vision
Rosie Perkins, Royal College of Music, UK

    Rethinking 'career' for musicians 12
    Zooming in on 'subjective career' 14
    Subjective career in practice: *Jack* 16
    Implications for musicians and conservatoires I: The need for space and reflection 20
    Implications for musicians and conservatoires II: Developing aspects of subjective career 21
    Closing remarks 23
    References 24
    Further reading and information 25

Chapter 3: Musicians made in the USA 27
Training, Opportunities and Industry Change
Angela Beeching, New England Conservatory, US

    Defining success 27
        Today's musicians profiled: Success redefined 28
        The job market: Supply and demand 31
    The size and scope of the US music industry 33

The changing culture and audience for classical music 33
Technology changing the profession 34
The need for skilled teaching artists 34
Music schools in America 36
The high price of education 37
The music curriculum 38
Career development programs 40
Entrepreneurship training 41
Conclusion 42
Advice for young artists (do's and don'ts) 42
References 42
Further reading and information 43

Chapter 4: Composed and Improvised 45
The Transition to Professional Life
Janis Weller, McNally Smith College of Music, US
Adulthood redefined 47
Self-authorship and Allan's story 50
Composed and improvised: Two sides of the same coin 50
Self-Authorship 51
Career development improvisation: Luck, opportunity, risk and confidence . 52
Career development composition: Standing on the shoulders of giants 52
Know thy stuff: The epistemological foundation 53
Know thy self: The intrapersonal foundation 53
Know thy people: The interpersonal foundation 54
Practical suggestions for educators and career guides 55
Professionalism 55
Integrating communication 56
Senior recitals and other concerts 57
Teaching 57
Networking and Participation 58
The Internet and social networking 58
Conclusion 59
References 60
Further reading 61

Chapter 5: Staying Afloat 63
Skills, Attributes and Passion
Dawn Bennett, Curtin University, Australia
The music, creative and cultural industries 64

Employment and employability in Australia 66
    Universities and schools 66
    Opera companies and orchestras 67
Education and professional development in Australia 69
Essential skills and attributes 71
    Business and entrepreneurship 71
    Communication skills 72
    Performance and passion 72
Concluding thoughts 73
References 75
Further reading and information 77

Chapter 6: Musicians in Society 79
Making the Connection
Glen Carruthers, Wilfrid Laurier University, Canada
Classically trained musicians in contemporary society 81
Post-secondary music education in Canada 82
Music production and consumption in Canada 83
Traditional employment streams 86
    Playing in orchestras 86
    Teaching in universities 87
Marie: A case study 89
Conclusion 91
References 94
Further reading 96

Chapter 7: Change and the Challenges of Lifelong Learning 99
Rineke Smilde, Prince Claus Conservatoire, Groningen;
Change and the challenges of lifelong learning 99
The musical landscape and the professional musician 101
    Cultural policies 103
    Audiences 103
    Technology 104
    Teaching in music schools 104
    Community work and cross-arts collaboration 105
European music academies responding to change 106
    Systems of training 106
    Dealing with graduates' needs 106
    International mobility and opportunities through the Bologna process 109
Lifelong learning for musicians 110
    Musicians' learning styles 110

ix

  Musicians' leadership 111
 Isaac, Daniel and Wendy: Three lifelong learners 111
  Isaac 112
  Daniel 112
  Wendy 114
 Musicians' roles revisited 114
  A niche: Educational leadership 115
 Strategies for preparing future musicians 115
 References 117
 Further reading and information 119

Chapter 8: Reflections on the Protean Music Career 125
Michael Hannan, Southern Cross University, Australia

 My background 127
 Going into business 130
 Towards academia 131
 Putting music into words 132
 Teaching 133
 More study 134
 At last, a full-time job 135
 The academic career 138
 Concluding reflections 140
 References 141
 Further reading and information 142

Part II : Resources

Introduction 147
 Contents and activity types
  Part II Contents 148

Foreword 151

Section 1: From Self to Career 155

Chapter 1: Conceptualising Music Careers I 157

Chapter 2: Conceptualising Music Careers II 161

Chapter 3: Musician Profile I 167
 Trying things out

Chapter 4: Plotting your Preferences 171

Chapter 5: Workshop 173

Turning on the career light

Chapter 6: Discussion Topic 177
Embracing the 'e' word

Chapter 7: The Musician's Lifestyle Quiz 179

Chapter 8: Getting What you Want I 183
Deciding what you want

Chapter 9: Getting what you want II 185
Following your passion

Chapter 10: Musician Profile II 187
Following your passion

Chapter 11: Getting what you want III 191
Likes and dislikes, strengths and weaknesses

Chapter 12: Musician Profile II 193
Filling in the gaps

Section 2: From Career to Community   195

Chapter 13: Community I 197
Teaching artists at work

Chapter 14: Getting to know your Dream Job 199

Chapter 15: Community II 201
Finding your mission

Chapter 16: Transitioning to Professional Life 203
Introduction

Chapter 17: Transitioning I 205
From professional student to professional musician

Chapter 18: Careers Panel 211
How did you get here?

Chapter 19: Getting Inspiration from Others 213

Chapter 20: Reading and Reflecting on Musician Biographies and Profiles 215

Section 3: Survival Skills   217

Chapter 21: Musician Profile IV 219
Orchestral life

Chapter 22: Getting a Head Start 223

Finding your mission

Chapter 23: Challenge 225
Action plans

Chapter 24: Musician Profile V 227
Finding the sparkle

Chapter 25: Transitioning II 231
From awareness to innovation

Chapter 26: Transitioning III 233
Know thyself – temperament and personality

Chapter 27: Skills and Attributes I 235
Professionalism

Chapter 28: Skills and Attributes II 237

Chapter 29: Skills and Attributes III 239
Skills audit

Chapter 30: Expanding the Skill Set 241

Chapter 31: Challenge 247
Volunteering

Chapter 32: Transitioning IV 249
Practical strategies for transitioning into professional life

Chapter 33: Networking I 253
Building circles

Chapter 34: Networking II 261
Who else do you know?

Chapter 35: Networking III 265
Reflections

Contributing Authors 267

Acronyms 271

Synopsis 273

Index 275

Foreword

This book is a welcome example of the great improvement in career advice available to today's young musicians. When I was a student, there was almost none. I don't remember any tutor, either at music college or at university, asking me how I planned to make my living when I graduated. They waved goodbye to me with what now seems neglectful insouciance. I plunged idealistically into the music profession and spent a long time being gradually and painfully enlightened about how difficult it is to earn a living in this complex and mysterious field.

I was fortunate to fall in with a very enterprising group of musicians, *Domus*, who were intent on doing concerts in a different way and who taught themselves how to build a geodesic dome and take it around from place to place, putting it up where there were no concert halls, and presenting informal concerts of our beloved chamber music inside the dome (complete with travelling piano, stage and cushions). Sometimes we even made food for the audience.

This project illustrated both the good and bad sides of life as a musician. Good, because we all got tremendous satisfaction out of striking out in a new direction and making something happen. It was great to meet audiences who loved what we were doing and even said it had changed their view of classical music and musicians. But we also discovered how much tedious, time-consuming admin is involved in establishing something new, and of course we found that it was very costly to do something new with no funding. I hardly dare to remember what tiny sums of money were left when we divided up the takings at the end of each week. And we learned something I'd still say is true: that in music there is no reliable link between reputation and reward. You can become well known and even be greatly esteemed without ever feeling financially secure.

Music is unusual in that training often begins in childhood. By the time a musician graduates from college, they've already spent years intensively engaged in practice and performance. They're far further up the ladder of experience than their non-musician friends who, on graduating, embark on jobs where they will be novices, expected to train from scratch. Musicians, on the other hand, are often already sophisticated artists at this age, longing to launch themselves into concert life. As *Life in the Real World* points out, life at college gives an unrealistic impression of how many performance opportunities there are, and how easy it is to claim them. I speak from experience when I say that the first years 'out there in the real world' can be a lonely and scary time. Like many musicians, I imagined that playing beautifully in my solitary practice room would somehow be enough to bring me to the attention of promoters and audiences. I thought they should magically 'just know' that I was there, waiting for opportunities. These days, with technology at one's side, it may be easier to spread the word of one's talent, using Facebook, Twitter, YouTube and whatever networking tools come next, but it still needs organisation and vision.

It's good to learn from this book that music educators today are more and more aware of the need to equip young musicians with the skills needed to build diverse careers. In today's economic climate, 'portfolio careers' are a necessity in many professions, and music is no exception. As this book points out, musicians should be proud of all the transferable skills they acquire as by-products of their years in orchestras, bands and chamber groups. Rehearsals and public performances will have taught them an enormous amount, even if they may not realise it. They can think independently, they can work in a team, they have learned how to concentrate, they can work patiently towards a long-range goal, they know how to network, they have communication skills, they can present themselves well, they can organise complicated diaries, they know how to master nerves and anxiety, and they have (usually) learned the invaluable art of diplomatic language when talking to colleagues. All these would make them welcome in many fields of work, quite apart from music.

No matter how much we talk about 'career strategies', music is actually more a vocation than a career. Young musicians need to be aware of this, because they will need to love music enough to put up with its insecurities and its discouraging lack of career structure. It never has been a reliable profession and it probably never will be. Yet music carries with it a high degree of job satisfaction, perhaps more so than in many other professions. Music is a deep well, endlessly absorbing for the player, and satisfying to be engaged in because so many people love music passionately, and love musicians for bringing it to them.

Susan Tomes

One of the UK's foremost pianists, Susan Tomes was the first woman to study music at King's College, Cambridge. She is in demand as a recitalist and concerto soloist, and has recorded over fifty CDs, winning many international recording awards. She is particularly renowned for her achievements in chamber music. For sixteen years she was the pianist of the award-winning group *Domus*, and since 1993 has been the pianist of the *Gaudier Ensemble*. From 1995 until 2012 she was the pianist of the *Florestan Trio*, one of the world's leading trios and one of the most-recorded. This season her Mozart Series with violinist Erich Höbarth has been a great critical success.

Susan is the author of three books about performing music: 'Beyond the Notes' (2004), 'A Musician's Alphabet'(2006) and 'Out of Silence' (2010), which has been translated into Japanese by concert pianist Noriko Ogawa. Susan's books are studied on 'music in performance' courses at the universities of Cambridge and Oxford, and at the Open University. *The Times Literary Supplement* wrote that 'Susan has a particular understanding of humanity rare in writing about music'.

Susan is increasingly known for her teaching. She runs her own masterclasses each year in London, attracting international chamber groups, and gives masterclasses at all the UK's leading music colleges, as well as further afield. She has written and presented programmes on BBC Radio 3 and Radio 4, and she contributes articles on music to *The Guardian* and *The Independent*. She serves as a member of international juries, gives seminars, and writes a blog on her website, www.susantomes.com

Part I
How do we make Music Graduates Employable?

Chapter 1
Music, Musicians and Careers

Dawn Bennett, Angela Beeching, Rosie Perkins,
Glen Carruthers and Janis Weller

Introduction

Virtuoso harpsichordist Wanda Landowska once said: "the most beautiful thing in the world ... is precisely the conjunction of learning and inspiration" (in Sachs, p. 144). Around the world, dedicated educators and mentors strive to engage students in planning for the realities of working life. This delicate balancing act is compounded by the general lack of curricular time devoted to this vital conversation together with outmoded definitions of success that may have little relevance to students' individual strengths, interests and inspirations. This book is designed to help fulfil these needs.

The book addresses essential career issues faced by musicians in today's global marketplace. Written by an international team of educators the book explores identity formation, lifelong learning, transitions into and between work, entrepreneurship, changing workplaces and musicians' connections with society. Adopting the linking theme of professional identity, the book includes research data alongside musician profiles and practical tools and resources.

Life in the Real World illustrates a range of pedagogical approaches and perspectives in two distinct parts. In Part I, chapters draw from each author's location to position the discussion within the context of the music profession in multiple locations. We draw on multiple locations because while many training opportunities for musicians are clustered around centres of excellence, the jobs most certainly are not. The mobility of musicians has never been higher: one has only to look at the careers of conductors such as Sir Simon Rattle or performers such as Natalie Klein to see that it really is a global market, and that most musicians will travel for training or for work. It follows that an awareness of jobs, travel opportunities and international collaborations is essential to the aspiring musician.

It is not possible to cover all major centres of music activity within a single volume; but readers will note common elements of life as a musician, many of which can be applied well beyond the scope of our examples. The connections among chapters inform a broad view of music practice that we hope will engage students without crushing their dreams and ambitions. Part II contains tried-and-tested materials that support learning and teaching. The practical exercises, resources and information are designed for individuals, small groups or classes. Materials can be reproduced or adapted, and they can also be accessed online.

History repeating itself?

Why do today's musicians typically have diversified careers, working in multiple roles? Why does it seem as though there are so few performance jobs? What has changed? In fact, a quick look at history reveals surprisingly little change in the diversity of musicians' practice.

Musicians in the Middle Ages often worked as town watchmen, warning people of impending danger or ringing the church bells as required. They trained apprentices and provided entertainment, working with different groups of musicians and catering for the tastes of various audiences (Headington, 1980). From the 12th century, musicians' guilds protected the rights and incomes of their (limited) members; however, the salaries of musicians rarely covered basic living costs. To make up their income, musicians sought freelance performance work and undertook a myriad of other roles. Some worked as scribes, some as servants and teachers. Some even worked as spies, taking information from place to place and selling it to the highest bidder (admittedly, this is perhaps less common today). Itinerant (travelling) musicians had the worst deal: most of them lived outside of the social class system until the late Middle Ages. As such they were without legal rights and were not permitted guild membership. Despite their obvious need, they were often paid in the form of gifts rather than with money.

HISTORY REPEATING ITSELF?

Musicians sometimes worked as spies

In the 14th century, much more work became available within the court system and the church. In rare cases, civic (town) musicians were lucky enough to be appointed for life and they achieved a higher social status than musicians had ever enjoyed before. Moving on to the 17th century, musicians often worked as school music directors, organists and scribes; or as performance musicians within a court, municipality or the military (Bukofzer, 1978).

In the 18th century, ecclesiastical and court control lessened and the concert orchestra emerged. Noblemen kept their own court orchestras, which led to increased employment for instrumentalists. However, only the 'superstars' earned significant amounts of money (Petzoldt, 1983). Most performing musicians augmented their salaries with a variety of work including teaching and freelancing. Telemann, for example, supplemented his role as church director by producing concerts, serving on committees and composing the music for events such as weddings.

In the 19th century there were less court appointments, and many musicians sought patronage or set up businesses in publishing or the retail trade. Concerts became commercial ventures needing to make a profit, with musicians often at the centre of the concert organisation (Rohr, 2001). At the same time, virtuoso performers combined entrepreneurship with superb performance skills to create lucrative careers. Chopin, Liszt, Beethoven, Schubert, Paganini, Brahms and Berlioz all built sustainable freelance careers. Brahms earned most of his living as a freelance editor and arranger, whilst Paganini left a secure court position with the sister of Napoleon Bonaparte in order to freelance around Europe.

Despite this complex history in which musicians are shown to have forged diverse, creative careers in order to remain 'in business', success is still most often painted as a thriving performance career. The challenge for today's educators and mentors is to communicate the breadth and depth of musicians' careers and to equip musicians for a sustainable future. It is this challenge that has shaped the chapters in Part I of this volume.

Rethinking 'career' for music students: Identity and vision

Like the musicians of the past, new graduates must create both short-term and long-term strategies and implement them on the fly, often with little outside guidance. In Chapter 2, Rosie Perkins rethinks 'career' for music students by describing how students carve their identities and adapt their expectations as they move towards full participation in the professional world. Alongside the characteristics and opportunities for practice in the UK, the author draws on findings from the *Learning to Perform* project, which tracked students for three years as they prepared for a professional career in music.

Musicians made in the USA: Training, opportunities and industry change

Angela Beeching considers in Chapter 3 how the career opportunities of today's music students differ from those of their teachers. She profiles a number of musicians who have created entrepreneurial careers, and details the characteristics and skills needed to succeed. Written from an American perspective and providing practical information for musicians curious about study and work in the US, Beeching's chapter addresses career goals and training, the arts economy, supply and demand, and entrepreneurship.

Composed and improvised: The transition to professional life

'*Dans les champs de l'observation le hasard ne favorise que les esprits préparés*' - Luck favors the prepared mind, said Louis Pasteur. As music students approach the end of formal schooling and begin to transition into professional life, there are numerous ways in which graduates can enhance their chances for good luck. There is no magic formula for getting started or sustaining a rewarding career over time; however, vital attributes include clear-headed self-awareness, a flexible and adaptable outlook, a developing savvy for the music world as a whole and the interpersonal skills to pull it all together.

In Chapter 4, Janis Weller addresses strategies for creating Pasteur's prepared luck. Weller focuses on the ways young musicians can prepare for this exciting but perhaps undefined transition from a virtually life-long identity as 'student' to the emerging identity of 'professional'. The chapter addresses both reflective and practical methods to help prepare students for the move from the familiarity of student life to the vast, uncertain world of musicians' work. Weller exposes tremendous opportunities for the aspiring professional who is aware, prepared, curious, hard working and, yes, a little lucky.

Staying afloat: Skills, attributes and passion

Understanding the complex nature of careers in the arts is critical to the establishment of responsive university curricula in a wide range of subject areas. In Chapter 5, writing from Australia, Dawn Bennett illustrates that roles beyond performance and beyond music can be valuable and satisfying aspects of musicians' careers, and would often not be traded for additional performance work. Mirroring careers in the arts, general labour market trends have seen more people expand their work behaviours, competencies and connections in search of success that is determined not in the eyes of others, but in terms of self-identity, intrinsic success and meeting personal and professional needs. Two of the most common terms applied to these career orientations are *portfolio*, which refers to multiple concurrent roles, and *boundaryless*, which refers to work away from traditional organisational career arrangements. This can involve working with different employers, ignoring traditional hierarchies and career progression, or validating achievements from outside of the employment situation.

The adjective that perhaps best describes careers in the arts is *protean*, and Bennett explores this further in Chapter 5. Protean careers are so-named after the mythological Greek sea-god Proteus, who was able to change form at will in order to avoid danger. This is something increasing numbers of people need to do in order to remain employable. Stemming from the mythical sea-god Proteus, who was the first 'shape-shifter', the protean musician refers to one who does not limit his or her activities, but instead forges a career from diverse activities in music and is able to take advantage of new opportunities as they appear.

Musicians in society: Making the connection

Despite the history of diversified careers in music, what is expected of today's musicians—how they contribute to the musical life of their communities, how they reach larger and broader audiences, how entrepreneurial skills factor into their career success, and how technology enables them to reach a worldwide public—has altered what they do on a daily basis and over the course of a career. Writing from Canada, Glen Carruthers places musicians in a wide social context. As he demonstrates in Chapter 6, once society expects something different from its musicians, music students and the institutions that teach them need to respond. Alongside examples of work and training in Canada, his chapter invites consideration of some of these changes, and explores some of the ways in which students can be encouraged to make connections with their communities.

Change and the challenges of lifelong learning

As Rineke Smilde discusses in Chapter 7, professional musicians in Europe are similarly confronted with questions of how to function flexibly in order to exploit opportunities in new and rapidly changing cultural contexts. The chapter gives an overview of trends and changes in the European music profession and explores ways in which European higher music education reflects the challenges of these realities in light of new European educational policies and musicians' international mobility. The author addresses the impact of these changes for musicians, drawing on examples from biographical research into musicians' lifelong learning skills and attitudes.

Reflections on the protean music career

In this book we argue that it is not sufficient to define a musician as a performer. Rather, a musician is someone who works in the profession of music within one or more specialist fields. This perception of a musician as a multi-skilled professional working within a portfolio or protean career is a significant shift from the traditional view of the performer. It exposes considerable potential for careers based on personal strengths and interests rather than a pre-ordained hierarchy of success.

In the final chapter, Michael Hannan illustrates the life of a protean careerist in music. The chapter charts a career involving piano accompanying, music copying, composing for advertising, playing in rock bands, studying musicology, teaching music in a variety of contexts, writing for an arts magazine, working as a music lexicographer, playing in ensembles from other musical cultures and, finally, developing a degree program that trains contemporary musicians. Hannan reflects on the formal and informal learning processes that enable the development of new skills, and reinforces the business and communication skills essential for career progression.

In sum, each chapter offers an added dimension and new perspective on what it takes to be a successful musician in today's global marketplace. To help readers put these ideas into action, Part II provides practical exercises and resources for use with individuals and classes.

Concluding comments

How do we make music graduates employable? What is success? What does employment—or self-employment—look like? What is a musician? This book aims to encourage future and practising musicians to freely consider 'what kinds of musician' they would like to be. In doing so, we hope to kindle reflective and expansive thinking stemming from a holistic, inclusive view of what it is to be a successful musician.

We hope that the volume proves to be thought provoking and useful, and we welcome your contributions and feedback for inclusion in our future work. Ultimately, we hope that our thinking will encourage readers to consider what inspires them and the role that this inspiration could play within their futures – to plan lives, not just careers, in music.

References

Bukhofzer, M. (1978). *Music in the baroque Era* (4th ed.). London: Dent & Sons.

Headington, C. (1980). *The Bodley Head history of western music* (2nd ed.). London: Bodley Head.

Petzoldt, R. (1983). The economic conditions of the 18th century musician (H. Kaufman & B. Reisner, Trans.). In W. Salmen (Ed.), *The social status of the professional musician from the middle ages to the 19th century* (pp. 161-188). New York: Pendragon Press. (Original work published 1971).

Rohr, D. (2001). *The Careers and Social Status of British Musicians*. Cambridge: Cambridge University Press.

Sachs, H. (1982). *Virtuoso*. Bath: The Pitman Press.

Chapter 2
Rethinking 'Career' for Music Students

Identity and Vision

Rosie Perkins

The transition from school to conservatoire is a challenging time for musicians, not least as a result of the convergence of highly skilled peers[1] (Burt & Mills, 2006). Coming at a time when students are planning for their careers, the realisation that they are among many musicians striving for similar ends can be devastating, forcing a widening of expectations early on in the higher education journey. Coupled with dominant discourses placing performance as the pinnacle of success for a musician (Bennett, 2008), it is not uncommon for students to feel 'second-rate' if they redefine their career aims to include activities beyond performance. It is often during the years spent in higher education that students struggle to make sense of their place within the music profession, grappling with how they see themselves, how other people see them, and what this means for them in terms of their chosen profession.

---

1. In the UK, a conservatoire is a higher education institution offering undergraduate and graduate degree courses.

While notions of success are certainly changing, as portfolio careers become the norm for musicians (see Chapter 3), conservatoire students must still navigate through a fog of often-conflicting messages. Take instrumental teaching, for instance. There remains a dangerous precedent to evaluate musicians on whether they have 'made it' as a performer or taken the so-called 'second-best' route to becoming a teacher (Huhtanen, 2008). Yet, teaching is known to afford intrinsically musical benefits (Burt-Perkins, 2008) as well as a strong sense of achievement (Mills, 2004), and many conservatoires encourage and support teaching as part of student portfolios. Further, even students who express reluctance to teach often hope to emulate the careers of their own teachers, recognising their contribution as *teachers* as well as performers. Even in this short example we glimpse something of the complex field of expectations, hopes and hierarchies at play in the education of the professional musician.

It is not surprising, then, that many young musicians talk of the struggles they face when deciding the direction of their career, redefining their expectations of conservatoire life, or in accepting that their original aims might not, in the end, be realised. Musicians' time in higher education seems to be as much about working through issues such as these as it is about acquiring other, perhaps more tangible, skills and attributes. What can we do—as those working in teaching, policy, or research roles—to guide students through this process? How can we work with students to encourage them to reflect constructively on their progress and plans, to understand themselves and their aims and to graduate as self-confident and well-prepared musicians? This chapter draws on research conducted at the Royal College of Music London (RCM) to rethink what we mean by 'career' for musicians, the role that 'identity' and 'vision' play within this, and the practical ways in which we can help students to navigate their journey towards being professional musicians.

What follows is divided into four sections, which begin by addressing possible reasons for pursuing music professionally and unpacking what we actually mean by the word 'career' when it comes to musicians. The second section zooms in on the 'subjective' aspects of career, in particular musicians' identity and vision. This is then brought to life through the case study of RCM student Jack. The case study demonstrates how career choice subjectively impinges on identity, and vice versa. The final section offers ways in which musicians and those who educate them can utilise the thinking in this chapter for the benefit of future students. Many of these strategies are also included as resources in Part II.

Rethinking 'career' for musicians

Let us start by pondering—amongst all of the trials and tribulations of studying, finding work and paying the rent—the possible reasons behind a decision to pursue a career in music. As Janet Mills (2005) so eruditely points out, music is a right; it is fundamental to all our lives and brings human beings great joy. Perhaps it is the desire to share this joy with audiences across the world that spurs musicians on: the chance to share musical experiences with other people or to capture in music the feelings that we cannot otherwise express. Perhaps it is the idea that music can transcend conflict and bring communities together, or perhaps it is the thrill of coming off stage after playing a packed Wigmore Hall.

Whatever a musician's particular motivations, the point is that a career in music is not simply a '9-till-5' job, it is also a way of life (Cottrell, 2004) encompassing values, decisions, dreams and expectations, as well as the practical need to earn a living. An important decision has, in many ways, already been taken when a student elects to study music. Certainly, at the RCM, the vast majority of students aim for a career in music. The complexities come when students realise that they need to carve a niche, to compete with others in their field, to discover what it is that drives and motivates them: that a lifelong professional connection with music will require determination, pro-activity and flexibility.

To ask students what they aim to achieve in their career, then, is a question laden with assumptions. What do we actually mean by the word 'career' when we refer to musicians? In many professions the model of a regular, salaried, permanent role that one can develop as a (traditional) career over many years still holds true. For musicians it simply does not. We are reminded throughout this book that musicians will engage in portfolio careers that are varied and diverse and which lack formal structures for progression and promotion. For musicians, career is perhaps better described as something that "people use to organise their behaviour over the long term" (Young & Valach, 2000, p. 188) and that offers a form of meaning-making in individual lives (Cochran, 1991). Career is both objective and subjective (Poole et al., 1993). It is objective in the sense that a person is engaged in a particular activity for a certain amount of time, earning a certain amount of money. And it is subjective in that it includes how people identify with themselves and with others (Mills, 2004). Crucially, career is seen as being far more than a job; rather it is a way of life that "allows people to account for effort, plans, goals, and consequences, [and] to frame internal cognitions and emotions" (Young, Valach & Collin, 2002, p. 217).

In her extensive work on the careers of RCM alumni, Mills (2004, 2005) developed these ideas to address the inadequacy of existing models of career for musicians. The model illustrated in Figure 1 encourages us to think about career in four ways.

RETHINKING 'CAREER' FOR MUSIC STUDENTS

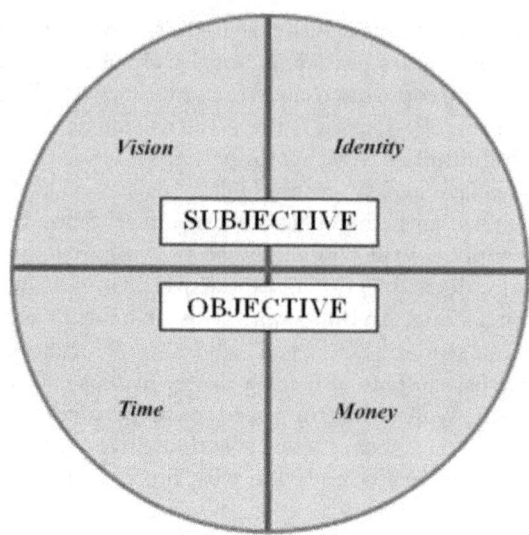

Figure 1: Conceptualising 'career' for musicians (Mills, 2004)

Objective facets of career include: (1) the *time* spent on different activities; and (2) the *proportion of income* generated from these activities (recognising that these may well be different). Subjective facets include: (3) how a person *identifies themselves* (how they see themselves); and (4) their *vision* for the future. Working with over 1,300 RCM alumni, Mills demonstrated the need to include all four facets when we consider musicians' careers, for they are indeed complicated and complex.

It is Mills and Smith's assertion (2002) that musicians who can align the subjective and objective factions of their career are those who will be 'successful'. It is likely to be a frustrated graduate, for example, who is aiming to be a workshop leader but spends his or her time playing orchestral music in order to earn a living. If we accept that Mills' model of career also provides a useful way of thinking about how we educate young musicians, we need to provide space within programs for the development of *both* objective and subjective facets of career. This chapter focuses largely on the subjective, demonstrating the significance of *vision* and *identity* to the lives of students. I argue that by supporting students as they work to bring the two career dimensions together, conservatoires can best prepare them for the realities of professional life. Resources to encourage students to think broadly about their developing objective and subjective careers can be found in Part II.

Zooming in on 'subjective career'

Identity—as one of the subjective facets of career—has become a frequently used concept in educational, psychological and music education writing (see, for example, MacDonald, Hargreaves & Miell, 2002). While this chapter does not attempt a theoretical or conceptual review, it is necessary to briefly delimit the ways in which I use and think about identity. In line with social constructionist thought (Berger & Luckmann, 1966), I take identity to be constructed in multiple social spaces as musicians move through their lives and interact with others. As MacDonald et al. (2002, p. 10) argue:

> Social constructionist theories suggest that people have many identities, each of which is created in interaction with other people, rather than having a single, core identity. These identities can be contradictory; for example, a musician can be a 'different person' on stage than when in solitary rehearsals, and be different again when engaged in each of a number of non-musical activities. In social constructionist terms, identities are also always evolving and shifting—each interaction can lead to new construction.

The key points here are that musicians can (and do) have *multiple* identities that, formed and reformed by their interactions with other people, are changing and fluid. Identity is thus not a singular or 'fixed entity' (Triantafyllaki, 2010) but rather taken to refer to shifting and multiple layers of understanding. As part of 'career', identity (hereafter used to reflect multiple and fluid identities) is something that people use "to justify, explain and make sense of themselves in relation to other people, and to the context in which they operate" (MacLure, 2001, p. 168).

The points above are vital as we consider how identity can be understood and developed in order to support young musicians preparing for a profession in music. Identity is what students *feel* they are, how they *feel* and *experience* their relationships with others, and how they *describe* themselves in relation to the music profession. But it is also closely linked to 'vision' (see Figure 1) in that it allows students to think about their aspirations and aims, or 'possible selves' (Hallam, 2009; Marcus & Nirius, 1986). In terms of career counselling, 'possible selves' are taken to "provide a link between one's self-concept and incentives for future behavior, an interpretive framework for an individual's current views of self" (Meara et al., 1995, p. 259). Taken together, identity and vision allow students to express and understand their sense of self as it shifts to reflect their activities, interests, and knowledge and as they work to construct and (re)align their expectations of what it means to be a professional musician.

Recent research in the UK has concluded that the need for time within conservatoire programs to enable students to develop a flexible identity is central both to developing expertise and in preparing for a broad career in music (Burt-Perkins, 2008). Identity formation does not emerge as an *addition* to the rest of the learning experience, but rather as a central part of the journey to becoming a musician. Indeed, Creech et al. (2008) found that amongst a portfolio of skills required for a smooth transition to the music profession, versatility is key. A flexible identity involves incorporating a wide range of skills, taking the initiative and gathering professional know-how, as well as allowing space for redefinition of goals. Or, to put it another way, it requires engagement in 'expansive' learning (Fuller & Unwin, 2003; see also Chapter 8): learning that includes stepping outside of the comfort zone and trying new things so that identity is challenged and broadened, and so musicians are open to new experiences and opportunities.

Through the lens of one student's words, the remainder of this chapter explores how subjective facets of career are developed in practice, providing examples of how identity formation works in everyday life, how (and why) this changes, how it helps in preparing for a career in music, and finally, how educational institutions can mediate and support students in this process. What follows is drawn from a longitudinal study of musical learning, *Learning to Perform*, of which brief methodological details can be found at the end of this chapter. The student, whom I call Jack, is an undergraduate pianist. In line with Bujold (2004), Jack's narrative is presented as a way of understanding his career, a technique used broadly within career research: "subjective careers evidenced themselves in the tales people told to lend coherence to the strands of their life" (Barley, 1989, p. 49).

Subjective career in practice: *Jack*

Focusing on the 'subjective' components of career, I now track Jack's vision and identity over a period of three years, examining how and why they shifted and changed over time. His journey is divided into five 'snapshots', each capturing different stages in his higher education. In addition to bringing to life the complex issues of subjective career, Jack's profile is useful as a discussion tool for students and teachers, for which guiding questions are included in Part II (tool 2).

VISION	IDENTITY
'My dream thing would be being a piano soloist but I think I have to be realistic and while the piano is really tough, it becomes really hard so I don't know ... I would love to teach. I would really love to teach'.	*'I don't know if the word exists— eclectic. I love contemporary music and chamber music and solo playing and academia and not only music academia. I don't throw myself in one direction, ignoring the others ... I don't consider myself as a pianist. I think as a person I am a pianist but it is more a job thing. You are a pianist if you earn a living out of it and I don't do that so music student would describe me more correctly'.*

Snapshot 1: End of first undergraduate year

In my first interview with Jack (see Snapshot 1), his words exemplify something of the confusion facing conservatoire students. While his 'dream' is to be a soloist, he immediately counters this by saying that he needs to be 'realistic'. On the one hand, Jack is demonstrating awareness that a solo performance career is not a reality for most graduates (Rogers, 2002), but his words also flag what seems to have become an embedded discourse amongst some conservatoire students: *I'd like to be a soloist, but it's not going to happen, so I guess I'll be happy to be a teacher.* When we couple this with his vision at that time, we see a gap between his 'dream' objective career (piano soloist) and his subjective career (eclectic student): there is a misalignment between his 'eclectic' loves and his vision of a rather narrower professional path. Perhaps the root of this disjunction is most evident in the distinction he makes between being a pianist 'as a person' but not as an earning professional. The subjective facets of Jack's career, and his desire to learn and develop broadly, appear here to be taking a back seat to the objective, which in turn appear to be constructed within dominant discourses of solo success that do not necessarily match Jack's own views.

VISION	IDENTITY
Hopefully I will have found my way into competitions so I can kind of be kind of recognised on the musical scale. If I haven't done well in any competitions, I haven't got much hope'.	*'I feel like a music student and even though I have got this big thing which makes me the soloist with the orchestra, I still don't feel like I'm this [amazing] pianist! I just feel like myself, just a music student, in London. That's it'.*

Snapshot 2: Beginning of second undergraduate year

In Snapshot 2, at the beginning of his second undergraduate year, Jack continues to aspire to a performance-based career, marrying recognition with competition success and embodying the sense of musical hierarchy (or, as he puts it, 'musical scale') within the music profession (see also Cottrell, 2004). In the days before we met for the interview, Jack had been offered a solo contract with an organisation in Europe, a role that would have secured him high-profile performance opportunities and taken him further towards the professional aspirations he held at that time. Yet he ultimately declined the offer, citing that to accept it—given his perception of the quality of the music he would be expected to play—would be to compromise the quality of his own musicianship. This 'critical incident' (Burnard, 2000) marks a notable change in Jack's career as he begins to explore what music making is about for him, and to reject predetermined notions of success (climbing the 'musical scale'). His description of himself as a 'music student'—despite the prestige of the 'big thing which makes me the soloist with the orchestra'—illustrates his realisation that to step nearer his anticipated goals may not actually change how he feels about, and thinks about, himself.

VISION	IDENTITY
'*Happiness. Whatever I do I want to be happy—not rich. [Interviewer: Do you see music as being part of that?] Yes. I can't live without it—whether it is for me or sharing with pupils or an audience. I can't live without making music. [Interviewer: So do you think it will be the only thing you do professionally?] No. I know that I will also need something more intellectual. Music is very intellectual. I like making music but I also like pondering music and writing about it because they explain the feelings and what you feel when you listen to music*'.	'*I would say musician rather than pianist but at the same time I would describe myself as open to broader horizons. I would not like to limit myself to musician*'.

Snapshot 3: Midway through second undergraduate year

As Jack's self-reflection continues, in Snapshot 3 we see a notable shift in his vision and identity. Here, he has moved away from his initial 'dream', aspiring instead to a career that will provide him with happiness, music making, and intellectual fulfilment. Jack has shifted from identifying himself as an aspiring soloist who has not yet reached his goal to describing himself as a musician, reflecting an identity linked with learning, thinking and writing about, and performing music. His vision is no longer tied to 'objective' notions of success such as competitions, but is instead centred on self-fulfilment through his love of music. At this point, his objective and subjective careers draw closer together: he sees himself and his 'possible selves' tying more closely with the professional roles that he seeks to undertake.

This trajectory is consolidated in Snapshot 4, where Jack alludes to the (perhaps tacit) pressure he felt to shape his aspirations towards solo work: 'I want to aim at doing what I want to do and never become bitter with what I am doing'. In an interesting metaphor on solo performance, Jack's description of music not being 'one island' reflects an identity that places value on wealth through knowledge and culture, as opposed to recognition or financial reward. Although he no longer aims to be a solo pianist, he does not speak of having 'given up'. Rather, he seeks a profession where he will have the time and space to continue developing his skills as a pianist *and* as a musician. The sense of struggle that was evident in Snapshot 1 has lessened here, as he builds confidence in his own dreams and eschews expectations that did not meet his own reality.

VISION	IDENTITY
'I want to try to be a better musician all the time. I want to never lose momentum —never lose motivation and I want to always strive never to become bitter because I have now worked hard enough to get where I want to get and I don't want to be in this two square metre little room all day and be thinking 'This isn't what I want to do'. I don't want to do that. If I am teaching, it is because I want to do that. If I am performing, it is because I want to'.	*'[I think you need to] bring everything together because music isn't one island. It is one piece and you have to know everything ... the world of culture is fascinating and it is one thing that makes you think that I don't have to be wealthy. It is the one thing that makes me realise that I don't need that much money and [to] have a wonderful home in Kensington. It is the one thing that makes me feel that I am really rich'.*

Snapshot 4: Beginning of third undergraduate year

We have seen Jack move from striving for a solo piano career to seeking a diverse and flexible role as a musician. In so doing, he had to reassess his vision and identity, work out what was important to him, identify his strengths, and ascertain what he actually wanted from his career. By the time he graduated a year later, he was secure in these subjective facets of his career and had a plan of action to ensure that his objective career (i.e. the activities that he undertakes) matched them.

Jack recognised, though, the difficulties he had faced in reaching this point. He explained to me, in Snapshot 5, that while he valued his versatility, he remained conscious of the pressure to excel as a solo performance artist:

I sometimes think that being versatile is not a strength at all. Perhaps people would like someone who is excellent at doing one thing and who devotes heart, soul and body to doing that one particular thing, which is not my conception of music for life. I am not the most gifted pianist. I haven't got the best technique in the world and I am not the best musician in the world either, but at least I am willing to improve, but I do realise how limited I can be. [Interviewer: And when you say your conception of a musician, what is that conception?] I don't know. It is just, I think ... I think that 90% of the people who audition for here, within the four years they are all hoping to be the world's most recognised musician and that flakes off as we go along and at the end of the time that we are leaving the RCM or we are about to leave it, it has completely crumbled and you realise what you can do around that and that can make you happy. In my case, it is doing different things. It is just about sharing for me. I have realised that piano solos are just not for me and I just don't enjoy that any more. I just like sharing and making people know and learn what music is about. That is what matters to me.

Snapshot 5: After graduation

The crucial task for Jack, then, was to identify *what would make him happy*. Tied up in this can be a host of struggles as industry expectations, conservatoire curricula, hopes and fears vie against the development of subjective identity and vision. Although difficult, these struggles are imperative to reaching an understanding of oneself as a musician; an understanding that is essential in the 'real world' of the music profession. Key points to take from Jack's story include the need to:

- Encourage and allow students to change;
- Support students as they develop their own ways of being flexible;
- Allow students to define success according to their own 'career'; and
- Create a culture where subjective and objective components of career are valued equally.

Drawing this together, Jack's story reminds us that an education in music involves the whole person and their developing sense of self, as well as their developing musical proficiency. The following section proposes ways in which educators may be able to support students as they navigate this journey.

Implications for musicians and conservatoires I: The need for space and reflection

We have experienced Jack's journey largely through his own words, and different readers will inevitably take away different lessons. In many ways, simply hearing his story can be informative, encouraging and affirming. There are, though, broader implications, supported also by other evidence presented in musician profiles throughout this book. Indeed, Creech et al. (2008, p. 329) argue that transition into the profession should be dealt with as a *process* rather than an event, so that higher education institutions "have support systems in place that foster self-confidence, interpersonal skills, perseverance as well as musical responsibility and autonomy". One such support system may grow from providing space for students to articulate their vision and identity, as well as to reflect on these as they change. In the busy lives of musicians such space is often lacking but, as Jack illustrates, it is vitally important:

LTP[Learning to Perform] ... interviews made me voice out hopes, feelings, ambitions that would otherwise have remained unspoken. Interview after interview it made me think about what my aspirations or fears at a given point were. It then made me construct a clearer picture of where I was heading to etcetera. In short it has—and in this it is cognate to AT [Alexander Technique]—made me be in touch with myself more. The effect of AT plus LTP was also to make me simply more open-minded—realising how much one can benefit from integrating this type of work in one's practice and more importantly in one's life.

Regular meetings, ideally with somebody removed from the central learning process and in a safe, non-judgmental setting, offer possibilities for students to 'voice out' the different facets of their careers. Not only can this stimulate student reflection and development, but it also has the potential to help educators understand and support students as they navigate through the transition to professional life. Figure 2 proposes a set of 'starter' questions that can form the basis of such meetings.

VISION	**IDENTITY**
• What are your aims for the future? • Where would you like to be in five years' time? In ten years' time? • Why do you want to achieve these things? • For how long have you wanted to achieve these things?	• How would you describe yourself? Why would you describe yourself like this? • How do you think others see you as a musician? How would you like to be seen? • Where do you see yourself fitting in the music profession? • What makes you happy?
TIME	**MONEY**
• How do you spend most of your time? • What different (musical or non-musical) activities do you do? • How is your time divided across the week? Are you satisfied with this? • How do you imagine spending your time when you graduate?	• Are you taking paid gigs, or earning money from teaching or other activities? If so, how does this reflect the time you spend doing the activity? Why do you do this? • Do you feel that your time is well rewarded? • How do you imagine earning your living when you graduate?

Figure 2: Operationalising 'career' for musicians

Once students have (some) responses to these questions, they can be better positioned to understand where they would like to be, where the gaps are, and what they can do to realise their ambitions. If possible, the same questions should be posed once per semester (or at other regular intervals), allowing students to reflect upon how their answers change over time. These questions are reproduced in Part II (tool 1).

Implications for musicians and conservatoires II: Developing aspects of subjective career

Once students have identified any gaps between their objective and subjective career intentions, or have realised that their aspirations are changing, how can they be supported in developing their career to meet their changing needs? Knowing that students seek to learn from their peers (Burt & Mills,

2006; Lebler, Burt-Perkins & Carey, 2009) it may be prudent to draw on previous students' experiences to provide advice to current and prospective students (see Chapter 4 for more discussion on alumni links). Working from the basis of Jack's story, and contextualised by other data from *Learning to Perform*, the following section provides exemplars of such advice.

- *Engage in as many musical and non-musical activities during higher education as possible.* This not only makes students better equipped for their portfolio career, but also enables them to discover and try new possibilities for their professional lives. In particular, students should be encouraged to pursue diverse activities outside, or in parallel with, their specialism, so that they create their own 'expansive' learning environment.

- *Do not be afraid to challenge your aims and plans.* Jack took the difficult decision to turn down high profile solo work because it did not fit with his musical aspirations. This decision forced him to reconsider what he actually *wanted* from his career. Students need to allow themselves space to think through and talk over what is important for them. It is crucial that, in doing so, they have the support of their instrumental teacher and other tutors. Professional development opportunities that introduce a range of teaching staff to the discussions presented in this chapter may also be valuable.

- *Take ownership of your learning.* Students need not scrap their dreams if they feel that they are becoming unachievable. They do, however, need to work out why they think they are unachievable, how they can redefine them and, crucially, how they can do this in a way that fulfils their ambitions. Systems must be in place to allow this to happen, including flexible programs that allow students to develop the professional skills they need at the time they feel they need them.

- *Work out what 'career' success means to you.* Whatever individual students see as success—whether it be working with disadvantaged children or playing at Carnegie Hall—they should be supported in pursuing their aims. But students should be cautioned to remember that, however they define success, they will still need to be diverse, flexible, and open-minded in order to respond to their career as it changes over time. A change of mind is not an admission of defeat. Rather, it is one of many reformulations of goals that musicians will encounter during their lives.

This sort of advice needs to run alongside a program that offers students practical opportunities to put newfound ideas into practice. Jack's story, as we would expect, differs in many ways to that of other students, illuminating crucial differences in lived experience and perceptions of career. Such differences highlight the need for flexible approaches to professional skills work, including provision on a case-by-case basis. If introduced at the right stage, professional skills training including, for instance, teaching experience, community work and entrepreneurship (see Chapter 3), enables students to work on the development of both their objective and subjective career.

Indeed, *Learning to Perform* concluded that a tailored approach appropriate to each individual's progress and stage of development is the most effective way forward (Burt-Perkins, 2008).

Closing remarks

It is a sorry state of affairs when students, asked about their career aims, answer: *I'd like to be an international star, but it's not going to happen.* Not only does this convey a notion of success that is largely irrelevant to the music profession, it also suggests that these young musicians may be dissatisfied with their careers even before they have graduated. Higher education is a time for self-development as well as more specialised education, and this should be no different for musicians. It is imperative that the gap between objective and subjective career is narrowed so that musicians are fulfilled by what they do; and it is during the years of undergraduate education that we have a perfect opportunity to do this.

We know that whilst many students *will* seek a career in performance, and *will* integrate performance into their working lives, relatively few will become internationally renowned for their solo work. If the benchmark for success is placed so high that few can reach it, most music students are set up to fail. It is this that leads students to doubt their abilities and to feel that they are 'failed performers' if they teach or embark on other non-performance activities. In reality the vast majority of music students are skilful, educated and accomplished musicians who will go on to a wide range of careers. It is nonsensical that success in music has become so aligned with reaching the very top echelons of one particular part of the industry. As Jack shows, success can also be concerned with making and sharing great music, achieving personal goals and, ultimately, achieving happiness. This chapter has attempted to provide a starting point for embedding vital support within music programs. Much more needs to be done to fully address the complex issues facing the music students of today.

Acknowledgement

This chapter was originally to have been co-authored with the late Dr Janet Mills. Many of the ideas presented here are referenced to her, or developed on the back of her thoughtful and rigorous thinking. Her contribution to this chapter and our broader knowledge of musicians' careers remains immense.

References

Barley, S. R. (1989). Careers, identity, and institutions: The legacy of the Chicago School of Sociology. In M. B. Arthur, D. T. Hall & B. S. Lawrence (Eds.), *Handbook of career theory* (4th ed., pp. 41-65). Cambridge: Cambridge University Press.

Bennett, D. (2008). *Understanding the classical music profession: The past, the present and strategies for the future.* Aldershot: Ashgate.

Berger, P. L., & Luckmann, T. (1966). *The social construction of reality: A treatise in the sociology of knowledge.* New York: Anchor Books.

Bujold, C. (2004). Constructing career through narrative. *Journal of Vocational Behavior, 64,* 470-484.

Burnard, P. (2000). How children ascribe meaning to improvisation and composition: Rethinking pedagogy in music education. *Music Education Research, 2*(1), 7-23.

Burt, R., & Mills, J. (2006). Taking the plunge: The hopes and fears of students as they begin music college. *British Journal of Music Education, 23*(1), 51-73.

Burt-Perkins, R. (2008). *Learning to perform: Enhancing understanding of musical expertise.* Teaching and Learning Research Programme Research Briefing 47. Available at www.tlrp.org.

Cochran, L. (1991). *Life-shaping decisions.* New York: Peter Lang.

Cottrell, S. (2004). *Professional music-making in London: Ethnography and experience.* Aldershot: Ashgate.

Creech, A., Papageorgi, I., Duffy, C., Morton, F., Haddon, et al. (2008). From music student to professional: The process of transition. *British Journal of Music Education, 25*(3), 315-331.

Fuller, A., & Unwin, L. (2003). Learning as apprentices in the contemporary UK workplace: Creating and managing expansive and restrictive participation. *Journal of Education and Work, 16*(4), 407-426.

Geertz, C. (1973). *The interpretation of culture: Selected essays by Clifford Geertz.* NewYork: Basic Books.

Hallam, S. (2009). Motivation to learn. In S. Hallam, I. Cross & M. Thaut (Eds.), *The Oxford handbook of music psychology* (pp. 285-294). Oxford: Oxford University Press.

Huhtanen, K. (2008). Constructing a conscious identity in instrumental teacher education. In D. Bennett & M. Hannan (Eds.), *Inside, outside, downside up. Conservatoire training and musicians' work* (pp. 1-10). Perth: Black Swan Press.

Lebler, D., Burt-Perkins, R., & Carey, G. (2009). What the students bring: Examining the attributes of commencing conservatoire students. *International Journal of Music Education, 27*(3), 232-249.

MacDonald, R., Hargreaves, D. J., & Miell, D. (2002). *Musical identities.* Oxford: Oxford University Press.

MacLure, M. (2001). Arguing for your self: Identity as an organizing principle in teachers' jobs and lives. In J. Soler, A. Craft & H. Burgess (Eds.), *Teacher development: Exploring our own practice* (pp.167-180). London: Paul Chapman.

Marcus, H., & Nirius, P. (1986). Possible selves. *American Psychologist, 41*(9), 954-969.

Meara, N. M., Day, J. D., Chalk. L. M., & Phelps, R. E. (1995). Possible selves: Applications for career counselling. *Journal of Career Assessment, 3*(4), 259-277.

Mills, J. (2004). Working in music. *British Journal of Music Education, 21*(2), 179-198.

Mills, J. (2005). *Music in the school.* Oxford: Oxford University Press.

Mills, J., & Smith, J. (2002). *Working in Music: Becoming successful.* Unpublished paper presented at the Musikalische Begabung in der Lebenzeitperpektive, University of Paderborn.

Poole, M. E., Langan-Fox, J., & Omodei, M. (1993). Contrasting subjective and objective criteria as determinants of perceived career success: A longitudinal study. *Journal of Occupational and Organizational Psychology, 66*(1), 39-54.

Rogers, R. (2002). *Creating a land with music: The work, education and training of professional musicians of the 21st century.* London: Youth Music.

Triantafyllaki, A. (2010). Performance teachers' identity and professional knowledge in advanced music teaching. *Music Education Research, 12*(1): 71-87.

Young, R. A., & Valach, L. (2000). Reconceptualizing career psychology: An action theoretical perspective. In A. Collin & R. A. Young (Eds.), *The future of career* (pp. 181–196). Cambridge, UK: Cambridge University Press.

Young, R. A., Valach, L., & A. Collin (2002). A contextualist explanation of career. In D. Brown (Ed.), *Career choice and development* (4th ed., pp. 206-254). San Francisco: Jossey-Bass.

Further reading and information

For more information on the alignment between objective and subjective career, see: Mills, J. (2004). Working in music: the conservatoire professor. *British Journal of Music Education,* 21(2): 179-198. Available at http://journals.cambridge.org/action/displayJournal?jid=BME

For further ideas on the integration of professional identity formation into conservatoire programs, see Huhtanen, K. (2008). Constructing a conscious identity in instrumental teacher education. In Bennett, D., & Hannan, M. (Eds.). (2008). *Inside, outside, downside up. Conservatoire training and musicians' work.* Perth: Black Swan Press (pp.1-11).

Described in the chapter, *Learning to Perform* was a three-year exploration of musical expertise that started from the premise that becoming a musician extends far beyond the practice room or composition studio. The project conceptualised learning holistically, seeking to understand the social, musical and personal parameters of developing as a musician and tracked students' career aspirations and identity as they progressed through their studies. From its inception, *Learning to Perform* placed importance on the need for student-centred research that connects with students' wants and needs. To this end, the project adopted a pragmatic perspective, working with mixed-methods in order to best answer its research questions.

At the heart of the research lay a longitudinal study of 31 students, who were tracked from either their first undergraduate year at the RCM until their third, or from their third undergraduate year until one year after graduation. Such in-depth study in a UK conservatoire is unique to the project, allowing us to collect 'thick' data (Geertz, 1973) that shed light on the types of tensions and confusions experienced in the course of a conservatoire degree. Specifically, these students were invited to attend nine semi-structured interviews over a three-year period, and to participate in the larger group of 276 students who completed one or more of six questionnaires over the course of the project, detailing their musical history, their identity, their career aspirations and their attitudes towards instrumental teaching.

Jack was amongst the 31 students tracked in more detail through qualitative enquiry. He is a male pianist and was involved in the project from his first year until the end of his third year. He has been chosen to represent the ways in which identity can change over the course of a higher education and the ways in which this is intertwined with success and vision, and thus should neither be seen as 'typical' of the RCM, nor as a basis for generalisation. Rather, he provides a 'real-life' example of identity formation, which may be useful to others. Jack was interviewed seven times. Each interview was conducted individually, recorded with permission and fully transcribed.

Learning to Perform was funded by the Economic and Social Research Council's Teaching and Learning Research Programme, RES-139-25-0101. For more information on the project, visit: http://www.tlrp.org/proj/phaseIII/L2P.htm

Chapter 3
Musicians made in the USA

Training, Opportunities and Industry Change

Angela Beeching

This chapter, written from an American perspective, offers a range of contemporary profiles that showcase the innovative career paths musicians are creating for themselves. These examples highlight some of the trends of today's emerging artists, who are typically entrepreneurial, technologically savvy and interested in exploring new ways to engage audiences and connect with their communities. The chapter also addresses the issues of supply and demand, the arts economy, work within the music industry, and how musicians are trained in the US. As a veteran music career counsellor at New England Conservatory, one of the top US music schools, I also provide practical information for musicians curious about studying or working in the US.

Defining success

The myth that fuels many musicians' dreams goes like this: 'If I practice really, really, REALLY hard, do everything my teacher tells me, go to the best school possible, compete and audition, then, with luck, and maybe with the connections my teacher has, I will *make it*'. For some, 'making it' means playing in one of the world's best orchestras, singing lead roles at the Metropolitan Opera or La Scala, or otherwise becoming an international 'star', touring the world and recording as a soloist or chamber musician. However,

"When musicians have a narrow view of the profession, they limit themselves in finding their own best career path", says bassoonist Ben Kamins, faculty at Rice University, former principal with the Houston Symphony and active freelance chamber player (in Beeching, 2010, p. 6). Others agree: "There is a misconception amongst music students that you get a job in an orchestra and you live happily ever after. It's incredible to get and keep that job, but it doesn't guarantee artistic satisfaction" (Careers Forum, 2007).

Music teachers and schools prop up young musicians' dreams by rewarding students with scholarships, ready-made performance opportunities and the relatively protective bubble of a college music degree program. In academia, students (and often faculty and staff) can be oblivious to the difficult realities and changes in the 'real world'. Unfortunately the bubble also keeps musicians uninformed about many non-traditional and entrepreneurial career paths.

Today's musicians profiled: Success redefined

What characterises the newest generation of professional musicians? What kinds of careers are they creating for themselves? How are they re-defining success? There follow a few examples of not-so-traditional approaches to music career success. These provide great springboards for discussion with students and colleagues.

Cellist Matt Haimovitz garnered national media attention several years ago when the *New York Times* ran a piece about his unorthodox national tour, which featured solo cello recitals played in rock clubs, coffeehouses and even a pizza parlour. He had become frustrated with the traditional concert experience and missed seeing his own generation in the audience. He wanted to reach out to new audiences with the music he was passionate about, from J.S. Bach to living composers and his own arrangements of rock standards. Haimovitz has championed performing in non-traditional venues. For his 'Anthem' tour of American works, Haimovitz performed Jimi Hendrix's improvisational version of *The Star-Spangled Banner* and recorded it live at the former New York City punk palace known as CBGB. Shortly after his initial forays into alternative spaces, Haimovitz hired a former singer-songwriter to find and book appropriate clubs for more extensive tours in support of his project.

Haimovitz and composer Luna Pearl Woolf later founded their indie classical label Oxingale Records, and have to date released over fifteen albums encompassing a wide range of artists and genre-blending, collaborative works. Recent projects include *After Reading Shakespeare*, featuring literary-themed solo cello suites by three Pulitzer Prize-winning American composers. Haimovitz toured the album in over 40 cities including exclusive appearances at Borders bookstores as part of *Borders on the Road*. Oxingale has also launched a YouTube channel, and on the label's website fans can download free ringtones of Matt's signature cellistic pyrotechnics.

Another example is the Boston-based pianist Sarah Bob, who had always been interested in the connections between contemporary visual art and music. She founded the New Gallery Concert Series in 2000 to present the two art forms in dialogue. Each concert is presented in collaboration with a corresponding visual art exhibition at the Community Music Center of Boston, where Sarah is on faculty. She selects the visual artwork and commissions composers to write musical responses to it. As of 2008 the series had hosted 26 concerts with over 123 musical compositions, 30 premieres and hundreds of works by over two dozen visual artists from around the world. The series includes works that span the spectrum of classical-contemporary, improvisation, electronic, jazz and avant-garde music, paired with sculpture, painting, indoor installations, photography and film. In describing the motivation behind her work, Sarah writes: "It's so exciting to be surrounded by so many incredibly enthusiastic and creative musicians and artists. To be responsible for stirring up an event with such people and to share that kind of energy is a thrill" (S. Bob, personal communication, December 5, 2008).

A third illustration is the Providence String Quartet, which developed an innovative urban residency, Community MusicWorks, over ten years ago in Providence, Rhode Island. Violinist/violist Sebastian Ruth founded Community MusicWorks on the conviction that musicians have an important public role to play in creating and transforming communities. Lauded by Alex Ross in *The New Yorker* magazine as a 'revolutionary organisation' the quartet lives, rehearses and teaches in an under-served urban neighbourhood that lacks after-school programs for young people as well as music education in the public schools. Ruth, a Brown University graduate, started the project with a US$10,000 grant from the university's Swearer Center for Public Service. Community MusicWorks is now funded through grants and private donations, and by 2009 their budget had grown to US$630,000. The organisation provides 100 neighbourhood children with lessons, plus the use of instruments and transportation to perform throughout the region. A substantial waiting list of students is evidence of the program's popularity with young people and their families (Community MusicWorks).

In terms of having an impact beyond their immediate community, in 2006 the organisation started a two-year Fellowship program that trains young professional musicians in the methodology of community-based performance and teaching careers. Fellows teach, perform and design programs alongside the members of the Providence String Quartet. The idea is that with this training, the Fellows can go out and start their own community-based programs in other parts of the US and the world.

These examples illustrate that one of the underlying trends of this new generation of musicians is a sense of mission: the urge to find new ways to connect music with audiences (see Chapter 6). Musicians are no longer content to perform in formal and traditional environments, disconnected from their audiences and from concerns in their communities. Today's musicians often have a sense of music as social force for change. These citizen-artists are exploring ways to find a sense of immediacy, connection and relevancy in their work (see the volunteering challenge in Part II).

As for vocalists, in America over the past ten years there has been a new wave of small, entrepreneurial chamber opera companies similar to those in Australia described by Bennett in Chapter 5. Organised on shoestring budgets, these chamber opera companies perform one-act operas with small casts and a few instrumentalists. Singers and composers eager to create new opportunities and reach new audiences have launched many of these enterprises. With more modest budget needs, the start-ups are often able to commission local composers and premiere new works, expanding the audience and the repertory.

Intermezzo Chamber Opera, the brainchild of tenor John Whittlesey, merges the musical and dramatic flavour of grand opera with the immediacy of art song, offering performances on a smaller, more intimate scale. Intermezzo focuses on contemporary 20th and 21st century chamber works (particularly by American composers) sung in English. Since 2003, the Boston-based Intermezzo has commissioned six works and has built a sizeable fan base, critical acclaim and a wide repertoire. Whittlesey, with a background in finances and a day-job consulting with hospitals, uses the full range of his musical and non-musical skills in realising this dream. From selecting repertoire and castings shows to raising the necessary funds, managing contracts, scheduling rehearsals and attracting audiences, it's an all-encompassing and rewarding venture.

For orchestral musicians, recent years have been difficult as a result of declining ticket sales, changing audience tastes, mounting expenses and a decline in funding. Yet there are bright spots in various communities where creative programming, savvy promotion and generous donors have brought success. Envisioning an orchestra that would showcase new works, the Boston Modern Orchestra Project (BMOP) was created in 1996 by conductor Gil Rose. At that time, many may have wondered whether Boston really needed another orchestra: not only was there the Boston Symphony, there was also an established set of local, regional and community orchestras plus numerous smaller ensembles specialising in new music, all vying for limited local media attention, audiences and arts funding. Despite all of this, Rose persevered. The orchestra, composed of top freelance musicians, performs five main stage programs a year plus community and smaller-venue concerts. BMOP has garnered rave reviews, developed a loyal fan base, premiered over 40 works, commissioned more than 20, and recorded more than 50. Rose provides yet another example of an entrepreneurial and ambitious musician pursuing a seemingly unrealistic dream, yet succeeding. He has found a niche, built an orchestra and an audience, and created work for dozens of fellow musicians and composers.

In geographic contrast to BMOP on the East Coast of the US, Gustavo Dudamel has a very different mission. The Venezuelan *wunderkind* became principal conductor of the Los Angeles Philharmonic in 2009. He was one of the youngest conductors to win a major US orchestra principal position. Dudamel is the most illustrious product of *El Sistema*, the remarkable national music education system that offers even the poorest Venezuelan children instrumental music training and participation in a network of youth orchestras. *El Sistema's* founder, Jose Antonio Abreu, describes *El Sistema* to be not simply about music education, but rather a social program for transforming lives and communities. And Dudamel is helping to create a version of *El Sistema* in his new hometown by providing music lessons and youth orchestra experiences to children in the most needy neighbourhoods of Los Angeles.

These examples highlight the fact that the arts are a testament to human ingenuity. Seeking to improve their communities, musicians are inspired to compose new works, create new instruments and record labels, devise music software and applications, launch ensembles, schools and performance series and, in the process, build new audiences and transform communities. They also contribute by becoming advocates and arts leaders serving on advisory boards to support local, regional or national arts initiatives. For today's musician, the essential challenge is to create a meaningful life's work and a liveable income in a highly competitive, changing marketplace.

The job market: Supply and demand

The problem with the status quo is that the majority of graduating musicians seek traditional jobs such as orchestral or college teaching positions. How many musicians are being trained in the US? The Higher Education Arts Data Service tracks information for the National Association of Schools of Music (NASM), which is the accrediting body for the majority of US music schools. For the 606 NASM institutions reporting for 2007-08, more than 110,000 students were enrolled in college-level music degree programs in the US and in that year over 20,000 graduated with music degrees (NASM, 2009). These figures illustrate that there are far more graduate musicians than there are 'traditional' jobs such as orchestral or college-level teaching positions.

For those desiring orchestral work in the US, the International Conference of Symphony and Opera Musicians (ICSOM) represents members of the 52 largest budgeted American orchestras, amounting to about 4,200 total musician positions. In a sample year, 2003, there were just 159 openings in ICSOM orchestras. The typical number of applicants requesting an audition for one of these positions ranges from 100-200. And while the top five US orchestras pay starting salaries of over US$100,000, the average ICSOM minimum salary in 2003 was only US$57,000 (ICSOM). The majority of orchestras in America do *not* offer full-time work and many only pay a per-service (hourly) wage. Smilde (Europe) and Bennett (Australia) paint a similar picture in this volume.

As for classical vocalists, the national service organisation, Opera America, surveyed its members in 2005-06 and identified 2,217 performances of 485 fully staged main season and festival productions in that twelve-month period (Opera America, 2007). Consider the number of singers competing for these 485 opportunities. In the 2007-08 year, according to the NASM, the combined number of sopranos in Bachelor's, Master's, and Doctoral performance degree programs nationwide was 4,820. As for the existing professionals, the sopranos listed in the *Musical America* 2009 directory, which lists professional singers with artist management (the ones most likely to be considered for soprano roles), numbered 860 (Musical America).

Regarding pay, the American Guild of Musical Artists (AGMA) negotiates singers' contracts with companies and publishes these with the agreed minimum salary levels. The minimum levels are probably closest to what the understudies, solo bit roles and chorus members are paid (salaries for leading roles are negotiated and vary widely). The Lyric Opera of Chicago has one of the largest annual budgets of any American opera company. Using examples from their 2007-08 season for weekly pay, understudies earned US$1,960; solo bit roles US$1,428; and chorus members with 0-1 year seniority were paid US$1,190 (AGMA). Productions generally have just three to five weeks of rehearsals. When pay is balanced against US professional opera companies' budgets (from US$100,000 to more than US$200 million), the range of annual budgets is reflected in the range of fees paid to singers. In some cases, pay is supplemented by employer contributions to pension funds or health-care programs. The majority of houses with more modest budgets offer a per-service rate for rehearsals and performances. For example, chorus members for the Boston Lyric Opera in the 2006-2007 season were paid US$146 per performance (AGMA).

Another sought-after career opportunity for music graduates is college-level teaching. The majority of full-time positions require a Doctoral-level degree and prior college teaching experience. Here, too, the market is flooded with qualified applicants: a single full-time opening can easily attract more than 100 qualified candidates. According to the College Music Society, as of 2009 the approximate number of full-time college-level music teaching positions in the US was 17,424 (personal communication, October 2009). To give an idea of how this aligns with position numbers, in 2008 the Career Services Centre at New England Conservatory (NEC) tracked the numbers of full-time US college music teaching opportunities for specific instruments. Taking the example of just two instruments within their study – cello and clarinet – it is possible to see the discrepancy between applicants and positions. NEC found thirteen openings for cello faculty and eleven for clarinettists during 2008. According to the Higher Education Arts Data Service, the total number of cellists enrolled in doctoral programs for 2008 alone was 155, and the total number of clarinettists 138 (NASM, 2009). Vacancies for other instruments are available on the NEC database (NEC, 2009) and they are sobering reading for those planning a college teaching career.

Salaries for college music teaching positions vary widely according to the type of institution and the level of teaching artistry sought. At top conservatoires and music schools, a handful of 'superstar' faculty members earn salaries in excess of US$200,000 (and they may earn more than the presidents of their institutions). In contrast, the more typical college music teaching positions offer starting salaries in the US$30-60 000 range. With part-time positions, adjunct faculty instructors earn hourly rates for private lessons; for class teaching, adjuncts may earn as little as US$2,000 - 4,000 per semester-long course. Although most Doctoral candidates aspire to full-time teaching positions, musicians often enter Doctoral programs with little understanding of the marketplace or the competition they will face for jobs. Unfortunately, many musicians at all degree levels graduate unprepared for the 'real world'.

The size and scope of the US music industry

The good news is that there are far more opportunities than simply the 'traditional' jobs. The US music industry encompasses a wide range of work, a vast number of jobs and enormous revenues. The industry employs roughly 295,000 people in the 'core' music industries, which in the US are defined as performers, ensembles, those working for publishing or record labels, and those doing studio and radio work, music instrument manufacturing and retail. There are another 899,000 people employed in the 'peripheral' music industries such as music schools, recording reproduction companies and those working as agents, promoters and venue managers.

A common theme throughout this volume is that most musicians have multi-layered working lives, often being active in multiple areas of what is termed the 'music industry'. While the phrase 'music industry' may conjure up an image of a well-oiled, organised machine, in fact the industry is a diverse, fluid and often ill-defined ecosystem.

According to 2005 data from the US census 'county business patterns' and the US census 'non-employer statistics', which counts self-employed musicians, the total annual revenue for the music industry includes US$3.1 billion from the core industries and another US$23.5 billion from the peripheral ones (personal communication, 2009). For individual musicians with diversified skills and interests, this means there is a wide range of 'real world' work opportunities: many musicians create careers that combine performance, teaching and work within the music industry where their knowledge and training is an asset.

The changing culture and audience for classical music

Still, the 'real world' today presents particular challenges for classical musicians. In the US, several generations of school children have grown up without in-school music education. And many of the immigrants coming to the US in recent decades have not arrived with a background or interest in western classical music. American newspapers are in decline, and coverage of classical music in the mainstream media is at an all-time low. Classical radio stations are now few and far between, and the recording industry is in free-fall as file sharing and technology have upended traditional record labels, distribution and promotion.

Faced with declining ticket sales and difficulties in raising funds, orchestras have encountered severe financial setbacks and some have gone out of business. As for performing arts series, many that 30 years ago programmed traditional recital and chamber music have now diversified to keep up with community and audience interests. These series now program jazz, world music and dance in attempts to appeal to the changing tastes of US arts consumers, leaving fewer performance opportunities for classical artists. Overall, in America the 'high arts' are generally marginalised, with pop culture the overwhelming dominant force. These factors outline the reasons that classical music as a whole is in transition.

Technology changing the profession

There are, however, bright spots in the professional music landscape. For example, despite dwindling audiences for classical music in general, there has been a renewal of interest in opera. According to the National Endowment for the Arts, opera attendance in the US grew by 35% between 1982 and 1992 and has continued to rise. The growth is due in part to the now widespread use of super-titles in concert halls, which has been a boon to American audiences new to the art form (Opera America, 2007). So technology is changing the profession. Musicians are using it to blur genres, to mix music from different traditions, and to connect with audiences in new ways.

Although traditional forms of distribution and compensation have been disrupted, a great deal of classical music is being downloaded. The same technological advances that have wreaked havoc in the recording industry have been a boon to independent artists and ensembles. Musicians can now afford to build their own fan bases, create their own labels and distribution systems, and promote their live shows and recordings. They are exploring new concert formats and ways to connect with their fans. Musicians and arts organisations are using Facebook, YouTube, Twitter and other social media to form more personal connections with fans (see also Chapters 5 and 8). And these days, audiences want to actively experience the arts. This is clear from the way arts consumers download, sample and explore music from all genres, using technology to connect with musicians, create mash-ups, collages and videos of musicians' works, and crossing genres and disciplines.

What do all these trends signal for today's musicians? Arts audiences have such a huge range of options that musicians have to be extremely entrepreneurial: they need to learn to develop their own fan bases, produce and market their own recordings and create their own professional niches. Above all, musicians must learn how to connect with audiences.

The need for skilled teaching artists

Over the past 15 years, orchestras, opera companies, festivals and concert series have invested in community education programs. These are aimed at helping audiences make a more direct and personal connection with music. For instance, orchestras in the US (as elsewhere) now typically offer pre- and post-concert talks, family concerts and interactive websites to engage audiences of all ages. In addition, soloists and chamber musicians engaged to perform in professional concert series are routinely asked to speak to audiences from the stage, introducing themselves and one or more pieces on the program (see also Chapter 4). This is part of the work that 'teaching artists' are called upon to do.

The term 'teaching artist' defines a relatively new niche and one of growing importance for musicians. Eric Booth, arts consultant and author of *The Music Teaching Artist's Bible* (2009) has defined a teaching artist as a 'practicing professional artist with the complementary skills and sensibilities of an educator, who engages people in learning experiences in, through and about the arts' (personal communication). According to the Association of Teaching Artists website (2010), "The Teaching Artist is an educator who integrates the creative process into the classroom and the community". Teaching artists work in a variety of settings: in primary and secondary schools, hospitals, prisons, shelters, community clubs, retirement homes and museums. As a result, many musicians make a significant portion of their income as teaching artists. The national organisation Young Audiences contracts 5,200 teaching artists (musicians, dancers, and actors) to present educational performances in schools in 33 state chapters in the US. Additionally, state arts agencies (funded by state taxes) often provide funding to subsidise partnerships between public schools and teaching artists. Musicians also independently book their own teaching artist work and create partnerships with community organisations.

The work is challenging and rewarding, and it represents the future as there will be an increasing need for skilled teaching artists. Many opera companies have young artist programs that focus on touring children's operas and other educational community programming. Orchestras offer contract work for players doing chamber music as teaching artists in the communities. The New York Philharmonic, the Philadelphia Orchestra and the San Francisco Symphony all hire outside teaching artist specialists to do this work in addition to involving their own orchestra members.

Teaching artist work can be far more involved and creative than simply introducing a work from the stage in a few sentences. The following is a terrific example of a professional ensemble that has built a community engagement partnership into a residency with a New York City public school.

The Four Nations Ensemble (an early music group with a core instrumentation of harpsichord or fortepiano, violin/s, flute and cello) has had long-term residencies working with inner-city New York schools in the Bronx and Brooklyn. At a presentation for Chamber Music America, Four Nations harpsichordist Andrew Appel described some of their residency project work. His description below comes from a presentation at a Chamber Music America conference in 1995. The passage is also included in Part II (tool 13).

Our approach is to engage students in a project that involves their skills and imagination and helps us, the musicians who are strangers in and unfamiliar with their communities. We ask a group of 9th or 8th graders to work as a marketing agency for our ensemble. (Those taking part have had some introduction to business and run a school store.) Four Nations doesn't know enough about them, their families and friends, and doubts if we can attract an audience to our programs of music. Their job is to get to know our product (classical music), get to understand the market (through surveys and interviews in their school), and develop an advertising campaign for classical chamber music that appeals to the market while remaining truthful to the product (truth in advertising).

There is never any pressure to 'appreciate' the music, only to observe and describe it. At the end of the school year, they present Four Nations in a concert. Tickets are available at the school store. The concert hall is managed by the students with the help of the school staff.

We have regular business meetings during the year to discuss the writing of copy and interpretation of the survey results. Here we can work on verbal, written and math skills. This is an important argument for the viability of the program. Posters, art, and copy are discussed as if we were employees of a major advertising firm. You might imagine that I offer lots of input. But, mostly I try and clear away the thicket of resistance to imagination. Decisions and materials must come from the students so that they can recognize themselves in each final product.

Concurrently, we begin working with other students in all grades, from Kindergarten to year nine. There are regular mini-concerts (15 to 20 this year) at which time we introduce them to the chosen repertoire. Our sessions include performances and then the sharing of responses, from emotional to creative. All the pieces on the 'big' concert program are heard throughout the year. In this way, students enjoy the pleasure of recognition – one of the most important in the appreciation of concert music.

How do musicians acquire the skills to do this work? Teaching artists need to be able to design, plan, and implement thought-provoking and compelling programs to specific age and interest groups. Musicians need guidance in creating appropriate interactive programs for third-graders as well as for adult audiences at senior centres, shelters and hospitals. Most musicians are not natural public speakers. And most musicians who earn performance degrees have very little training in pedagogy. Whether students or professionals, musicians need training, feedback and inspiring models in order to become first-rate teaching artists.

Music schools in America

To put career preparation efforts in context, it may be useful to describe the particulars of American higher education music programs. There are over 600 NASM member institutions nationwide, offering college-level degrees, certificates and diplomas in music performance. These conservatoires, colleges and university programs typically offer Bachelor's and

Master's degrees in music performance; some also offer the Doctor of Musical Arts degree (equivalent to the PhD) and various performance certificates or less academically oriented diplomas.

There are four types of US college-level music schools, as well as excellent schools of each type. Firstly, there are independent private conservatoires of music such as the Curtis Institute, the Manhattan School of Music, the Colburn Conservatory (one of the newest) and the New England Conservatory (one of the oldest). A second type is the music school within a private university, such as the Peabody Institute (of Johns Hopkins University, Baltimore), the Eastman School of Music (part of the University of Rochester, New York) and the Shepherd School of Music (at Rice University, Houston, Texas). A third type is the school of music at a public (state-funded) university, such as the Jacobs School of Music at Indiana University (Bloomington), University of Michigan School of Music, Theatre and Dance (Ann Arbor) and the music department at the State University of New York at Stony Brook. The fourth type comprises *schools of the arts* that offer degrees and training in a range of art disciplines (theatre, dance, visual arts and music), such as the California Institute of the Arts, North Carolina School of the Arts and the University of the Arts in Philadelphia, and the Juilliard School in New York City (where, dance, drama and music are taught).

American music schools attract many talented students from other countries. International students are drawn by the prestige and reputation of particular schools and by the opportunity to study with specific faculty members. The tradition of excellence in US music schools was amplified after World War II when waves of European and Russian musicians fled their home countries to seek refuge and build careers in the US. These immigrants found or created work for themselves in orchestras, opera companies, recording and film studios, as well as by teaching. The new American music entrepreneurs created many more performing arts groups, founded festivals and performing arts series, taught several generations of American musicians and helped build audiences.

Some of the world's most revered music teachers work in the US at American conservatories, and international students comprise 30% or more of the total student body. This shows that international talent has profoundly enriched musical life in America and continues to do so. International musicians who tour the US enhance and enliven concert series, expand imaginations and provide possibilities for inspirational collaborations. This is a gift not only for American audiences and communities, but also for aspiring young music students.

The high price of education

Unfortunately, college education in the US is extremely expensive. Undergraduate programs at private colleges generally cost (with tuition and living expenses) upwards of US$50,000 per year, so a four-year degree can cost US$200,000. To pay for college, US students and their parents must balance family savings and scholarship assistance with part-time student jobs as well as student loans. The national average for undergraduate debt (for all majors) is US$20-30,000, whereas graduate students leave school carrying a US$40-50,000 debt. International students are rarely eligible to borrow money in the US, so their need for scholarships and family support is even greater.

College education is expensive in the US because schools are not primarily funded by the national government, as they are in many other countries. In America, tuition fees vary greatly, depending in part on the type of school in question. *Private institutions* are typically high-tuition schools because they are budget-dependent on tuition, donations and grants. Less expensive *state universities* are funded with state tax revenue, which subsidises their lower tuition fees. However, some private conservatories and universities have substantial scholarship endowment funds to offset tuition. The US music schools offering full scholarship assistance include Curtis, Yale University's graduate program and the Colburn Conservatory. But for many musicians, the crucial deciding factor in their choice of schools is not the price tag but the studio instructor; musicians are often willing to go into serious debt in order to study with a particular musician.

The high cost of American music education makes more sense when viewed in the context of the country's arts economy. In America, unlike many other countries, the federal government does not primarily support the arts and social service sectors. Instead, most US arts institutions (orchestras, opera companies, and music schools) are designated as 'non-profit' (or 'not-for-profit') organisations. This designation is a tax-exempt status for those arts, social and religious organisations whose core mission is to serve or improve society. The tax-exempt status allows these entities to supplement their earned income (from ticket sales or tuition fees) with charitable donations in order to raise the necessary funds for their work. Non-profit organisations compete for funds from individual donors as well as from corporate, community and public foundations. Just as performing arts organisations' earned revenue from ticket sales only covers a third of their budgets, tuition at music schools typically covers only a fraction of the total cost. Arts organisations must raise substantial sums of money each year in order to operate and remain viable and competitive.

The music curriculum

US music schools today offer a much wider variety of degrees and coursework than was available 20 years ago: degrees are offered in music performance and education, and many schools offer music business/industry, recording engineering and production, music therapy and arts administration degrees. Schools offer training in classical, jazz and many other genres. Some schools also have specialised certificate programs available, either as stand-alone curricula or as programs that can be completed in conjunction with another degree. Examples of specialised certificate programs include the Eastman School of Music's arts leadership Program, Manhattan School of Music's graduate orchestral studies degree program, and the music-in-education concentration at New England Conservatory. Despite all these changes, the core curriculum for US undergraduate music performance degrees has essentially remained the same over the past 100 years.

The original model, based on European conservatoires, was the three-legged stool of performance, music theory and music history. The heart of a music performance program is, understandably, performance studies. Studio lessons, large and small ensembles, rehearsals and concerts are the primary focus for music students. The undergraduate curriculum generally includes two years of theory study using the very same ear training, solfège and species counterpoint taught to past generations. Music history is also typically taught in two years, by dividing the history of western classical music into four semester-long segments and using a combination of lectures, listening recognition ('name that tune'), exams and written papers. The rest of the curriculum comprises electives and liberal arts requirements such as Science, Mathematics, and English courses. These requirements can vary greatly at different institutions. As US schools grapple with how best to prepare musicians for tomorrow's careers, many schools are offering (usually as electives) courses and programs in world music, improvisation, music technology and career development. Booth (2009, p. 21) reflects that

> ... the technical training of musicians in conservatoires and university programs is at the highest level ever ... [however] the weakness is that the students, the world and the professional field are changing faster than the training programs. This creates a tension between the skills being prioritized and those needed to live a full, rewarding life in music.

Beyond performance, other necessary skills are numerous. Included below is a list of those skills and traits (attributes) typically found in successful musicians. These make useful discussion points with students and are further explored in Chapter 5 (Bennett).

- Initiative
- Resilience
- Perseverance
- Optimism
- Interpersonal skills
- Creative problem-solving
- Organisational skills
- Planning skills
- Ability to see opportunities and obstacles
- Ability to give and receive constructive criticism
- Knowledge of one's strengths and shortcomings

Not every successful musician possesses all these strengths, but successful musicians typically possess many of them and then often collaborate with others who can supply the missing ingredients. Successful musicians learn both how to compensate for what they lack and how to capitalise on their strengths. The good news is that musicians can develop these abilities by pursuing self-directed projects. And most music careers are, in fact, built project by project. A related discussion along with activities on building skills and attributes is included in Part II.

Claire Chase, flautist/co-founder of the successful ensemble ICE (International Contemporary Ensemble), sums up the experience of being a musician-entrepreneur:

> *Our generation of young musicians, despite the economic challenges that we face, is experiencing an unprecedented freedom. We can do anything we want to do. We can produce our own concerts, release our own albums, create our own communities and our own movements, and we don't need a lot of money to do this. We just need great ideas, we need a spirit of adventure, and we need each other (thick skin is good to have, too)*
> (Orchestra Musician Forum, 2008). See Part II, tool 19 for discussion.

Claire is a terrific spokesperson for the next wave of musicians and the opportunities available. Still, not every musician is so well prepared and able to take on entrepreneurial projects. The question, then, becomes how music schools best prepare musicians for the profession and what kinds of professional learning programs work best.

Career development programs

American music schools have been using a variety of ways to address changes in the industry, in part because of increased student and parent demand for more targeted career assistance. Because of the packed requirements of the undergraduate music performance degree, career preparation coursework is generally included as electives, certificate options or, where possible, inserted into other existing courses as pet projects by inspired faculty. At the undergraduate level, US schools offer a range of career preparation assistance that may include:

- Music career development courses (required or elective)
- Career workshops/seminars
- Career advising
- Alumni networking/mentoring
- Music technology seminars
- Entrepreneurial project assistance (mentoring and seed money for projects)
- Pedagogy courses and mentored teaching experience
- Community/audience engagement projects
- Community service requirements
- Internships

More and more US music schools are offering career development workshops, courses and services. Many music schools in the US have hired specialised faculty to teach, and staff to manage, these offices. Career development programs are aimed at connecting students with career options and assistance. This ranges from goal setting and job searches to self-promotion, grant writing and performing in the community. But music students look for guidance, feedback and role models throughout their education. In casual conversations, master classes and rehearsals, there are countless opportunities for all faculty and staff to help, whether or not there is formalised career development. The essential career development assistance that musicians need means encouraging them to:

- Explore opportunities across the music industry
- Articulate their career goals and project ideas
- Assess their strengths and weaknesses
- Plan and follow through on action steps to move forward toward their career goals

The transitioning tools in Part II, together with the series of challenges at the end of this chapter, are excellent examples of how these discussions can begin.

Entrepreneurship training

Entrepreneurship has been a staple of US college business degree programs for more than ten years and it is now finally reaching music degree programs. There are already many music business and industry degree programs in the US offering entrepreneurship-related coursework. More recent is the inclusion of entrepreneurial courses and workshops within music *performance* degree programs. For example, the University of Michigan supports the student-initiated Arts Enterprise Club, a collaborative project between the School of Business and the School of Music, Theatre and Dance. This project has inspired Arts Enterprise chapters at Bowling Green State, University of Wisconsin Madison and others. There is also entrepreneur programming supported by the Kauffman Foundation at Eastman and Oberlin. The University of Colorado, Boulder, houses the Music Entrepreneurship Center, and there are newer entrepreneurship initiatives at Indiana University, the University of South Carolina, Manhattan School of Music and New England Conservatory. Links to these projects are included at the end of this chapter. Music entrepreneurship training often includes:

- Overviews of the music industry
- Case studies of music ventures
- Social entrepreneurial projects (projects to benefit communities)
- Feasibility studies
- Business plan creation
- Group projects
- Traditional music career development coursework such as:
    - Creating promotion and marketing materials
    - Interviews with alumni/music entrepreneurs
    - Case studies in audience development
    - Fundraising
    - Grant writing; and
    - Developing and delivering project presentations

Conclusion

There are far too many talented, experienced and deserving musicians for the number of traditional full-time competitive performance and teaching jobs. Consequently, musicians need to cultivate *more* than just performance skills. Because of changes in audiences and culture, musicians need to be able to communicate well with audiences as well as to design and implement interactive performance programs. Further, musicians need entrepreneurial skills and abilities in order to create opportunities for themselves and create their own career paths.

Advice for young artists (do's and don'ts)

Don't:

- Rely solely on opportunities your teacher or school provide
- Pin all your hopes on winning competitions, finding artist management, or landing a full-time orchestra position or university teaching job. There are many other ways to create success in music
- Rely on the advice of just one teacher or advisor. Instead, get a range of opinions;
- Study or perform only traditional, standard repertoire
- Imagine that success is determined only by how many hours you practice

Instead, *Do:*

- Search for opportunities: take auditions and apply for programs, festivals, grants, fellowships
- Find a mentor(s) with whom you can discuss practical career issues and projects
- Work as an intern with an arts organisation to learn about the business side of a career
- Develop teaching artist skills and get involved in audience and community engagement projects
- Explore how technology can help your career: create a website or MySpace musician profile, or use another social networking tool
- Find a project to commit to, and get going on it

References

Beeching, A. (2010). Beyond talent: Creating a successful career in music. 2nd ed., New York: Oxford University Press.

Booth, E. (2009). *The music teaching artist's bible: Becoming a virtuoso educator.* NY: Oxford University Press.

National Association of Music (NASM). (2009). *Higher education data service* report (Data Summaries, 2008-2009).

New England Conservatory. (2009). Bridge: Worldwide Music Connection online database of opportunities. Retrieved Oct. 28, 2009, from http://www.necmusic.edu/career.

Further reading and information

American Guild of Musical Artists (AGMA): http://www.musical-artists.org/agreements_opera.html, 2009.

Arizona Commission on the Arts (Eric Booth): http://www.azarts.gov/artists/teachingartists.htm.

Arts Enterprise Club: http://www.artsenterprisemi.com.

Boston Modern Orchestra Project (BMOP): http://www.BMOP.org.

Careers Forum, Rice University Shepherd School of Music: http://music-careers.rice.edu, 2007.

Community MusicWorks: http://www.communitymusicworks.org.

El Sistema music lessons and youth orchestra experiences in the neediest neighbourhoods of Los Angeles: http://www.fesnojiv.org, and http://www.grammy.com/blogs/educationwatch-dudamels-discoveries-benefit-el-sistema.

Entrepreneurs in Music, featuring the writing of Claire Chase: http://www.polyphonic.org.

The Four Nations Ensemble: http://www.fournations.org.

International Conference of Symphonic and Operatic Musicians (ICSOM), affiliated website: http://www.orchestrafacts.org.

Intermezzo Chamber Opera: http://www.intermezzo-opera.org.

Musical America: www.MusicalAmerica.com.

New Gallery Concert Series: http://www.newgalleryconcertseries.org.

Opera America: Quick Opera Facts, http://www.OperaAm.org, 2007.

Oxingale Records: http://www.oxingale.com.

The Association of Teaching Artists: http://www.teachingartists.com/whatisaTA.htm.

The Orchestra Musician Forum, Virtual Discussion Panel: "Entrepreneurs in Music" http://www.polyphonic.org (Mar. 24-April 4, 2008).

Young Audiences: http://www.YoungAudiences.org.

Chapter 4
Composed and Improvised

The Transition to Professional Life

Janis Weller

'The real art of conducting consists in transitions'. Gustav Mahler

Whether conducting an orchestra or conducting one's life, transitions can be significant challenges as well as highly rewarding opportunities. Learning to recognise and negotiate career transitions requires a conscious awareness of skills and strategies that can maximise possibilities as well as smooth the bumps along the way. While there are stellar examples of music colleges that thoughtfully prepare their students for the transition into a professional career, many music graduates enter this exciting and critical time of life largely by playing it by ear (no pun intended) and hoping for the best.

This chapter addresses several transition issues for young musicians and suggests ideas for approaching these topics within higher education institutions. The chapter first frames the evolving nature of musicians' work and its connections to 21st century cultural shifts (as described throughout this book) in relation to the changing nature of life stages, particularly the increasingly vague notion of reaching 'adulthood' in 21st century western societies. According to Burland and Davidson (2002, p. 123), the transition from higher education into the work-world and, by extension, into adulthood as it is traditionally understood, "is considered the most significant of the life-span changes". Recently, a new life stage called 'emerging adulthood' has been proposed. Emerging adulthood, a time between the traditional life stages of adolescence and young adulthood, spans the college years and the transition into professional life. The chapter will provide perspective on this 'significant and stressful' time of change for aspiring young artists.

The second part of the chapter analyses the professional transition of one young musician, Allan, using Baxter Magolda's theory of self-authorship. Drawing on a term first coined by Kegan in 1994, Baxter Magolda (2004, p. 8) defines self-authorship as the "capacity to internally define a coherent belief system and identity that coordinates mutual relations with others". Allan's experiences demonstrate a growing self-confidence that successfully balances his academic training (what I call the 'composed' elements of his evolving career) with his ambition, people skills and ability to assess musical as well as professional risks (the more 'improvised' elements of his work). Self-authorship and the concept of emerging adulthood will offer two related lenses for examining the young musician's transition to professional life.

The chapter concludes with some practical approaches for integrating career and school-to-work transition ideas and strategies into an existing music school culture. While an increasing number of music schools are designing career-oriented courses, diversifying their career centres and even establishing institutes for entrepreneurship (see Chapter 3), the majority of music colleges in the United States continue to train young musicians using primarily traditional curricula, values and expectations (Cutler, 2009). The challenges of altering or adjusting those time-honoured traditions may be financial, curricular, political, personal or institutional. But even in the most traditional environments, educators with an interest in assisting their students with career issues can still provide meaningful counsel and opportunities. Particularly when the curriculum and the budget cannot accommodate career-specific courses or other professionally focused offerings, strategies must be developed to consciously engage soon-to-be-alumni in career reflection and skill building.

Transition is the psychological process people go through to come to terms with the new situation. Change is external, transition is internal (Bridges, pp. 3-4).

Of the many large and small transitions made throughout a lifetime, few are as profound or have a larger impact on an individual than the graduation from higher education. Eagerly anticipated and sometimes also dreaded for its open-endedness, preparing to leave school is exciting for many students and overwhelming for others. After almost a lifetime with the self-identity of 'student', these young graduates transition into the so-called 'real world' and are expected to function effectively on personal, professional and social levels, often with little specific guidance.

One marker of the traditional notion of adulthood is employment within a chosen field. This is often a persistent expectation even among today's music students as they approach graduation, in spite of overwhelming evidence that substantive performance 'jobs' *per se* are in very short supply. The do-it-yourself nature of many, if not most, musicians' careers presents a dichotomy between expectations and reality. As Beeching illustrates in Chapter 3, with the current recessionary economic climate this situation has been exacerbated. For traditional organisations such as symphony orchestras and opera companies, which are struggling financially, an already tight audition market has become more difficult. Graduates in many disciplines are unable to find enough entry-level work to support themselves: "Among 2009 US college graduates, 80 percent moved back home with their parents after graduation, up from 77 percent in 2008, 73 percent in 2007, and 67 percent in 2006" (collegegrad.com, 2009). These are disturbing numbers across the general population that reflect a significant shift in the process of transition to independence in traditional-aged college graduates.

However, young musicians who possess musical artistry as well as discerning non-musical skills may have a slight edge in the employment arena. As described in Chapter 1, the reality of a portfolio career is not only the model for today's young musicians but has also been the pervasive norm for musicians throughout history and across many cultures. For the savvy young musician, opportunities to begin building an entrepreneurial career have never been better, and may even provide advantages in the new economic climate within which they are required to operate.

Adulthood redefined

The term 'adult', or even the idea of a time of life called 'adulthood', is a relatively recent concept not commonly used until the late 19th century (Gillis, 2008; Hunter, 2009). In western societies we tend to assume that the lifespan of an individual is a progressive, continuous process from one stage to the next: infancy, childhood, adolescence, adulthood and, finally, old age. An individual is presumed to march dutifully from one stage of life to the next, not always smoothly or clearly, but generally in a linear progression. But this is an early modern view, further developed within the emerging field of psychology in the late 19th and early 20th centuries – with the theories of Erik Erickson, Sigmund Freud, Carl Jung and others. While useful and largely appropriate for much of life in the 20th century, dramatic changes to personal, social and work lives in the 21st century mean that these tidy divisions are becoming inadequate to describe the human lifecycle. For musicians and other creative individuals, the divisions may be even less appropriate.

In order to provide some context for a discussion of the transitions to adulthood, it is useful to look briefly at perspectives on the life span in pre-modern life. For most of human history (especially as recorded in the west), an individual's life account was based more on his or her place in society than on the individual's particular age. That is, an individual's chronological age (measured in horizontal time from birth) was largely unimportant until after the Industrial Revolution. Instead, one's suitability for a given role was determined by social station in life (a vertical measurement) as well as the ability to successfully accomplish a task or job (Gillis, 2008). For instance, if an individual was able to successfully accomplish the job of a soldier, it did not matter if the individual was twelve, 20 or 40 years old. Similarly, Hunter (2009, p. 2) explains that in the medieval church, the age of reason and accountability was the tender age of seven. The attainment of the ability to tell right from wrong essentially determined an adulthood of sorts. From medieval times to the modern era, marked roughly by the French and American Revolutions and the beginnings of the Industrial Revolution in the late eighteenth century, life was tenuous and often short, with high mortality rates at all ages but especially in childhood. Formal education did not have distinct economic consequences at the time, so it was limited to a small number of elites.

Since social status was more important than age *per se*, appropriate to their rank everyone was expected to contribute actively to the household. With the rise of industrialisation and the resulting wage-based surplus economy, there began a dramatic social shift that led to a more linear, developmental worldview, a 'chronologisation' of society (in Gillis, 2008). Birth and death rates improved such that a more linear progression of life evolved into distinct stages that centred on family and work. Mandatory schooling followed. Rituals began to mark developmental stages more distinctly, and ultimately a shift to a time-of-life, age-based level of maturity—adulthood—emerged.

> *The loss of social consensus over the meaning of adulthood means that the very category of adulthood has become opaque* (Hunter, 2009, p. 9).

What does all this have to do with young musicians entering professional life in the twenty-first century? Particularly since the end of World War II and the GI Bill that followed, strongly time-based, linear societies such as those in the US typically present distinct career tracks that start with formal education, followed perhaps by an internship and then an entry-level job with a clear ladder for advancement. By the end of the first decade of the twenty-first century, fragmenting of traditional career trajectories is significant in many professions. Factors such as global economic instability, the off-shoring and on-shoring of workers and, in many fields, profound global interconnections, have blurred the cultural and social makeup of the workforce.

Whilst this broadly general model has certainly expanded and continues to evolve, young musicians have always launched and sustained careers that are not necessarily linear or driven by age, culture or geography. Many receive formal training through higher education. But with a curious similarity to pre-modern times, the music sector has always noticed and rewarded those who are ready to perform, regardless of their chronological age or level of education. Whether it is Mozart, Michael Jackson or the latest young violin prodigy, the field (and the market) recognises musical talent and stage charisma. At the end of a long musical career, concert pianist Alfred Brendel gave a stunning series of concerts on his 'final' tours at age 76; and guitar legend Les Paul had a popular weekly gig in a New York jazz club right up until his death at age 94. Clearly, while many musicians' careers change and evolve over time, musicians are not necessarily limited (or driven) by the passage of time or steps on the advancement ladder, as is often true in more traditional careers such as banking, medicine or law.

In the early years of the 21st century, many authors and researchers have been grappling with these shifts in lifespan stages, recognising that the transition to adulthood in the traditional sense seems to be changing significantly. Whether termed 'emerging adulthood' (Arnett, 2004), 'quarterlife crisis' (Robbins & Wilner, 2001; Wilner & Stocker, 2005; Vanrenen, 2007) or even such odd mash-ups as 'adultolescence or kidults' (Hunter, 2009), the postponing of traditional 'adult' roles is pervasive in western societies. Labelling such as this significantly affects both personal and societal perceptions and expectations of transitions to career and life after formal education is completed.

'Emerging adults', a term first coined by Arnett (2000), proposes a new developmental stage in the life span of individuals in western cultures, roughly from the age of eighteen through to the late twenties. Earlier in life, individuals in adolescence share common situational characteristics: for instance, most live with parents and attend high school. Traditionally, young adulthood follows adolescence and is classically defined as taking on so-called adult responsibilities such as full-time work, marriage, home buying and starting a family (Arnett, 2004). Arnett's extensive research of young American people within varying socio-cultural and socio-economic groups indicates that emerging adulthood is a much more widespread phenomenon than the traditionally understood move from adolescence directly to young adult.

Having left the dependency of childhood and adolescence, and having not yet entered the enduring responsibilities that are normative in adulthood, emerging adults often explore a variety of possible life directions in love, work, and worldviews. (Arnett, 2000, p. 469)

Arnett (2004) maintains that emerging adulthood is not merely a time of transition to adulthood itself, but rather a distinct period of identity exploration and instability that is highly self-focused and transitory, yet full of hope and possibilities. Rather than primarily a time of angst and transition (Robbins & Wilner, 2001), emerging adulthood also seems to provide opportunities for the exploration of self and the world with an openness to possibilities not yet jaded by experience. The next section builds upon these rich elements of emerging adulthood through the concept of achieving 'self-authorship'. In order to demonstrate its importance as an activity sustaining a music performance career, I share and examine Allan's story.

Self-authorship and Allan's story

Composed and improvised: Two sides of the same coin

It's a weird thing. You not only have to be a good musician, but you also have to be a person that's easy to work with and responsible, and then you also have to have this fun, creative side that sets you apart from the other people. And then you have to be a smart business person, and then you have to be really lucky to get the good gigs. (Allan, personal communication)

Spontaneously and in a nutshell, Allan ticks off a remarkably insightful and thorough list of attributes and situations that could help launch and sustain a music performance career. After graduating with a Bachelor of Music degree in bass performance, Allan was only two years into his professional career. How did he gain such savvy in such a short time? Allan's journey toward self-authorship can be described as "a coherent belief system and identity" that marks a mature relationship with one's self and with the larger world (Baxter Magolda, 2004, p. 8).

During my interviews with young performing musicians, two primary sub-themes pertaining to both artistic growth and career development emerged. Simply put, some components of life, art and career (such as formal education and temperament) are less flexible and more regulated throughout our lives. As individuals, we are often guided by our innate characteristics and temperament and by the structures provided by others, notably the educational systems we travel through. It can be handy to think of these factors as 'composed' parts of our lives. However, other elements including luck, opportunity and risk have strong aspects of chance and highly flexible elements that can be seen as the more 'improvised' parts of life. While seemingly opposites, these themes are also closely interrelated and can help provide a framework for connections and transitions between formal education and professional life.

In the following section, Baxter Magolda's (2004) theory of self-authorship is used to analyse first the improvisatory theme and, second, the composed theme, using the lens of self-authorship to look at Allan's artistic growth as well as his career development. For Allan, purely artistic considerations and those relating specifically to career were for him tightly interwoven. The analysis is thus integrated, much as Allan does in his own life.

Self-Authorship

Baxter Magolda (2004, p. xxii) defines self-authorship as

> ... the capacity to internally define a coherent belief system and identity that coordinates engagement in mutual relations with the larger world. This internal foundation yields the capacity to actively listen to multiple perspectives, critically interpret those perspectives in light of relevant evidence and the internal foundation, and make judgments accordingly.

This description beautifully portrays, in academic terms, the artistic process of a performing musician. In building 'a coherent belief system' based on a historical foundation and vocabulary of musical skills and awareness (the 'composed' elements), performing musicians develop an internally defined musical identity "that coordinates engagement in mutual relations" with other players (some of the 'improvised' elements), whether in a symphony orchestra, a jazz combo, or any other musical group (Baxter Magolda, 2004, p. xxii). Listening critically as well as responding to an ever-changing reality in the moment of performance, musicians must be intimately connected to both their internal musical identities and those of colleagues. Whilst simultaneously staying connected to their own musical identities, in running a successful professional as well as a musical life, musicians apply these same principles by responding to the rapidly evolving marketplace of the music sector.

Two years into his post-college professional career, Allan blends the composed and improvised, educational and experiential, artistic and professional business of a musician's work:

> *When you're a student you're studying what everyone has done before you and what something's supposed to sound like or what the rules are. And then once you become a professional, if all you do is sound like the people before you or follow all the rules, you're not going to be that desirable a musician. The second you cross over that line of following your teacher's instructions and stuff, it's almost developing who you are and adding your own characteristic to music and making sure it's something like ... if you don't have any character, anything that makes you unique or you, you're not gunna get called for anything.*

Along with the necessity of developing a unique and individual style, Allan recognises the links between a strong musical foundation that encompasses a variety of core musical skills, and an essential awareness and connection to the artists that came before as well as the musical styles they performed. In this brief explanation, Allan sums up an important balance between the 'composed' parts of a musician's training and work, and the 'improvised' elements that begin to set one apart as an independent artist. The result of this balance defines the player's musical self-authorship and in the process elevates both the artistic product and, ultimately, the player's employability as a unique and interesting musical artist. Self-authorship also provides a foundation for tapping into the improvisatory elements of a musician's work.

Career development improvisation: Luck, opportunity, risk and confidence

An improvisatory career development cycle, which can be imagined as a variable spiral of potentially escalating possibilities, helps musicians create and recognise so-called lucky moments and opportunities (see also Chapter 8). Willingness and eagerness to embrace artistic and personal risks that result from 'luck' and opportunities is a first step. At the early career stages, where success is somewhat relative and self-defined, the budding professional creates, or takes advantage of, opportunities to develop confidence. As confidence increases, the player builds his or her self-assurance to try again. This then escalates the cycle, ideally by gradually accepting bigger risks with higher stakes. Allan says:

> *The luck thing comes down to being in the right place at the right time, essentially ... I got a really amazing experience when I got to play with Cliff, Bobby, Dave and some other amazing players. That was a huge great experience that taught me a lot, because it was one of the tougher gigs I've ever been on because those guys are just like old and wise and smokin' and I was just in over my head. I kept up, but it was still definitely an experience that taught me a lot and I was just happy to be able to do that. But I got that merely on the fact that I picked up the phone down in the receptionist's office, and it was Jay calling to get a hold of Terry. And he couldn't get a hold of Terry, and when I picked the phone back up and said, 'do you want Terry's voice mail?' He said, 'Nooo, I'm just trying to find somebody to sub for me for this show,' and I was like, 'I can do it.' And then he just gave it to me.*

Even at an early stage in his career, Allan's developing self-authorship allows him to assess lucky opportunities and the risks they may entail. With growing confidence, Allan not only embraces artistic risks but also can evaluate his performance and measure the benefit-to-risk variable, helping to appropriately prepare him for subsequent opportunities that test his musical expertise. With increasing confidence, Allan can apply both his formal training and his growing 'street-smarts' gained through on-the-job experiences, to the challenges he encounters in his developing professional career.

Career development composition: Standing on the shoulders of giants

Musicians in all styles and genres need vast knowledge and skills built on historical models and theoretical underpinnings. For many musicians, this knowledge and skill base is acquired through many years of formal study and practice, including recognised training and degree programs and/or ongoing mentoring relationships. Allan clearly incorporates a strong foundation in the composed theme in addition to his proclivity toward the improvisational: *"There are some standard ... idiomatic styles, or just certain licks that are ways to play something and if I hear the groove I can know this guy would've played it like this. You have a foundation".* The intrapersonal element of developing a personal musical voice has an important role, even in the composed world of education and training. One needs the knowledge and a skill base in order to let go and develop a personal contribution, regardless of performance medium, style or genre.

In order to more fully understand self-authorship, the next section analyses each of the three primary components of self-authorship—epistemological foundations, intrapersonal foundations, and interpersonal foundations—using the framework of Allan's early career experiences. These three foundations are central to musicians' development as viable artistic and career-oriented professionals. And all three factors must come together in developing a mature self-authorship. By these measures, Allan already seems well on his way.

Know thy stuff: The epistemological foundation

Musicians must "view knowledge as contextual" (Baxter Magolda, 2004, p. 8) and must integrate both foundational and contextual knowledge and skills in performance. Am I playing Mozart or Mahler? Classic rock or hip-hop? Jazz or funk? This requires core skills and knowledge as well as a sophisticated understanding of each genre or style. As Allan says: *"You have to have like these specific things that you learned and you have them memorised so well that you don't have to worry about it"*. But later he acknowledges that this alone is not enough:

> *You get this instinct every once in a while, when you're playing, when you wanna play some cool lick or you want to add something to the song... and if you hesitate for a second on that, you will miss the chance to add it to the song, and then you're not doing you, your band, or the music any justice ... you have to trust it and just go with. I've never once had it fail me. Trust it, because it's always right. Especially when there aren't any rules you have to follow any more, it will always be right because that instinct is you, and that's how you think the song will sound. Once I learned to follow that instinct I guess, that was kinda where I started. That was a turning point for me.*

Here, Allan blends his epistemological (composed) knowledge base with the potential excitement of a musically risky (improvised) moment in order to create something new and artistically satisfying. Whether in a string quartet or jazz combo, this ability to take 'book learning' and meld it in the moment with artistic risk, combines the composed and improvised themes and blends the epistemological foundation with the second element: the intrapersonal foundation.

Know thy self: The intrapersonal foundation

The intrapersonal foundation is a way to "choose (one's) own values and identity in crafting an internally generated sense of self that regulates interpretation of experience and choices" (Baxter Magolda, 2004, p. 8). For a performing musical artist, the development of an original and unique musical voice is one way the intrapersonal foundation can be directly translated. It is not sufficient to merely mimic other players or rely simply on impressive technical facility. True artists also have a distinctive voice that well grounded in technique, skill and knowledge, but unique to each individual. For Allan, the opportunity to express himself more personally was an important positive direction after graduation: "*I noticed that I didn't have my instructors there to tell me what I was doing was wrong. All of a sudden I was allowed this ability to play what I felt was right and nobody could tell me otherwise ... that's when I started getting more creative with my playing*". Significantly, he also said:

> I believe that everyone has a voice, and it just depends what you do with it. ... I've been successful if I've shared my voice with enough people to have even in the slightest way added to the music industry or music as a general thing ... what do I have that I can bring to the table that can make me, you know, not better than the rest, but able to shine with the rest?

Allan grounds the development of his original voice closely with his epistemological knowledge by recognising the importance of both. Interrelated as he crafts his career, both of these foundations are dependent on the professional relationships of the third foundation: the interpersonal.

Know thy people: The interpersonal foundation

A lot of my instructors ... they gave me a lot of professional advice ... like I had questions about what should I do, how should I poke my head into this world? ... and they just gave me lots of advice ... They even like, gave me gigs before, like they couldn't do it and they'd call me up. And that was a great help too, 'cause that's like getting your foot in the door that you normally wouldn't have ever gotten.

The third developmental foundation of self-authorship focuses on the role of interpersonal relationships. For Baxter Magolda (2004, p. 8) this foundation is more than 'people skills'. In describing the interpersonal foundation of mature, self-authored relationships, she emphasises that authentic and respectful interdependent interaction allows the individual to "take others' perspectives into account without being consumed by them", another critically important skill for musicians. In today's entrepreneurial world of a professional life in music, who you know and who knows you is a vital centrepiece to career launching and career sustaining.

I talked to my high school band director [and asked] what it's like, because you know, that's what you did. And he told me it was probably going to be one of the hardest things you'll ever do in your life ... and I agree, it's been pretty difficult, but he was really nice about it too.

Allan frequently emphasises the central importance of interpersonal skills:

> That's one thing that people don't think ... they need as a musician, is the ability to mesh well with others ... if you don't mesh well with the other people, then you're not going to keep the job ... I think a lot of musicians just don't seem to get that. They have some like serious attitudes when they get a big gig and then they just get fired because no one wants to work with them if you're acting like that.

Even before he graduated, Allan's eagerness to seek out mentors and ask them about professional life helped him create musical and personal/professional relationships that led directly to professional opportunities. Allan is observant and savvy and quick to adapt personally as well as musically, again illustrating his developing self-authorship and professional improvisatory career skills. Along with an easy-going adaptability to interpersonal situations, his confidence and openness build upon his composed foundation of formal educational relationships to serve him well in the early stages of his career.

Self-authorship is an exciting concept for examining and clarifying individual growth, identity and development. In this section, I have explored some of its applicability as a model for both artistic growth and career development in a young professional musician. The various facets of the composed and improvised themes combine with the three elements that make up mature self-authorship to create a complex, interwoven web of connections that come together to support and create both the transition from school to career and the potential sustainability of that evolving career.

Practical suggestions for educators and career guides

Our music curriculum is very full of required courses. How can we offer career training too? Isn't it our job to prepare students musically and then they're on their own? Won't the truly talented and motivated do just fine? (Faculty comments, unpublished)

While some conservatoires and music colleges have embraced a commitment to providing career training and support for their students, those schools are still in the minority. As Cutler writes (2009, n. p), music schools that address careers directly "... show a commitment to producing *working artists*, as opposed to simply outstanding ones" who are likely to be unprepared to deal with professional realities of the 21st century. Cutler's perspective expresses a significant opportunity in the ways higher education could approach the art, craft and business of music.

Core musical, educational and curricular traditions and values are not easily altered in higher education, and many in the field would argue they should not change. Discussions become heated, missions and outcomes are debated, and budgets and credit hours are considered. The dilemma is how educators and career guides who believe in the importance of career preparation can support and prepare their students for a successful transition into the professional music world without making any huge adjustments to time or to financial resources. The following section offers strategies found from personal experience to be highly effective in this regard.

Professionalism

We can recognise, model, train, practice and reward universal attributes that will help graduates succeed in life, regardless of their career or personal goals. This can be achieved by encouraging and expecting self-responsibility and personal accountability: the foundational attributes of professionalism. The inherent tasks and challenges of majoring in music help students develop a strong work ethic (for example, extensive individual daily practice and study) with follow-through and task completion (public performance, publication etc.), all of which encourage striving for excellence. Overt connections to the transferability of these music-related skills to taking-care-of-business are not necessarily a given. And educators can both identify and expect a growing ability in students to make these connections.

Starting at a very young age, music students have extensive experience with interpersonal communication and collaboration. Music is, after all, the ultimate team sport. Again, music students may not make connections to the ways these skills can support and drive their budding careers without specific observations from educators, teachers and mentors. Highly developed skills and habits fostered in the formal study of music are often generalisable traits that are very useful in adult life. These broad aspects of 'professional behaviour' and work readiness are, similarly, attributes of successful musicians in the musical sides of their lives. They are necessary traits for achieving the level of accomplishment that graduating music students have attained. We can help students recognise that these are also transferrable skills, vital for successfully building and expanding the business side of a career as well as the musical elements.

A recent study by The Centre for Professional Excellence, reported in the online journal *Inside Higher Ed* (Moltz, October 23, 2009), interviewed human resource professionals and business leaders about the need for professionalism in the workplace. Among the most important attributes noted were:

- Accepts personal responsibility for decision and actions;
- Is able to act independently; and
- Has a clear sense of direction and purpose.

The study noted the need for colleges to put a particular focus on imparting these traits to their students. In the DIY world of entrepreneurial musicians, these expectations are central to success and career sustainability. Yet this work ethic may not be self-evident to 'emerging adult' musicians accustomed to structured learning environments where teachers determine precise requirements, due dates and grading rubrics.

The following section considers practical strategies for encouraging student growth in these areas without formally expanding the curriculum.

Integrating communication

Music students are often single-minded in their pursuit of musical excellence. While this is an important characteristic for fully developing an artist's potential, it can also lead students to discount the value of studies and activities perceived as not directly related to winning the next audition. As Bennett states in Chapter 5, the "ability and confidence to communicate effectively" using both written and verbal skills is "imperative to a musician's practice, whether in a performance or teaching role or in running a freelance business". Clarity of thought and writing, and an articulate speaking style, pay dividends throughout a career. Here are a few ideas for integrating high communications standards into music studies:

- Reinforce the importance of these skills through personal examples, artist stories and relevant assignments;
- Require well-written bios and program notes for student recital programs;
- Set expectations for professional, respectful email correspondence (no text-ese, profanity or sloppy grammar);
- Provide opportunities for students to practice oral presentation in class and in performances. Many presenters and concert venues expect a casual performance style. Audiences enjoy hearing a few words from an artist during a performance, especially when remarks are delivered with style, panache and humour;
- Encourage the prompt return of phone calls, emails and other correspondence. In a crowded and competitive field, an eager, quick response will attract attention; and
- Encourage students to make professional use of the vast communication potential of Internet-based new media. This may require an attitude adjustment away from the purely social uses of new media (more on this below).

Senior recitals and other concerts

In addition to the musical preparations, expect students to fully produce their recital. From securing dates, equipment and personnel to promotion, programs and hospitality, students will gain skills in the full performance experience and responsibilities they will encounter once they are on their own. Learning to balance the challenges of musical and administrative preparation and planning is essential for the day-to-day real world even if students are fortunate enough to have management. In addition, 'service learning' performances such as those in the local community, especially for underserved populations in schools, senior centres, hospitals, hospices and rehabilitation facilities, not only provide independent performance opportunities with musical and production requirements, but also connect students with the powerful role that music can play in the lives of individuals and community.

Teaching

Interested students can be encouraged to build a small private teaching practice while still in higher education as well as to explore their interest in teaching. Ideally, a course or two in pedagogy should support this venture. A student-run organisation or club can meet together with a faculty advisor to discuss challenges and opportunities of both the pedagogic and business elements of studio teaching. Students' studio instructors can also be good networking resources.

Networking and Participation

Networking and participation feature throughout this book because building strong professional and personal contacts is a central element of creating a successful career (see for instance Chapter 8). However, networking requires particular skills and there are a number of things that can encourage students to take some risks and experience new people and contexts. For instance, students can:

- Be active participants in their music school, not exclusively holed up in a practice room day and night;
- Attend concerts on and off campus and perhaps volunteer to work backstage or host a reception at performances;
- 'Shadow' a teacher for a day to better understand his/her life in and out of school;
- Join professional organisations – an excellent way to build contacts;
- Make an effort to meet faculty they do not yet know, forming new contacts for their future careers and practising their communication skills. Taking a walk around campus or having a cup of coffee together are simple ways students can initiate and connect with faculty in non-academic settings before graduation; and
- Set up a system that works for them to keep track of contacts. In addition to the ever-present mobile phone method, musicians need to save their contact lists in a safe environment. Some will prefer an old-fashioned hard-copy method like an address book. Regardless of format, easy accessibility for use and updating is critical.

In addition to their musical roles, faculty and guest artists can regularly model professional life through storytelling from their own experiences in classes, lessons and rehearsals.

The Internet and social networking

In addition to interpersonal connections, faculty can encourage students to begin shifting their social networking activities to professional uses. While the specific tools themselves (MySpace, Facebook, Twitter and so on; see also Chapters 3 and 8) will continue to change and evolve at a rapid pace, the important role of the 'who you know and who knows you' concept can be expanded and nurtured very effectively online. While college students are frequently linked through these sites socially, I have found (especially among performance majors) frequent resistance to using the sites in professional ways. There is no doubt that social networking sites can consume vast amounts of time if not carefully managed. But they also offer an unprecedented opportunity to build networks of colleagues, audiences and other supporters. Whether posting a senior recital on Facebook or developing a full-blown electronic press kit, these are vital avenues for all 21st century musicians.

Whilst some faculty members may shudder at the thought of staying connected to vast numbers of alumni, social networking tools also provide very simple ways to follow the evolution of former students' careers over time. Maintaining connections can help those of us in higher education better understand our students' needs and future paths, whilst continued contact positions graduates as ideal mentors for current students.

Conclusion

The stories throughout this book evidence that students with motivation and drive get a head start on their professional careers even prior to graduation. Some of that early career activity can happen within the music school environment, by building awareness and shifting attitudes from the regulated structure of formal education into a gradually developing professional mind set. Although it can be challenging to take on additional tasks while wrapping up a college degree, soon-to-be graduates who have firm dates and projects on their calendars after graduation do not face a suddenly blank calendar after the big day. An interesting project, auditions, some private students or an already planned concert or recital can all help create a stream of continuity into professional musical life.

As we remember former students who went on to successfully launch professional careers, we can consider what distinguished those individuals during their student years. Was it talent? Work ethic? Perseverance? Resilience? Optimism? What are their stories? Were some less-than-stellar students able to craft successful careers while other music school stars fizzled out soon after graduation? We can learn a lot about the changing musical work scene by staying in touch with graduates and perhaps inviting some back to campus to talk with current students, incorporating what we learn into conversations and curriculum.

The case study '*self-authorship and Allan's story*' has been adapted as a resource for use with students and is included in Part II, tool 16.

References

Arnett, J. J. (2000, May). Emerging adulthood: A theory of development from the late teens through the twenties. *American Psychologist, 55*(5), 469-480.

Arnett, J. J. (2004). *Emerging adulthood: The winding road from the late teens through the twenties.* New York: Oxford University Press.

Baxter Magolda, M. (2004). *Learning partnerships: Theory and models of practice to educate for self-authorship.* Sterling, VA: Stylus Publishing.

Bridges, W. (2009). *Managing transitions: Making the most of change* (3rd ed.). Philadelphia, PA: Da Capo Lifelong Books.

Burland, K., & Davidson, J. W. (2002). Training the talented. *Music Education Research, 4*(1), 121-138.

Collegegrad.com (July 22, 2009). 2009 College graduates moving back home in larger numbers. Retrieved July 22, 2009, from: http://www.collegegrad.com/press/2009_college_graduates_moving_back_home_in_larger_numbers.shtml.

Cutler, D. (2009, September 27). How arts schools prioritize career development. Message posted to http://blog.entrepreneurthearts.com/2009/09/27/how-arts-schools-prioritize-career-development/.
Cutler, D. (2010). *The savvy musician: Building a career, earning a living, and making a difference.* Pittsburgh, PA: Helius Press.
Gillis, J. (2008). Life course and transitions to adulthood. *Encyclopedia of children and childhood in history and society.* Available at: http://www.faqs.org/Ke-Me/Life-Course-and-Transitions-to-Adulthood.html.
Hunter, J. D. (2009). Wither adulthood? (Report). *The Hedgehog Review,* 11.1 (Spring, 2009): 7(11). Expanded Academic ASAP. Gale. University of St. Thomas Libraries. 14 Sept. 2009. http://galegroup.com.ezproxy.stthomas.edu/itx/start.do?prodld=EAIM Gale document number: A201105955.
Kegan, R. (1994). *In over our heads: The mental demands of modern life.* Cambridge, MA: Harvard University Press.
Robbins, A., & Wilner. A. (2001). *Quarterlife crisis: The unique challenges of life in your twenties.* New York: Tarcher/Putnam.
Vanrenen, B. (Ed.). (2007). *Generation what? Dispatches from the quarter-life crisis.* Canada: Speck Press.
Wilner, A., & Stocker, C. (2005). *The quarterlifer's companion: How to get on the right career path, control your finances, and find the support network you need to thrive.* NY: McGraw Hill.

Further reading

Bayles, D., & Orland. T. (2001). *Art & fear: Observations on the perils (and rewards) of artmaking.* The Image Continuum: California.

Chapter 5
Staying Afloat

Skills, Attributes and Passion

Dawn Bennett

A recurring theme throughout this book is that a clear self-image and professional identity are essential attributes for graduates seeking to apply their knowledge to the development of a sustainable career. Underpinning this are the core skills and attributes that make graduates career ready. Research has revealed much about the working lives of classically trained musicians, who tend to include both skilled and unskilled work within a portfolio of roles (Burland & Davidson, 2004). From this research we know that the most common activity for musicians is teaching, and that very few people work solely in performance. We know that music work is diverse: for instance, two-thirds of musicians work both within and outside of music. We know that musicians share their expertise, and that less than half are paid for all of their music work. We know that over 80% of musicians teach, 70% perform and 30% run ensembles. And we know that almost all musicians include work that is self-employed (Bennett, 2008; Huhtanen, 2004; Metier, 2001).

The above descriptors are a far cry from the general use of the term *musician* to describe a performer, and the discrepancies between performance work and musicians' work can be overwhelming for the aspiring musician. Until, that is, we ask whether musicians develop non-performance work merely to pay the bills, or whether other factors are considered. As this chapter reveals, one of the most exciting aspects of musicians' careers appears to be the seemingly never-ending potential for stimulating, exciting and diverse roles. These roles, beyond performance and even beyond music, often would not be traded for additional performance work.

In the early stages of their training, performance majors are likely to have a narrowly defined self-identity in line with the priority afforded to performance ambitions (see Chapter 1). For performance majors in particular, it is important to challenge preconceived notions of career by providing opportunities to reconcile romanticised ideals with realistic experiences in which 'possible selves' (Marcus & Nirius, 1986) can be explored. This includes opportunities to question and examine existing hierarchies. Whilst established musicians and teachers will understand the relevance of non-performance skills, fostering awareness and providing meaningful learning experiences for students remain particular challenges within already crowded curricula.

Consistent with other chapters in this volume, this chapter draws on the location of the author to contextualise its arguments. Australia is the sixth largest country in the world and has the lowest population density, which gives the impression that it is a far cry from the hustle and bustle of Europe or the US. However, the six states and two territories that make up Australia are home to musicians who represent a wide diversity of nationalities, music and traditions. To some extent, Australia has negotiated its marginal position in relation to the global music sector by developing a distinctive sector that celebrates its relative distance from other major centres of activity.

In 2006, 2.9 million people in Australia undertook paid and unpaid work in culture and leisure activities and an additional 2.5 million people participated in these activities as a hobby (Australian Bureau of Statistics, 2008). It is important to note that national census collections around the world tend to refer only to a person's main job. As a result, much of the activity undertaken by multi-tasking artists is not captured. Taking this into account, in Australia it is likely that some 167,000 people currently earn some income from music. Given that the Australian population is projected to rise by one-third to 33 million within the next 50 years it is reasonable to expect that by 2060 there will be at least 220,000 people earning some income from music, with six million people working in culture and leisure. There are ample opportunities within all of this for musicians who are flexible and creative.

The music, creative and cultural industries

Although most musicians plan careers directly connected with music, the reality is that most sustain their careers within an increasingly complex, competitive and diverse cultural environment (as other chapters in this volume indicate). Whilst economic measurement of the arts is beyond the scope of this chapter, it is important to contextualise music activity at least in terms of general scope and size so that students understand the enormity of the sector in which they will work.

In Australia, for example, the full range of music activities and industries that make up the music sector was conservatively estimated in 2005-2006 to be worth AUD$6.8 billion, or just over 3% of Australia's gross domestic product (Guldberg & Letts, 2005). The music sector, thus defined, includes related activity in performance, composition, recording, film and television, education and training, venues, manufacturing, trade and technology, research and information and health.

In 2002, the United Kingdom National Music Council (NMC) analysed the economic value of the UK's music industries utilising the categories of composition, musical instruments, performance, artist earnings, recording, retailing, distribution and education and training. The Council identified domestic expenditure on music sector goods and services of £4.9 billion (NMC, 2002). In 2007, UK music industry exports alone were worth £1.3 billion (Live Performance Australia, 2008). The Recording Industry Association of America (RIAA) estimated the world music market in 2004 to be worth US$40 billion (RIAA, 2004) and, not surprisingly, the trade value of music sales has since declined at a rate consistent with the global decline in trade value. The trade value of digital music sales, however, is estimated to average 21% worldwide and continues to grow (Canadian Heritage, 2010). Indeed, since peer-to-peer (p2p) file-sharing site Napster emerged in 1999, music sale revenues have dropped 25% globally. As with the Australian example given earlier, there is also the value added by music to numerous industries such as recreation and culture, manufacturing, retail and wholesale trade, communication and education. These data are important not only in relation to advocating music's cultural and social value and its broader economic impact, but also in terms of exposing the opportunities for musicians beyond music.

Music forms part of much larger industry sectors to which terms such as the *creative* or *cultural* industries are applied. Although there is no internationally agreed definition for the creative industries, the UK definition is widely accepted and describes

> those industries that are based on individual creativity, skill and talent. They are also those that have the potential to create wealth and jobs through developing intellectual property. This includes advertising, architecture, the art and antiques market, crafts, design, designer fashion, film and video, interactive leisure software, music, the performing arts, publishing, software, computer and video games, television and radio. (Department of Culture, Media and Sport, 2006)

In 2004, the combined creative industries in the UK represented 8% of the UK economy (National Endowment for Science, Technology and the Arts (NESTA), 2006). The *cultural industries* are often even more broadly defined than the creative industries and most often include film and video, motion pictures, television, art galleries, libraries, archives, museums, botanic gardens, music and theatre, performing arts venues, and services such as education. Musicians, therefore, work within a large and diverse industry sector; and their creativity, specialist and generic skills are transferable across the creative and cultural industries and beyond (Bennett, 2007). This exposes a wealth of opportunities for musicians prepared to draw on and develop their strengths and interests, passions and resources in search of intrinsic satisfaction. Taking Australia as their context, the following sections examine education and training, employment and employability. In particular, they highlight the relevance of skills and attributes essential to the development and maintenance of a career in music. Whilst I draw on the Australian context, differences between Australia and other locations are often matters of scale (see, for example, different perspectives on employment and employability in the US (Chapter 3), Canada (Chapter 6), and Europe (Chapter 7).

Employment and employability in Australia

In 2003 there were 188 instrumental graduates from Australian BMus performance degrees in classical music: 113 orchestral instrumentalists, 59 pianists and organists and 16 classical guitarists. This is a very small number when compared to other countries such as the US (which has 20,000 music graduates each year; see Chapter 3), but then so is the number of jobs. For example, in Australia there are less than 600 full-time orchestral performance positions and only 48 full-time performance positions for vocalists within opera companies. Approximately one-third of Australia's orchestral musicians come from overseas, a further one-third are trained overseas, and a random sample of 50 Opera Australia singers suggests that just over half were born in Australia. The downside of this for graduates is the realisation that there is global competition for Australian positions. The upside, of course, is high standards and a wealth of experience. The Faculty of Music at the University of Melbourne (one of few Australian institutions to release graduate destination data for music) reports that almost 50% of its 2006 graduates were working within education, 20% in retail, 14% as music therapists and a further 14% in arts organisations. The data illustrate just a few of the destinations for music graduates and the diversity of skills and attributes needed to successfully engage with these roles. Again drawing on the Australian context, the following section looks at the two most common activities for musicians: performance and teaching.

Universities and schools

Academia provides full-time employment for a number of artists and musicians who juggle their creative practice with the demands of teaching, grant-getting and research. The vast majority of music lecturers and instrumental tutors work on a casual basis, and are paid from AUD$60 per hour for instrumental and vocal teaching and around AUD$100 per hour for lecturing work, although some institutions pay considerably more. With only 24 or 26 teaching weeks in an academic year, no holiday pay or sick leave and, for many employees, no superannuation, casual lecturing is unlikely to be a musician's sole source of income. As elsewhere, instrumental and vocal teachers are selected for their performance expertise and most often come from the ranks of orchestras or chamber ensembles.

Conditions can be somewhat more stable within the public (state) school system, wherein graduate teachers earn from AUD$50,000 per year. Instrumental teachers enjoy the same conditions and benefits as classroom teachers. The downside of working within the school sector is the lack of flexibility in terms of committed teaching time, which can make it difficult to accommodate other, less flexible employment such as performance work. Nonetheless, many teacher-performers manage to successfully juggle both roles. As elsewhere, there are also myriad opportunities for instrumental, vocal and ensemble teachers within the private school system as well as in community music schools and private studios, often home based. Graduates need to be aware that the vast majority of these positions are structured as hourly or part-time contracts, and that many will not provide payment during school holidays. They can, however, be fairly flexible. Musicians working in many smaller schools offer tuition on a self-employed basis. Musicians should always seek legal advice to ensure that insurances and other obligations are in place, as these can be the responsibility of the individual rather than the school.

Opera companies and orchestras

A growing number of Australian music companies cater for niche markets, and these companies contract musicians for short seasons. Sydney's Pinchgut Opera, a chamber opera company that presents little-performed operas in intimate settings, is one such example. Although the company utilises a common core of voices for the chorus of each opera, Liz Nielsen, Chair of Pinchgut Opera, explains that they "work on a season-by-season basis and have no full-time contracts. Depending on the [musical] work, we contract about twenty-five professional singers each season. This means that we are able to get the best singers for the particular roles in the opera we are presenting" (personal communication). Instrumentalists are employed in the same way. Each year, the Melbourne-based Chamber Made Opera produces two creative developments and three operas, including two extant touring productions. It specialises in the commission and presentation of chamber theatre written by living artists. Again, vocalists and instrumentalists "are all contracted specifically per performance during the rehearsal, production and performance period" (personal communication, 2008). Larger opera and theatre companies have also moved towards a seasonal employment model. Even the state companies State Opera South Australia, Queensland Opera, West Australian Opera and Victoria Opera rely entirely on singers contracted on a seasonal basis. This is similar to the story in the US (Chapter 3) and in the UK, where the only full-time professional choir is that of King's College, Cambridge.

Full-time orchestral positions exist somewhat precariously within nine Australian orchestras, which each employ sessional (casual) musicians to augment their numbers according to the program (Table 5.1). Performers commence at the lowest salary rate unless prior experience can be demonstrated. The performers in most ensembles move to a new pay level every year or two until the top level is achieved following ten or more years of service. Some ensembles, such as Opera Australia, work on the basis of a 25% increase in salary over ten years. Most employment agreements include a number of Sunday calls and some overtime in addition to touring. Orchestral managers can expect to earn about AUD$85,000 per year, and similar roles in production or marketing attract salaries of about AUD$70,000 depending on the size and type of organisation.

Table 5.1: Full-time performance positions in Australia

	Full-time positions	*Salary range for tutti players/chorus members**	*Top rate for section leaders*
Instrumental			
Adelaide Symphony Orchestra	67	42,821 – 54,126	66,092
Australian Chamber Orchestra	15	83,842	NA
Melbourne Symphony Orchestra	87	59,428 – 77,255	91,518
The Queensland Orchestra	79	43,945 – 55,545	67,823
Sydney Symphony Orchestra	89	72,761 – 88,761	112,780
Tasmanian Symphony Orchestra	45	43,669 – 55,197	67,399
West Australian Symphony Orchestra	80	46,205 – 58,401	71,310
Australia Opera and Ballet Orchestra	69	56,324 – 70,405	84,486
Orchestra Victoria (full/part-time)	69	44,902 – 56,754	69,928
Repetiteurs	6	46,968 – 71,123	NA
Vocal			
Opera Australia	48	48,800 – 62,462	NA
Combined total	651		

*Salary data, shown in Australian dollars, are drawn from 2008 employment agreements. The estimated number of people earning some income from music in 2006 was 167,000.

As Table 5.1 illustrates, approximately 0.4% of Australia's 167,000 musicians hold full-time performance positions with a single employer, and we know from previous research that the majority of these full-time musicians engage in multiple activities beyond their full-time roles (Bennett, 2008). Orchestral musicians, for example, often hone their skills and find creative freedom in chamber music and other performance settings.

Teaching and other interests are commonly pursued for their intrinsic satisfaction as well as for the supplementary income they provide. Within this complex working environment, the practice of musicians from around the world highlights the importance of particular core skills and attributes. As illustrated by the musician profiles in Part II, identifying and acquiring these essential skills and attributes results in more options and greater career control. However, maintaining control means that musicians must continuously learn or enhance their skills to meet each new challenge. The following section looks at the provision of some of these skills.

Education and professional development in Australia

Education and professional development are essential and constant features of musicians' careers as they strive to become and remain employable within an environment characterised by the knowledge economy, globalisation and technological change. In 2006, Australian census data report that almost 1.1 million people in Australia (5% of the population) had completed training in the arts or culture, and a staggering 1% of the population (215,000) people had completed some form of formal music training. Music is the most commonly offered university arts discipline in Australia, with some 159 undergraduate and 120 postgraduate courses attracting 5,500 enrolments each year. Despite its prevalence, there is no single collection of data relating to music education and training, music courses, student numbers or graduate destinations. I draw the following information from various sources including Lancaster's (2004) Different Beats survey of post-secondary education in Australia; my studies of performance-based BMus degrees, musicians and employment (Bennett, 2008); data from the Australia Council Research Centre and the Knowledge Base of the Music Council of Australia (2005 – 2011); and numerous Australian arts associations and organisations. (Links to these sources are included at the end of the chapter)

Almost 95% of the musicians who have contributed to my research over the past twelve years had undertaken formal education and training. Almost half of them had studied at graduate level, and a Bachelor of Music degree was by far the most common undergraduate course. Australian university degrees follow the English system rather than a liberal arts model. In line with increasing pressure to offer a diverse range of degree options, in 2008 there were 66 Bachelor of Music (BMus) degrees in Australia with specialties in music therapy, composition, arts management and piano performance. There was one degree in applied business in music industries; ten double degrees in music and education; three Bachelor of Arts degrees in music; and 21 double degrees in which music was offered alongside other subjects such as psychology, commerce, law and general science. In contrast, initial results from a more recent audit of 2010 enrolments (unpublished) show a reduction in the number of undergraduate awards, despite an increase in the number of enrolments. Traditional BMus awards continue to attract the highest number of enrolments. Respondents reported only 40 degrees in music, half of them with variations on the title 'Bachelor of Music'. There are also new awards in performing arts, popular/contemporary music, music studies and creative arts/industries. The number of music education awards had decreased to six, only one of which was a double degree in music and education. There was also an increase in the number of technology/multimedia programs, all with different titles.

In a few universities it is possible to build the double degree of one's own choice. The logistics of timetabling a double major in, say, nuclear physics and viola performance are, of course, a nightmare. But it seems to be an appealing option among the undecided and for students whose parents favour the 'get a real job' approach. The trend towards double majors and generic arts degrees is international, and it provides interesting options for both undergraduate and graduate study. Given their overwhelming popularity, the question is to what extent specialist performance degrees prepare graduates to forge and sustain careers in music.

In 2004, analysis of the content of Australia's 24 classical music performance degrees revealed that despite growing evidence of the broad requirements for sustaining a career in music, entry requirements and core curricula in Australia are largely performance-based, and crucial skills in small business and pedagogy receive very little (if any) compulsory course time. Practising musicians advocate the inclusion of career development, teaching skills and small business skills in addition to music technologies and internships. Their feedback can in fact be quite critical: for example, "preparation for a career in classical music as a performer is often too focused on the art and not enough on the business, social and cultural conditions that performers must be a part of" (in Bennett, 2008, p. 70). Not surprisingly, teaching, small business and performance are the overwhelming focus of the professional development undertaken by musicians. Ironically, these essential aspects of musicians' practice are often much better represented in non-degree courses and in degree programs with a focus on contemporary music.

Compulsory units within Australian Technical and Further Education (TAFE) courses focus on generic skills that are absolutely vital to the careers of all musicians: for example, business studies, occupational health and safety, music industry knowledge and negotiation skills. Existing competencies are recognised so that students can focus their attention on particular areas of their development, and specialist studies such as those in performance are included as elective units. For this reason, many university graduates turn to TAFE. Whilst TAFE study has traditionally provided an alternative pathway to university, there are currently over four times as many students progressing from university to TAFE than from TAFE to university. Recent change in the Australia Higher Education sector mean that TAFE colleges are increasingly offering degree-level courses in direct competition with universities, so there are interesting times ahead.

Graduate study is increasingly popular in the arts. Graduate Diplomas in performance, composition and education are generally one-year courses. The Graduate Diploma in Education is the equivalent of the British Postgraduate Certificate in Education and qualifies graduates to work as music teachers. Most Australian courses focus on classroom teaching, but recent legislative changes have resulted in a growing number of courses that focus on instrumental or vocal pedagogy. In 2006 there were 32 Masters Degrees in performance, music therapy or composition and two Masters of Education degrees with a major in music. The Doctor of Musical Arts (or Creative Arts) is offered by many institutions and includes coursework, creative work and an exegesis (thesis) of around 50,000 words. Doctor of Philosophy (PhD) study is based on the English model of pure research (sometimes including creative research) undertaken over a period of three to four years and resulting in a thesis of approximately 80,000 words (or less if a creative component is included). In *Different Beats* (2004), Lancaster found that graduate study in Australia centred on performance/creative practice and musicology (88%), composition (81%), technology (73%), music education (73%) and ethnomusicology (63%).

Essential skills and attributes

Business and entrepreneurship

Nadel (1998) once noted that an architect is not a designer of buildings but a business person whose product is architecture. Similarly, musicians can be seen as business people whose product is music. As one musician explained, "people like music, but they don't realise how much business sense is needed to maintain a music career" (Bennett, unpublished interview, 2004). Indeed, countless musicians and artists miss out on funding and opportunities either because they do not consider themselves to be running a business or because they do not have the skills to effectively manage their business.

The term entrepreneur comes from the French word *entreprendre*, which means to take action. Although often associated with risk-taking, entrepreneurs tend to be creative, disciplined planners with a passion for what they do. Planning quietly for as long as required, they act when they are ready and they are prepared to accept the consequences. However, whereas people in many fields become entrepreneurs once they are established and have developed expertise and professional networks, artists need to be entrepreneurial right from the start. The development of an entrepreneurial mindset emerges as a vital component of musicians' training (refer to Chapter 4).

An Australian study of final-year arts students found that most are unable to recognise and articulate the core employability skills they have developed, such as the ability to 'work as part of a team' or to 'work independently'. Ironically, the same study found Australian business to be very aware of arts graduates' employability skills: "employers seek Arts graduates specifically for the valuable range of generic skills they do typically possess" (Delves, 2008, p. 22). As other authors have noted, running a small business involves time management as well as financial management, effective marketing and careful planning to define and meet both short-term and long-term goals. The relevance and early development of these skills can often be illustrated through discussion of activities that are already familiar to students. Organising a performance, for example, can involve working with teams, negotiating with venues and musicians, marketing and promotion, writing grant applications, understanding contracts, meeting insurance obligations, writing invoices and keeping financial records. Despite their transferability to many different fields, few artists include these valuable skills on their résumés.

Communication skills

Sixty-two percent of the UK musicians who participated in Roger's 2002 study reported communication to be the most important skill within their practice, and Traasdahl (1996) found the same to be true among popular musicians. Communication skills are imperative to every musician's ability to create networks, liaise with clients, manage group situations such as rehearsals, and 'sell' a music product or service (see Chapter 8 and also Part II resources on building networks and connections). The ability and confidence to communicate effectively is imperative to a musician's practice, whether in a performance or teaching role, or in running a freelance business. Lack of confidence in this area is one of the major barriers faced by graduates, who are often ill-equipped to find or recognise opportunities for work and experience. Just like written communication skills, the tact, forethought and confidence required for effective verbal communication are refined through experience. It is not possible to get this experience within the solitary confines of the practice room, but it can be developed in every unit with effective modelling, peer teaching and mentoring activities, open rehearsals and presentations. As suggested in Chapter 3, time-efficient strategies include inviting students to consider outside gigs and other activities to be part of their formal learning. This is effective in further developing communication skills, sharing expertise across the group, and learning more about the activities in which students are engaged.

Performance and passion

At the heart of most musicians' practice is a love of performance. As one musician articulated, performance skills are "essential to maintain the drive necessary for me to exist as a musician" (Bennett 2005, unpublished interview). However, performing is often not about being in the spotlight. Rather, it is about making music with others. As such, performance skills are just one of many skill sets, and making the link between performance and other activities is vital. Whether or not they are 'good enough' to get into a performance degree or to succeed as a soloist, enjoyment and satisfaction will for many people be found in organising events, teaching, researching, performing in a group, managing projects, writing about music or making recordings.

The insights above were recently brought home to me when I began what should have been a session dealing with performance anxiety by asking a class of undergraduate performers to raise their hands if they 'live to perform'. Only one hand was raised, which was astounding because there had previously been much discussion about careers and aspirations, much of it performance-centred. After some time I asked the students a question that has since proven to be the most effective career discussion question I have encountered: 'What do you love to do?' The students responded by talking about their many and varied strengths and interests in a different way than ever before, and it occurred to them (and to me) that few people had ever actually asked them what they enjoy doing. The discussion was enlightening because it bypassed the usual artistic hierarchies and prompted students to place themselves, rather than music, at the centre of their future careers. Attributes such as confidence, adaptability to change, motivation, resilience, inner strength and passion are just as important as essential skills. Passion is often the force behind successful careers and is perhaps the most crucial attribute of all. Without a passion for music, a career is unlikely to succeed and is almost certain to be unhappy. This is perhaps where the focus on performance within formal music education and training is most concerning.

Concluding thoughts

This chapter has outlined skills and attributes that are essential to the development and maintenance of a career in music. It can be hard to demonstrate to students the relevance of each skill set, and yet it is essential for students to explore them. Strategies and tools that have proven effective in stimulating student interest include journals, drawings, discussion groups, mentoring programs, career profiling of musicians and professional internships. In her conclusion, Beeching (Chapter 3) reminds us that musicians need to create both their own opportunities and their own career paths. And Perkins (Chapter 2) advocates the importance of including "flexible programs that allow students to develop the professional skills they need at the time they feel they need them".

This chapter began by acknowledging that providing students with meaningful learning experiences within an already crowded curriculum is a particular challenge. Nonetheless, and within these constraints, meaningful discussion can be stimulated with the use of pertinent questions about what musicians most love to do, their interests within and beyond music, their strengths and talents, and their passions. For example:

1. What are your most rewarding experiences inside of music?
   What was rewarding about them?
2. What are your most rewarding experiences *outside* of music?
   What was rewarding about them?
   How do they relate to those things you most enjoy within music?
3. What things would you like to try or to develop more fully?
4. What would you like to learn more about?
5. What are the strengths of your character?
6. What are you good at?
7. What are you passionate about?

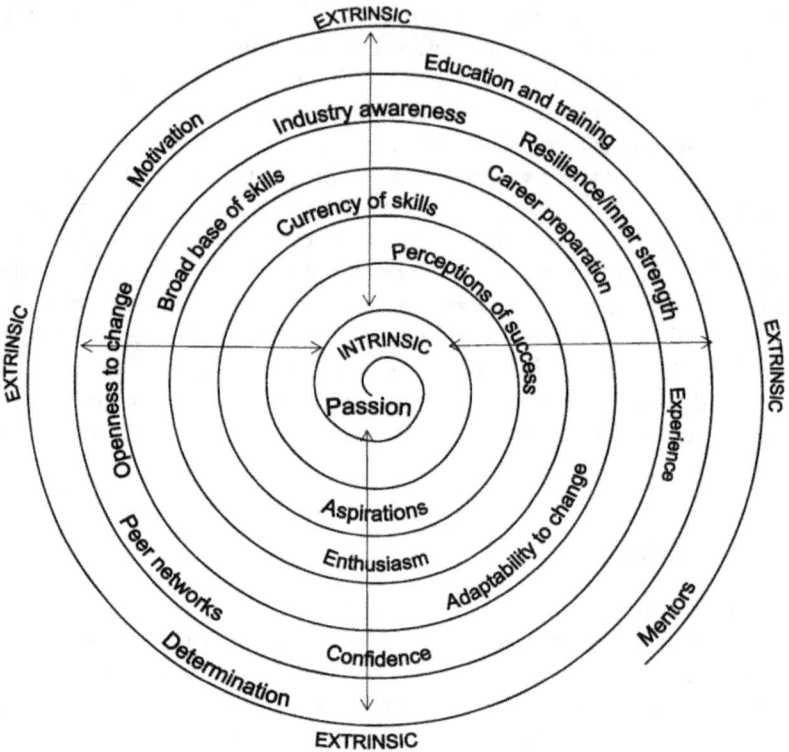

Figure 5.1: Conditional Matrix of Intrinsic and Extrinsic Influences (Bennett, 2008)

The answers to these questions are likely to frame future career decisions and will be fundamental to developing an emerging professional identity and clear self-image. I tend to address them singly or within themes, often accompanied by musician profiles (or guest musicians) and accessible readings. They work well both within class and as online discussion topics, as do each of the elements of the matrix above.

Part II includes five musician profiles for use as discussion tools. The first comes from an Australian violinist who lived in Europe for many years. Angie's work in Europe and Australia spans orchestral and chamber music performance, teaching, and a quartet which combines poetry, stories and music to provide innovative concerts and workshops for children and adults. Angie's varied career has been underpinned by her overwhelming passion for music. Passion also underpins the second profile, which comes from an Australian pianist who describes the excitement found in continually developing and combining new goals and interests. Since the interview, pianist Jan has taken a position in a university outside of Australia and is currently taking the region by storm!

The remaining three profiles come from European musicians who were in the first ten years of their professional careers at the time of the interviews (2008). The first of these (profile 3) comes from European pianist Dominik Falenski, who was born in Berlin and is now based in Denmark where he is finishing his Masters degree. He begins by talking about how he came to be a pianist, and then describes the different experiences that have shaped how he views his career both now and into the future. The next profile is from Danish freelance trumpeter Jeppe Uggerhoej, who graduated from his Bachelor degree one year prior to the interview. He talks about how he is building a career in music, the need to be able to perform in different genres, and trying different things to work out what he might want to do in the longer term. Jeppe's profile highlights that being musically multi-lingual is increasingly important. The ability to work in multiple settings and genres increases opportunities for performance, and the enjoyment to be gained from them is enormously beneficial to the interpretation of classical works.

The final profile comes from a young European trombonist, who asked not to be identified. The musician secured his first principal position in 2002 while in his final undergraduate year, and he has since secured a position with one of the world's leading orchestras. He describes life in an orchestra, the 'sparkle' that makes orchestral work enjoyable, getting ahead, and his future career plans.

The musicians who have generously shared stories of their lives in music offer some valuable insights, not least of which are that learning is continuous and that careers continuously evolve. They demonstrate that careers in music are much more than a job: successful musicians are those who follow their passion and develop their strengths and interests to forge sustainable careers. The stories further emphasise that intrinsically satisfying careers require musicians to surmount the existing hierarchy in which performance is the pinnacle of success, and to think instead about individual strengths, likes and dislikes. The more students see this in their teachers, peers and heroes, the more they will start to develop it in themselves.

References

Australian Bureau of Statistics. (2008). *Culture and leisure.* Retrieved October 26, 2008, from www.ausstats.abs.gov.au/ausstats/subscriber.nsf/0/E3A2D45541A868B2CA2573E900101F72/$File/49020_2008.pdf.

Bennett, D. (2007). Creative artists or cultural practitioners? Holistic practice in Australia's cultural industries. *Journal of Australian Studies, 90,* 133-151.

Bennett, D. (2008). *Understanding the classical music profession. The past, the present, and strategies for the future.* Oxon, England: Ashgate Publishing.

Burland, K., & Davidson, J. (2004). Tracing a musical life transition. In J. Davidson (Ed.), *The Music Practitioner: Research for the Music Performer, Teacher and Listener.* Farnham: Ashgate.

Canadian Heritage. (2010). *The Canadian Music Industry 2008 Economic Profile*. Quebec: Canadian Heritage.

Delves, L. (2008, January). *The arts skills summary: Building employability awareness in arts students.* Paper presented at 'Preparing for the graduate of 2015', the 17th Annual Teaching and Learning Forum, Curtin University of Technology, Perth.

Department of Culture, Media and Sport. (2006). *Creative industries*. Retrieved March 15, 2008, from www.culturalpolicies.net/web/unitedkingdom.php?aid=426.

Guldberg, H-H., & Letts, R. (2005). *A statistical framework for the music sector [electronic resource]: for the Statistics Working Group of the Cultural Ministers Council: a scoping study.* Statistics Working Group Secretariat, Cultural Ministers' Council, Dept. Communications, Technology and the Arts: Canberra. Retrieved August 10, 2009, from http://nla.gov.au/nla.cs-ma-an40176436.

Huhtanen, K. (2004). Once I had a promising future (facing reality as an ex-promising pianist). *Australian Music Forum, 10*(3), 21-27.

Lancaster, H. (2004). Different streets, different beats? *Sounds Australian, 64*, 3-7.

Live Performance Australia. (2008). Submission to review of export policies and programs. Submission to the Department of Foreign Affairs and Trade, May 2008.

Marcus, H., & Nirius, P. (1986). Possible selves. *American Psychologist, 41*(9), 954-969.

Metier. (2001). *Orchestral research final report.* Retrieved October, 2004, from http://www.metier.org.uk/metierMedia/orchestral.pdf.

Moltz, D. (October 23, 2009). Are today's grads unprofessional? *Inside Higher Ed*. Retrieved March 15, 2010, from http://www.insidehighered.com/news/2009/10/23/professionalism.

Nadel, H. (1998, March). *Exploring ways to strengthen a practice for long-term growth.* Retrieved March 20, 2002, from http://www.isdesignet.com/Magazine/Mar'98sprep.html.

RIAA. (2004). Year end report. Retrieved June 10, 2009, from <news/marketingdata/default.asp>.

Rogers, R. (2002). *Creating a land with music*. London: Youth Music.

National Music Council. (2002). *Counting the notes: The economic contribution of the UK music business*. London: National Music Business.

NESTA. (2006). *UK creative industries face threat from emerging nations.* Media release, NESTA, April 25. Retrieved June 16, 2009, from www.nesta.org.uk/press-release-archive/view/1153.

Statistics Canada. (2004). *Profile of the culture sector in Atlantic Canada*. Ottawa: The Cultural Statistics Program, Tourism, and the Centre for Statistics in Education.

Traasdahl, J. O. (1996). Rhythmic music education in Denmark. In G. M. Oliva (Ed.), *The ISME Commission for the Education of the Professional Musician 1996 seminar. The musician's role: New challenges* (pp. 67-74). Lund: Universitetstryckeriet, Lund University.

Further reading and information

There are 300 qualified music therapists registered with the Australian Music Therapy Association and most work in multiple part-time or casual positions. The Association can be found at: www.austmta.org.au

TAFE (technical and further education) training packages come with toolboxes of resources. The music training package and tools are found at: www.ntis.gov.au/Default.aspx?/trainingpackage/CUS01

The Knowledge Base of the Music Council of Australia contains a wealth of information under the headings of statistics, context, creation and support. The Knowledge Base is at: www.mca.org.au/web/component/option.com_kb/

Many arts organisations run professional development courses: for example the UK-based Artists' Professional Development Network (www.apd-network.info) or art:21 in the US (www.pbs.org/art21/education/professional/index.html). Musicians can also find help in the form of single-unit enrolments at universities and colleges. Outside of the arts there are small business support networks and business incubators that offer free help, support, training and limited infrastructure. See, for example, Business Enterprise Centres in Australia (www.becaustralia.org.au).

For more music research in Australia, see The Australia Council's Research Centre at: www.australiacouncil.gov.au/research/arts_sector/reports_and_publications/arts_rippa

See also the Bibliography of Australian Music Education Research Project (BAMER), at: http://www.deakin.edu.au/arts-ed/education/music-ed/bamer/

For further reading on non-traditional career orientations, see: http://wfnetwork.bc.edu/encyclopedia_entry.php?id=249

See also: Bennett, D. (2009). Academy and the real world: Developing realistic notions of careers in the performing arts. *Arts and Humanities in Higher Education, 18*(3), 309-327. http://ahh.sagepub.com/cgi/content/abstract/8/3/309

Australian Ensembles

The following are links to Australian ensembles mentioned within the chapter.

Adelaide Symphony Orchestra	www.aso.com.au
Australian Chamber Orchestra	www.aco.com.au
Australian Opera and ballet Orchestra	www.opera-australia.org.au
ChamberMade Opera	www.chambermade.org.au
Melbourne Symphony Orchestra	www.mso.com.au
Opera Australia	www.opera-australia.org.au
Orchestra Victoria	www.orchestravictoria.com.au
Pinchgut Opera	www.pinchgutopera.com.au
The Queensland Orchestra	www.thequeenslandorchestra.com.au
Sydney Symphony Orchestra	www.sydneysymphony.com
Tasmanian Symphony Orchestra	www.tso.com.au
West Australian Symphony Orchestra	www.waso.com.au

Searching for jobs and opportunities

Performance positions are listed on the websites of the organisations listed above. The Music Council of Australia has free weekly employment bulletins. These include jobs and opportunities in education, performance, composition, administration and community development. See: http://www.mca.org.au/web/content/view/143/6

Chapter 6
Musicians in Society

Making the Connection

Glen Carruthers

Musicians in society and the extent to which musicians' identities are moulded by interaction with the world around them are central to any discussion of careers in music. It is these interactions that form the subject of this chapter.

The literature on music and musicians in society from the past 75 years is extensive and varied, from Adorno's abstruse writings on popular culture (Adorno & Simpson, 1941), through easy-to-read forays into social history like Loesser's *Men, Women and Pianos* (1954), to many wide-ranging studies from the 1970s, including Raynor's two sweeping historical overviews (1972, 1976) and books by Shepherd et al. (1977) and Small (1977). There are many books from the 1980s and 1990s by Shepherd (1991), Frith (1996) and others, as well as countless more recent writings.

The tendency nowadays to situate music and musicians within social contexts extends across all disciplines. For example, mainstream musicology, in response to the new musicology of the 1980s, refocused much of its attention in the late 20th century from 'the work itself' to music *in situ*. This approach, encouraged by Kerman's rallying cry for a less positivistic, more critical musicology (1985), is now evident in almost all serious writing about music from popular magazines to scholarly journals. Textbook histories of music, too, devote more attention with each new edition to locating music within social and historical environments. The root issue, as other chapters in this book make plain, is identity: the identity of musical artworks, of the musicians that create and perform them, and of the audiences that enjoy them.

In light of the rethinking that characterised all fields of music study in the previous century, it is not surprising that identity became a major preoccupation in musician training. Music career development officers rethought their goals and methods in designing courses and workshops, and music educators now emphasise the practical application of skill sets students acquire in the classroom. Put simply, music students and the institutions that serve them are increasingly looking outwards for career planning and curricular direction and guidance.

What students expect of music teaching institutions has changed markedly in recent years, and reflects not only the new roles musicians play in contemporary society, but also changed personal and professional values. At one time, students enrolled in music degree programs had a clear idea of how they wished and expected their careers to unfold. This model usually mirrored their teachers' careers and career expectations, which in turn reflected the priorities and proclivities of their teachers' teachers. This continuum remained largely unchallenged from the inception of widespread institutionalised music teaching in the 19th century through to the closing decades of 20th century.

There was something flawed in this longstanding model of career preparation and development. For one thing, it worked backwards: teachers drew on their own experiences to identify the skills they believed their students required. Teachers then devised courses and programs to develop and hone these skills. That the world may have changed appreciably in the intervening years was not really considered. For another thing, this model was predicated on the assumption that real career outcomes would mirror anticipated career outcomes. Students who played or sang brilliantly would have brilliant careers, students who played or sang adequately would have adequate careers, and so forth. But these assumptions were often belied by experience.

There are many possible explanations for this disconnect between career expectations and outcomes. For example:

- Students and/or their teachers harboured unrealistic career expectations;
- The training students received did not properly prepare them for their careers;
- Students weren't choosing careers; rather, careers were choosing students;
- What students thought they wanted was not really what they wanted; or
- What society expected of musicians was not what musicians were prepared to offer.

This last explanation highlights a danger inherent in aiming for a ready-made career in music: students are positioned to be followers who fit into the world around them, rather than leaders who initiate social change (Carruthers, 2009).

When the gap between anticipated and actual career outcomes is unpacked, redundancies and lapses in musical training come to the fore. Although curricula may include too much of some things (perhaps history and theory) and not enough of others (perhaps entrepreneurship and music technology), curricula reflect much larger issues. What, for example, is it that musicians contribute to the communities in which they live and work? How has this changed over the years? How can students be prepared to meet these new challenges?

Classically trained musicians in contemporary society

The world has been changing so rapidly and so dramatically that much of what once seemed irrevocably true is now known to be false. Music curricula can no longer presume that classically trained performers will devote most of their time and energy to playing classical music to paying audiences. The age of the one-trick classical music specialist (an invention of the 19th century) has, except in the most exceptional circumstances, come and gone. Even classical recitalists, for instance, are expected to have good business acumen, a flexible repertoire, and communication skills that facilitate interaction with audiences on- and off-stage.

Until the 1970s, best practice in arts and arts education meant specialisation. An emphasis on skills acquisition in support of a solo career placed human capital at the centre of musical learning. Training aimed to produce better musicians, because better musicians were poised to succeed in a highly competitive milieu. Emphasis was on the individual and on the skills necessary to play or sing well, and all else was meant to serve this primary goal.

This view of musical training changed in many institutions in the late twentieth century. The primacy of European concert music was challenged and community music programs shifted emphasis from the individual to the group, as the democratisation of music teaching and learning transformed the music profession. In a broad sense, emphasis continues to shift in conservatoires and schools of music from developing better musicians to the exclusion of all else, to training musicians to help build better lives for themselves and others.

Advances in technology played an important role in this change. The role technology plays in fostering and sustaining community cannot be over-estimated, and technology encourages inclusiveness in music making at every turn. School children are able to produce increasingly sophisticated music with the aid of powerful software. More and more people have access to the world's music on demand through the Internet. In other words, since music production and consumption are ubiquitous, the role of the musician has evolved apace. Accordingly, intending music teachers interrogate anew the role music plays in the life of a well-rounded child. Intending musicologists know music's 'meaning' is inseparable from its context, from the time and place in which it is conceived, captured, transmitted and received. Intending performers would do well to debate these larger issues too, to be prepared to serve society's interests meaningfully and to play a transformative role in a rapidly changing world.

The reality is that musicians in Canada (as elsewhere), including those trained specifically as performers, deliver a range of services to the communities in which they reside. Versatility – once considered dilettantism – now provides musicians with a competitive edge. For this reason, versatility cannot be cultivated coincidentally or collaterally. Rather, it must be intentionally taught and learned. Early on, students must begin to acquire a mix of musical, academic, technological, entrepreneurial and networking skills, any combination of which can be called upon at a particular point in time.

Music students themselves have long been ahead of the curve, devoting considerable time and energy to extra-curricular activities that help build networks. Students perform in churches and bars, teach in commercial music studios, work in retail music stores, play at weddings and funerals, direct choirs, market bands (their own and others') and volunteer at youth and senior centres, sometimes for pay, sometimes for service-learning credits, and sometimes simply because it's the right thing to do. These activities reflect opportunities that exist in the professional world. By engaging in a range of activities, students develop an awareness of the roles and responsibilities musicians assume in contemporary society.

Post-secondary music education in Canada

In Canada, post-secondary music training occurs mostly at colleges and universities. The exception is the province of Québec, which follows a more continental model in which conservatoires, colleges and universities operate side-by-side.

Music programs in Canada range tremendously in size. In 2007-2008, Bishop's University in Lennoxville, Québec, employed three full-time and fifteen part-time faculty members to serve a total of 45 music students. At the opposite end of the spectrum is McGill University in Montréal, which in the same year employed 50 full-time and 150 part-time faculty members to serve 825 undergraduate and graduate music students. Five of the largest music programs in Canada (Montréal, McGill, Western, Toronto and British Columbia) had a combined teaching complement in 2007-2008 of 185 full-time professors and 460 part-time instructors, teaching over 3,000 music majors. There are more than 40 other colleges and universities in Canada offering degree programs in music.

This wealth of choices makes for rich, varied possibilities for advanced music study in Canada. For some students the intimacy of small classes, a supportive cohort of musical peers and an emphasis on student/teacher interaction, make smaller programs the obvious choice. For students who value competition, networking opportunities and the pace and opportunities provided in major urban centres, larger schools are a better choice. Ideally, by selecting carefully, students can find programs that offer the best of both worlds.

It is worth noting that the cost of post-secondary study in Canada is comparatively low. Provincial governments heavily subsidise post-secondary education and, even for international students (who usually pay a hefty premium), tuition is still far lower than in the US. Since education falls under provincial jurisdiction, the levels and scope of support available to international students differ widely from one part of the country to another.

Because post-secondary education is not nationalised, enrolment figures and other information must be gathered from a wide variety of sources. Certainly, student numbers have increased dramatically since the 1960s. This trend was evident as early as 1970:

> Statistics show that the rise in enrolment within music faculties and departments surpassed the rise in general university enrolment at the undergraduate level: from 1960 to 1970, enrolment overall grew 277% from 114,000 to 315,722, whereas music enrolment grew 486% from 397 to 1,928. (Green & Vogan, 1991, p. 410)

In ensuing years, enrolment has continued to increase. By one estimate, in the year 2000 there were more than 6,500 students enrolled in post-secondary music programs across Canada (Carruthers, 2001). Accounting for attrition, and assuming that most students are enrolled in four-year programs, there is a graduating class each year of more than 1,000 music students nationwide. For example, in 2000, 1,257 students graduated in Canada with an undergraduate degree in music (Job Futures National Edition, Services Canada Website, 2007, p. 1).

Music production and consumption in Canada

The production and consumption levels of music in Canada are clearly relevant when considering a career in music in this country, although students rarely elect to become professional musicians on the basis of supply and demand. As Carl Morey wrote almost 30 years ago in *Careers in music: A guide for Canadian students*:

> I doubt that anyone decides to take up or reject the study of the oboe after checking a market survey on the country's oboe requirements of the next twenty-five years! Whatever it is that drives us to become musicians simply does not take such statistics into account. (Green *et al.*, 1986, p. 177)

Nonetheless, students understandably want assurances that employment opportunities exist for them. Although the world of music is changing no less in Canada than in other western nations, the picture remains reassuring.

What is the state of music production and consumption in Canada? What are the chances of securing work in this vast country and what do jobs pay? Much can be gleaned from Statistics Canada's surveys of the Canadian population aged fifteen or older (website addresses are supplied at the end of this chapter). Telephone surveys were conducted in 1992, 1998 and 2005, so it is possible to identify longitudinal trends. The number of Canadians attending popular music concerts has remained more-or-less constant over the years, but a small but perceptible growth in the number of Canadians attending classical music concerts is evident. In 1992, 8.4% of Canadians attended classical music performances. In 1998 the figure was 9% and in 2005 it was 9.5% (2.5 million). Because Canada's population has been growing, these percentages represent a sizeable increase in real numbers. For instance, while the number of Canadians listening to all genres of recorded music increased 2.2% between 1992 and 2005, the increase in actual numbers was 25.8% once population growth is factored in (Hill Strategies, 2007).

An increase in music consumption is mirrored by a surge in music production as well as in cultural industries and services generally. The number of Canadians employed in the arts and culture sector increased substantially in the 1980s and 1990s, and in some areas the increase was dramatic. The number of Canadians employed full-time in sound recording and music publishing, for instance, increased 14% in only five years (from 1996 to 2001). In other areas, the statistics are less impressive. The number of Canadians employed full-time as performing artists increased only 3% over the same period. However, as a percentage of the total workforce, in 2001 many more Canadians were employed in the arts and culture sector compared to the previous five years, although growth was most conspicuous in support services (Singh, 2004). Growth was especially evident in the 1980s, when "cultural sector employment grew twice as fast as the total workforce" (Durand, 2004, p. 3). This trend continued through the 1990s: "while the total number of employed workers in Canada grew 20% between 1991 and 2002, the growth in employment in the culture sector was significantly higher at 31%".

The Conference Board of Canada reported in August 2008 that the Canadian cultural sector (although not necessarily the demand for oboists!) continues to grow dramatically:

> The arts and culture industries that make up Canada's culture sector employed about 616,000 in 2003, which represented 3.9 per cent of national employment. ... The Conference Board of Canada estimates that the culture sector accounted for 1.1 million jobs in 2007. (Conference Board, p. iii)

This translates into an impressive economic footprint "valued at CAN$84.6 billion in 2007, constituting 7.4 per cent of Canada's real gross domestic product" (Conference Board, p. iv).

The likelihood of securing employment in the arts and culture sector in Canada today is good, but there are challenges. Employment opportunities for music graduates are not as good as in some other industry sectors, and income levels are not generally high. In 2007, musicians with an undergraduate degree in music had average annual earnings of CAN$23,700, but the average earnings of graduates from other undergraduate programs was CAN$36,000. Average unemployment of music graduates was 12%, whereas average unemployment of graduates from other undergraduate programs was 8%.

These somewhat sobering statistics do not mean that young musicians, given the opportunity, would wish they had elected different studies and careers. While job satisfaction is not as high as it might be, the overwhelming majority of music students do not regret their educational choices. Table 6.1 encapsulates data collected by the Canadian government comparing the satisfaction levels of music graduates to other graduates. These figures suggest that, whether working within the field of music or not, music graduates continue to value their music training a great deal.

Table 6.1: Satisfaction of music graduates compared with graduates of other programs at the same level. (Job Futures, 2007, p. 2)

Question	'Yes' responses	
	Music graduates (%)	Other graduates (%)
Would you make the same educational choice again?	88	78
Are you satisfied with your work?	77	89
Does your work directly match your training?	37	52
Do you feel over-qualified for your work?	29	34

Although, as noted, employment income in the Canadian arts and culture sector is not high, it does vary considerably from profession to profession. The average income of conductors, composers and arrangers actually dropped from CAN$30,381 in 1995 to $27,381 in 2000, which represented a decrease of 10% in constant 2000 dollars. Over the same period, the average employment income of instrumentalists and singers (represented by the American Federation of Musicians and, in the case of opera singers, Actors' Equity) rose 17%, from CAN$13,718 in 1995 to CAN$16,090 in 2000 (Singh, 2005, p. 4). Despite gains in some areas, "earnings data show that most culture occupations are ranked in the bottom half (averaging less than CAN$30,000 annually) of all types of earners in Canada" (Luffman, 2001, p. 4). For this reason, and because variety and breadth have their own appeal, many musicians combine a primary focus on performing with one or more other occupations. A focus on two traditional employment streams – playing in orchestras and teaching in universities – highlights developments occurring across the spectrum of music careers in Canada. It is to these two employment streams that the chapter turns next.

Traditional employment streams

Playing in orchestras

Orchestras Canada provides advocacy, professional development and networking for orchestral musicians, boards and administrators, and represents more than 80 Canadian orchestras. Several are amateur or community orchestras, others are orchestras with a professional core only, and still others are full professional symphony orchestras. A few, such as the internationally renowned Tafelmusik, are period instrument ensembles.

One of *Orchestras Canada* services is an online, open access job postings site. A snapshot of postings between January and April 2008 gives an idea of opportunities in Canada. During this period, a total of sixteen positions in strings were auditioned (ten violin, three viola, two cello, one bass). Positions were available in British Columbia, Alberta, Ontario and Québec, but none were open in Saskatchewan, Manitoba or eastern Canada. Only one position in winds, brass and percussion was vacant anywhere in the country (2nd bassoon in the Toronto Symphony Orchestra). The fact that there are not large numbers of full-time, permanent positions available does not mean that professional playing opportunities do not exist. What it does mean is that orchestral musicians, like orchestras themselves, must rethink their career expectations.

In 2002 *Orchestras Canada* commissioned an independent study of the state of Canadian orchestras. Phase 1 involved a report based on stakeholder interviews (Chandler & Ginder, 2003, April 30) and Phase 2 comprised a national conference held in June 2003 thematically linked to the Phase 1 findings. Phase 3 constituted 30 recommendations based on findings in the Phase 1 report (Chandler & Ginder, 2003, July 30). A bias in favour of 'the good ol' days' is evident from the following statements in the initial report:

> With a few notable exceptions, musicians in Canadian orchestras are poorly paid relative to their training and experience. This, coupled with a reduction in the number of services and/or musicians, has led to an increase in moonlighting both inside and outside the musical milieu. This, in turn, cuts into practice and rehearsal time. (Chandler & Ginder, 2003, April 30)

These observations are predicated on the conviction that professional performers fulfil the singular function of performing music for others to enjoy. This view accords with the belief that, in the life of a professional musician, activities besides practising, rehearsing and performing are intrusive and unwelcome.

This model is less viable now than ever before. It has inherent limitations from the musician's perspective (a single job that is not especially well-remunerated) and has serious limitations from the audience's perspective (music is something that others do for you). It does not connect readily with generations of young people weaned on interactivity. For people in their teens or twenties who are accustomed to obtaining services on demand, a passive evening at the symphony listening to music written, programmed and performed by others may hold limited appeal. This is one reason why orchestras worldwide are engaged in crucial self-reflection.

As orchestras rethink themselves in order to attract new audiences, so musicians must rethink themselves, not only to increase job prospects, but also to garner greater job satisfaction. Growing numbers of practising musicians who once expected to spend their careers playing in professional orchestras are expanding their horizons, particularly in the direction of freelance work. This is especially true of players in (or in close proximity to) large urban centres. In and around Toronto, for instance, playing opportunities in musical theatre, opera, ballet, new music and films abound, but such employment is likely to be part-time and seasonal. What these opportunities provide, as well as additional income, is the diversity many musicians desire. Playing for 30 or 40 years in one orchestra that will have its ups and downs financially and artistically may not resonate with musicians who seek to engage life on their own terms rather on terms imposed by someone else. Professional self-determination is attractive to many players.

In addition to diversifying their performing portfolios, many orchestral musicians elect teaching as a supplementary source of income and, often, as a source of creativity and professional stimulation. Although part-time teaching positions at conservatoires, colleges and universities and private teaching are always options, full-time teaching at post-secondary institutions is attracting orchestral players in increasing numbers. At one institution, two of three candidates recently short-listed for a clarinet teaching position were orchestral musicians looking to change careers. One was in her early thirties, the other in his fifties, but both were seeking challenges, opportunities, stability, benefits and income beyond what orchestras can currently offer. Examples of the pro-active diversification of musicians can be seen in Chapter 8 and in the musician profiles included in Part II.

Teaching in universities

The availability of university teaching positions in music varies considerably from year to year. In Canada, postings in *University Affairs* (published by the Association of Universities and Colleges of Canada) and the *CAUT Bulletin* (published by the Canadian Association of University Teachers) reflect the numbers and kinds of positions available. In November/December 2007, for example, seventeen university teaching positions in music were advertised, most with a start date of summer 2008. Some positions involved studio instruction, while others involved classroom teaching; one position was administrative. The majority were probationary, tenure-track appointments, while a few were term replacements for professors on parental, sabbatical or administrative leave. Specialisations were as follows:

- Positions involving studio teaching (including composition and conducting): clarinet, violin, violin/viola, collaborative piano, composition, jazz piano, jazz bass, jazz voice, and orchestral conducting; and
- Positions not involving studio teaching (including administration): department chair, ethnomusicology, media studies/popular music, music cognition, music therapy, and theory.

Four positions were in Western Canada, ten were in Ontario and two were in Québec. No positions were open in British Columbia or Alberta and only one position was available in Eastern Canada.

Working conditions are generally excellent for university-based musicians in Canada. The standard teaching load is less than eighteen contact hours per week (usually 15 or 12) and the teaching year normally comprises two four-month terms (September to December and January to April). Unless spring or summer teaching is assigned as part of a standard teaching load or as remunerated overload, faculty members are free during May to August to perform, study and teach at summer music programs.

While orchestral musicians are not required to teach (although most do), university-based performers are expected to maintain active professional performance profiles. When performance academics apply for tenure and promotion, panels consider the status of venues in which the applicant has performed; whether broadcasts were local, regional or national, whether concerts were self-presented or part of an established series; whether recordings were distributed nationally or internationally; and whether they appeared on commercial or independent labels. At most universities, a high level of ongoing professional engagement is expected of all faculty members.

Besides teaching and performing, service to the community is required of Canadian performance academics. The distribution of responsibilities has traditionally been 40% teaching, 40% research (or, in practice-based disciplines, performance/creation) and 20% service. A tendency to view these activities as co-dependent signals widespread change. The old model of teaching, research or performance/creation and service was based on two assumptions: 1) that it is realistic and useful to separate these activities; and 2) that it is realistic and useful to rank them hierarchically. Because connectivity between academia and the wider community is gaining more traction all the time, an integrated and balanced approach to the assessment and evaluation of teaching faculty is burgeoning in Canada. In other words, the role performance academics play in the community is as important as the role they play within the university.

To this point we have considered ways in which traditional employment opportunities for musicians, namely playing in orchestras and teaching in universities, are changing. The following case study will show that out of this situation is emerging a new kind of career.

Marie: A case study

As orchestras and universities as well as recording companies, publishing firms and other partners in the music industry evolve to keep pace with globalisation, with a new world economy and with a new world order driven largely by technology, the advent of protean musicians reflects changed societal and personal values. As other contributors to this book have shown, this new kind of career is now common. For reasons ranging from personal preferences to the demands of the labour market, countless musicians are now involved, sequentially or simultaneously, in a breadth of professional activities. Indeed, the ability to shift back and forth within a range of undertakings is highly valued in the marketplace. It is not unusual for this mix of activities to fluctuate frequently in response to internal (or personal) and external (or social) stimuli. The ultimate goal for many musicians is to integrate personal and professional lives so that a fulfilling career in music unfolds in the company of one's partner, family and friends. Perkins further explores intrinsic career satisfaction in Chapter 2.

The following case study exemplifies how an identity that is uniquely satisfying and satisfyingly unique can be constructed from myriad professional opportunities. Choices that inscribe identity are made throughout one's career. It is rare that musicians today land in a particular job and remain there for the course of their careers without exploring opportunities within a fairly wide envelope of professional possibilities. This case study also provides useful fodder for discussion with students, since the subject, Marie, is by turns reactive (she makes the best of extant situations) and proactive (she creates new situations), which speaks of a non-prescriptive professional self-image.

Marie, who graduated with her Bachelor of Music degree in 1998, has followed a protean path. For two years after graduating she volunteered as the conductor of a community choir, was the volunteer accompanist and assistant conductor of a second choir, and coached musical theatre productions at high schools. She sang backup for a singer-songwriter and this required frequent touring and recording. In the final year of her degree, Marie had been a founding member of a women's chamber choir, with which she continued to rehearse and perform after graduation. She sang in a church choir and in other choral groups, and performed in two operas by a local composer. She taught voice and accompanied singers on piano. Her principal source of income was music related but did not come from performing: she worked full-time in the university music library, where she had been employed part-time while completing her degree.

In 2001 Marie became a founding member of the Canadian Chamber Choir, a nationally auditioned ensemble that undertakes one or two projects annually in different regions of the country. These projects involve rehearsals, concerts and workshops. As volunteer executive director of the choir she developed financial plans and organised national tours. She arranged auditions, managed the choir roster, developed budgets, prepared grant applications, initiated a fundraising strategy and created promotional material for the choir's website and press kit.

With her husband Jackson and three friends, in 2001 Marie also founded an alternative roots band, the Dust Poets, with which she sings and plays accordion. The group tours extensively in Canada and the US. Dust Poets gave its first overseas concerts in the UK in September 2010 and has released four CDs. The group is mostly self-managed, so Marie and Jackson assist in organising recording projects, writing grant applications, making tour bookings, and handling publicity, bookkeeping and merchandise sales. Marie also appears on an as-needed basis with other bands. In total, in the four years since obtaining her undergraduate degree Marie was involved in about two-dozen distinct and ongoing musical activities, all of which contribute to a rich and complex musical identity.

In 2003 Marie moved to Toronto, where Jackson was beginning his Master's degree. She was accepted into the Elmer Iseler Singers, a renowned professional choir with which she sang for three seasons. In 2007, Marie and her husband moved to Winnipeg, where Jackson is employed at Manitoba Music, an association that promotes growth and sustainability in the provincial music industry. Marie volunteered at the Winnipeg Folk Festival and was subsequently hired as its Education and Outreach coordinator. In that role she developed and oversaw outreach programming, worked with volunteers, and shared responsibility for front-office management and reception. All the while she continued to tour and record with the Dust Poets and Canadian Chamber Choir.

When I asked Marie if I could include a sketch of her career in this chapter, she made the following observations:

> *The thing I was starting to tell you about the other day is the idea that having a variety of musical experience gives you a musical 'edge': that each experience informs the way you approach every other one, and gives you all kinds of varied perspectives that you wouldn't have playing only one genre of music or one instrument. Take Crystal, who has chosen a classical clarinet career [she's now a university professor in Canada]: she's played in a mariachi band, played baritone sax in a jazz band, sung in a women's choir, played and sung in Kitchen Women [an alternative roots group] and studied accordion as a kid, and she would definitely credit all of this other stuff with giving her 'edge' as a clarinettist. For me, having chosen to keep more than one of these balls in the air professionally I see ways that my classical training informs my folk performing (and vice versa) all the time, and actually that's a huge part of what makes the Dust Poets distinctive. And not to take this into a discussion about what it takes to be a superstar performer (is it 'edge', or is it singular focus?), a very real truth is that being willing to diversify makes for a more sustainable career and keeps life interesting!*

Marie's success can be attributed to talent, ability and exceptional adaptability. She has spent much of her career to date engaged in musical activities of her own making, while at the same time working for other musicians and musical organisations. She has always been, simultaneously, a performing musician across several genres and an administrator. Her career will undoubtedly continue to take twists and turns she could not possibly have anticipated and for which her formal education provided only informal preparation. She fits perfectly the model of a musician who creates her own opportunities, who adapts quickly and easily, and for whom performing is one component of a spectrum of professional activities. In this way she typifies a successful modern musician.

Conclusion

Marie's career has been driven by a complex matrix of circumstances and aspirations that have required self-reflection every step of the way. It demonstrates that curricula must be designed in consultation with professionals like Marie and must foster meaningful community engagement from the first year of study.

The most obvious means by which these objectives can be achieved is community service learning and service-learning-like activities, as well as by involving university-based research institutes in curricular design. If students are engaged in the communities in which they live, as well as given credit towards their degrees either by means of course credits or at least annotations on their transcripts, a sense of belonging to the community will accrue that becomes integral to professional identity. Curricula that include opportunities for students to participate musically in the community, and to see first-hand the effects that music making and teaching have on the community, will go a long way not only towards helping students forge an identity relevant to today's world, but also towards cultivating the incentives and tools to embrace lifelong learning that can help students remain relevant to tomorrow's world.

Similarly, when students become involved with research institutes and government agencies the relevance of their studies can be underscored. There are, for instance, two research institutes at Wilfrid Laurier University in Ontario that intersect with that institution's curricular objectives. The Manfred and Penny Conrad Centre for Music Therapy Research (opened in September 2003) and the Laurier Centre for Music in the Community (opened in March 2008) partner with organisations and individuals in the community and extend a bridge between the university and community along which students are situated as participants and observers. Community outreach can thus link research to praxis. There is a wealth of other programs in Canada that are designed to do precisely this, including the Community Arts Practice Certificate at York University in southern Ontario.

Experiential learning, which as is shown elsewhere in this book is hugely advantageous to students, is fundamental to music programs. But the programs in existence tend to 'preach to the choir' in that they attract students, teachers and researchers who have already recognised the role the arts play in a social milieu. The majority of music students, especially performers, rarely interrogate larger social issues, and it is with this cohort in mind that new curricula can be developed. A few examples from Brandon University and Memorial University of Newfoundland, one in the middle of Canada and the other at the Eastern extreme, are illustrative. Whether the focus of a program is performance, theory, music education, digital arts media or something else, curricula can encourage students to:

- Investigate their emergent identities by unpacking the role music and musicians play in society. Dialogue in lessons and classes is a first step, but identity modules in, for example, music history classes, can ensure a moderated design instead of hit-and-miss opportunities to explore social contexts. For example, students in a Baroque music history class at Brandon University wrote essays on Vivaldi's ubiquitousness as elevator/restaurant/mall music and explored why this might be so. Is it something inherent in the music itself? Do we harbour a distorted perception of this superficially formulaic repertoire? Or, rather, is our view of Vivaldi linked to the way we perceive music's purpose today? Such topics invite students to look at old music in a new light, situating repertoire in a contemporary setting relevant to their own experiences. It is one thing to recognise that something is so; it is another to ask why;

- Participate in service-learning activities that encourage interaction between students and community partners. Memorial University of Newfoundland has an ambitious Opera RoadShow that takes the School of Music's Opera Workshop to Newfoundland outports. The opera students engage in school and community workshops and performances:

    > Professional training is the primary activity of the opera workshop program [and] the Opera RoadShow is a vibrant component in the professional development of its artists. Outreach is also an opportunity to give young audiences access to a new and powerful way of using their voices that expands creative communication in all aspects of their lives. (Memorial University website)

    At Brandon University, the Rural Development Institute has supported tours by student ensembles to rural and northern regions to engage in community, school and other outreach initiatives. By reaching out now, modes of behaviour are adopted that can inform professional careers later on;

- Interact with professionals engaged in sociological and related research in such areas as community development and popular culture. At Brandon University, a course in the 'Sociology of Folk, Blues and Roots Music' does precisely this: "drawing from theories of popular culture this course examines folk music traditions as a social phenomenon. Topics include: the social type of the singer/song writer; marginality and artistic expression; the subculture of folk traditions; song writing, social problems and social control" (Brandon University website). Courses similar to this in all genres of music can be easily imagined;

- Develop lifelong learning skills that will serve students' needs as their careers inevitably take unanticipated twists and turns. Professional development courses that examine successful career trajectories (such as Marie's protean career) will help students appreciate how constantly reviewing and updating their professional skills and attributes is a prerequisite to ongoing success;

- Develop knowledge and experience of formal and informal musical practices in the wider community. In Brandon University's Introduction to Community Music course, students "work towards a personal understanding of what Community Music means globally" by researching local, regional, national and international Community Music practices. "The course examines sociological, cultural, historical, political and pedagogical issues related to Community Music" (Brandon University website). This course, which is available to all streams of the undergraduate music program, is of value to all music students since musicians cannot thrive except in community with others.

The key to helping intending and practising professional musicians find their place in society, and engage productively in a complex network of stakeholders, is to design curricula that require self-awareness, self-reflection, community outreach and social interaction from the very first stages. Students themselves cannot be expected to make these connections entirely without guidance. An observation made by Carl Morey almost 30 years ago remains relevant today:

> It is true ... that most young people have a very limited set of ideas about what a musical career might be when they start musical training, and it frequently happens that with experience they come upon a facet of musical life that pulls them away from their original plans for the perfectly good reason that they are more attracted to the alternative. (Morey, in Green *et al.*, 1986, p. 178)

Students often have a definite but unrealistic idea of the shape and direction their careers might take. More often than not this involves a single locus of activity. This is not surprising since in discrete curricular streams at most universities, performers are separated from music educators, performers and music educators are separated from music theorists and historians, and so forth. But in recent years, nodes between disciplines have attracted more attention. Awareness of the means by which performing and non-performing activities successfully merge in a balanced career has resulted in a restructuring of music programs. Interdisciplinary studies that include a mix of theoretical and practical modules are now common, and students are graduating with increasingly robust skill sets. As well, consumer demand for engagement and reciprocity is reshaping the performing arts as a vital means of building, asserting and sustaining community. This is integral to urban renewal. Many educational institutions, orchestras, opera companies and other musical organisations are taking their responsibility to the community seriously and are working assiduously to anticipate societal needs.

There is, however, an inherent pitfall in trying to anticipate what skills musicians might need in the future. Institutions, and the students trained by them, run the risk of limiting themselves to the imaginable, when it is the unimaginable for which future generations of musicians must be prepared. This is the real challenge for all musicians: to remain relevant in the midst of constant flux (Carruthers, 2009). Teachers, administrators and bureaucrats must ensure that arts curricula and policies remain current and reflect a society whose shape and character could not reasonably have been anticipated even a generation ago. One thing is certain: for the foreseeable future, professional musicians will be galvanised and communities will be animated not by entrenchment, specialisation, isolation and privilege, but by adaptability, all-roundedness, reciprocity and democracy. These characteristics form the basis of enlightened curricular reform that will serve the interests of today's students tomorrow.

References

Adorno, T. W. (1962/1976). *Introduction to the sociology of music.* New York: Seabury Press.

Adorno, T. W. & Simpson, G. (1941). On popular music. *Studies in philosophy and social science, ix,* 17-48.

Brandon University Website. 2009-2010 General Calendar. Introduction to community music. Retrieved November 10, 2009, from http://calendar.brandonu.ca:8080/servlet/calendar?book=u-grad2009&key=30369&full=.

Carruthers, G. (2009). Reactive and proactive reform in post-secondary music schools. *Ecclectica Online — The Arts Edition.* Retrieved August 8, 2009 from http://www.ecclectica.ca/issues/2009/1/.

Carruthers, G. (2008). Human, social and creative/community capital in the training of professional musicians. In D. Bennett & M. Hannan (Eds.), *Inside, outside, downside up: Conservatoire training and musicians' work* (pp. 37-47). Perth: Black Swan Press.

Carruthers, G. (2001). A status report on music education in Canada. In S. T. Maloney (Ed.), *MUSICANADA 2000: A celebration of Canadian composers/Un hommage aux compositeurs canadiens* (pp. 86-95). Montréal: Editions Liber.

Chandler, D., & Ginder, J. (2003). Soundings: Towards a better future for Canada's orchestral community. Retrieved February 7, 2008, from https://www.securewebexchange.com/oc.ca/password/CCopusEmployment.php.

Chandler, D., & Ginder, J. (2003). Soundings: Recommended actions in the short term. Retrieved February 7, 2008, from https://www.securewebexchange.com/oc.ca/aboutUs/PHASE_THREE_Recommendatios.pdf.

Conference Board of Canada. *Valuing culture—measuring and understanding Canada's creative economy.* Retrieved November 5, 2009, from http://www.torc.on.ca/documents/08-152_CanadasCreativeEconomy.pdf.

Durand, M. (2004). The culture sector labour force: Has the 1990s boom turned to bust? *Focus on Culture* (Quarterly Bulletin from the Culture Statistics Program), *14*(3), 1-8. Retrieved February 7, 2008, from http://www.statcan.ca/english/freepub/87-004-XIE/0030287-004-XIE.pdf.

Frith, S. (1996). *Performing rites: On the value of popular music.* Oxford: Oxford University Press.

Green, J. P. & Vogan, N. F. (1991). *Music education in Canada: A historical account.* Toronto: University of Toronto Press.

Green, T., Sauerbrei, P., & Sedgwick, D. (Eds.). (1986). *Careers in music: A guide for Canadian students.* Oakville, ON: The Frederick Harris Music Co.

Hill Strategies Research Inc. (2007). A profile of the cultural and heritage activities of Canadians in 2005. *Statistical Insight on the Arts, 5*(4). Retrieved January 31, 2008, from http://www.canadacouncil.ca/NR/rdonlyres/510379DB-37C1-4C70-934A-197D8670CD72/0/Cultural_activities2005.pdf.

Job Futures. (2007). National Edition, Services Canada Website. Retrieved November 5, 2009, from http://www.jobfutures.ca/fos/U051.shtml.

Kerman, J. (1985). *Contemplating music: Challenges to musicology.* Cambridge, Mass.: Harvard University Press.

Loesser, A. (1954). *Men, women and pianos: A social history.* New York: Simon & Schuster.

Luffman, J. (2001). Labour market outcomes of arts and culture graduates. *Focus on Culture* (Quarterly Bulletin from the Culture Statistics Program), *12*(3), 3-9. Retrieved January 31, 2008, from http://www.statcan.ca/english/freepub/87-004-XIE/0030087-004-XIE.pdf.

Memorial University of Newfoundland website. Opera Workshop/Opera RoadShow. Retrieved November 10, 2009 from http://www.mun.ca/music/ensembles/opera.

Opus (Orchestras Canada job postings website). Retrieved February 7, 2008, from https://www.securewebexchange.com/oc.ca/password/CCopusEmployment.php.

Raynor, H. (1976). *Music and society since 1815.* London: Barrie & Jenkins.

Raynor, H. (1972). *A social history of music from the Middle Ages to Beethoven.* London: Barrie & Jenkins.

Shepherd, J. (1991). *Music as social text*. Cambridge: Polity Press.
Shepherd, J., Virden, P., Vulliamy, G., & Wishart, T. (Eds.). (1977). *Whose music? A sociology of musical languages*. London: Latimer.
Shepherd, J. & Wicke, P. (1997). *Music and cultural theory*. Cambridge: Polity Press.
Singh, V. (2005). Earnings of culture workers: Findings from Canadian census data. *Focus on Culture* (Quarterly Bulletin from the Culture Statistics Program), *15*(2), 1-5. Retrieved February 7, 2008, from http://www.statcan.ca/english/freepub/87-004-XIE/0020387-004-XIE.pdf.
Singh, V. (2004). Economic contribution of culture in Canada. *Culture, tourism and the centre for education statistics. Research Paper No. 23*. Retrieved February 7, 2008, from http://www.statcan.ca/english/research/81-595-MIE/81-595-MIE2004023.pdf.
Small, C. (1977). *Music—society—education*. London: Calder.

Further reading

Bowman, W., Ed. (2006). The future of university music study in Canada (a collection of seventeen articles on Canadian post-secondary music education). *Ecclectica Online*. http://www.ecclectica.ca/issues/2006/2/.
Callon, G. J. (2007, July 27). *Career opportunities in music*. Acadia University Website: http://plato.acadiau.ca/courses/musi/callon/CAREERS.HTM.
Carruthers, G. (2008). Educating professional musicians: Lessons learned from school music. *International Journal of Music Education*, *26*(2): 127-135.
Carruthers, G. (2006). Universities and the music-learning continuum. *International Journal of Community Music*, *D*, pp. 1-17. www.intljcm.com/.
Department of Canadian Heritage (2006). *The Canadian music industry 2006 economic profile*. http://www.pch.gc.ca/pgm/fmusc-cmusf/pubs/prfl/prfl-eng.pdf.
Shepherd, J., Ed. (2000). Music studies in the new millennium. Special issue of the *Canadian University Music Review/Revue de musique des universities canadiennes*, *21*(1).
Statistics Canada Service Bulletin (2007). Sound recording and music publishing. http://www.statcan.gc.ca/pub/87f0008x/87f0008x2009001-eng.htm.
What can I do with my studies [in music]? Student Academic Success Service, University of Ottawa. http://www.sass.uottawa.ca/careers/studies/arts/finearts/music.php.

Websites for Canadian organisations

Association of Universities and Colleges of Canada: http://www.aucc.ca/
Brandon University Rural Development Institute:
    http://www2.brandonu.ca/organizations/RDI/
Canadian Association of University Teachers: http://www.caut.ca/
Canadian Chamber Choir: http://www.canadianchamberchoir.ca/
Dust Poets: http://www.dustpoets.com/
Elmer Iseler Singers: http://www.elmeriselersingers.com/
Laurier Centre for Music in the Community:
    http://www.wlu.ca/page.php?grp_id=29&p=9042
Manfred and Penny Conrad Centre for Music Therapy Research:
    http://www.wlu.ca/page.php?grp_id=29&p=10526
Manitoba Music: http://www.manitobamusic.com/
Orchestras Canada: http://www.oc.ca/
Statistics Canada: http://www.statcan.ca/menu-en.htm
Tafelmusik: http://www.tafelmusik.org/
Toronto Symphony Orchestra: http://www.tso.on.ca/season/index.cfm
Winnipeg Folk Festival: http://www.winnipegfolkfestival.ca/wp/
York University Community Arts Practice Certificate:
    http://www.yorku.ca/web/futurestudents/programs/template.asp?id=613

Chapter 7
Change and the Challenges of Lifelong Learning
Rineke Smilde

This chapter addresses music developments in Europe and what these might mean for those working in the sector. When looking at issues such as musical life and careers, international mobility, and training for professional musicians, Europe should not merely be defined as consisting of the countries that are members of the European Union (EU). Rather, Europe in a musician's sense encompasses the whole conglomerate of those 47 countries that work together on implementing the Bologna Process in higher (music) education. Some of the research that is drawn upon in this chapter covers the Bologna Process participants, whilst other research addresses the countries of the EU (currently 27 member states).

This chapter traces developments in musical life in Europe and what this means for the careers of the musicians; how post-secondary music academies align with this; and how the concept of lifelong learning can play a key role in addressing the challenges. Drawing on biographical research, the chapter concludes with observations on musicians' lifelong learning. Based on that research, the chapter considers strategies for implementing a 'lifelong learning environment' within music academies.

Change and the challenges of lifelong learning

Musicians in Europe face major changes in the social-cultural landscape and corresponding changes in the music profession. This rapidly changing cultural life is leading to a shift in the nature of musicians' careers. As elsewhere, whereas in the past a professional musician might acquire a secure job in, for example, a music school or an orchestra, that is no more the case. One of the reasons for the decrease in formally organised jobs within Europe is ongoing change to state funding for the arts. As classical music organisations lose dominance and other music styles gain popularity, cultural life is being organised in a different way (Prchal, 2006). As a consequence, musicians in Europe have evolved more flexible career patterns and there is a greater need for transferable skills in areas such as self-management, decision-making and business.

Just like musicians in other locations, European musicians most often combine several professional activities, functioning in different cultural contexts and in varying roles. Their professional environment has also become increasingly international. In fact, by far the most important development in the European music profession is the emergence of the portfolio career in which musicians are increasingly self-employed, entrepreneurial and mobile. Rarely employed in one job for life (or even one job at a time), the European musician is increasingly an entrepreneur with simultaneous or successive, brief and/or part-time periods of employment, often within different areas of the economy. This overlapping of activities makes it rather difficult to provide an accurate picture of the music industry throughout Europe (Rogers, 2002).

Whilst exact figures of musicians holding a portfolio career are not known, alumni research from a number of European music academies suggests that the increase of protean careers is substantial. As in Australia (Bennett, 2008) the most common combination of roles is that of a performer and a teacher. A portfolio career does not mean that a musician has not been employable; rather, it reflects societal change and creates exciting challenges. As expressed by Myers (2007, p. 4):

> The role of portfolio careers in sustaining the professional lives and energies of musicians carries important implications for lifelong musician education and learning. Moreover, the fact that at least a portion of these successful musicians has grown to see themselves as adding value to the larger society, rather than expecting society to sustain their isolated and detached musical prowess, indicates the need for early grappling with the question of what it means to be a musician in contemporary society. Structured opportunities for students to think analytically about this question is a positive way to consider that careers will likely involve a complex of intentional and complementary initiatives supported by lifelong learning for a cross-section of knowledge and skills. That is a very different message from the frequently unspoken subtext that if one expects to survive as a musician, he or she will necessarily piece together a potentially random group of jobs that have the cumulative effects of compromising lofty ambitions and perpetuating the view that one is undervalued.

Indeed, more and more European musicians are challenged to collaborate with practitioners in other arts and non-arts sectors (business, health care, young offenders, educational projects and so on). This presents important opportunities for generating new kinds of artistic work.

Despite the increasing professional demands on musicians, the standards of performance excellence keep rising such that there is an ongoing demand for higher artistic and educational quality. The question arises as to how future professional musicians (and the institutions training them) can deal with the requirement of such new competences. Functioning successfully as a professional musician is not an easy task. Clearly, as Beeching points out in Chapter 3, being talented and having many artistic skills is not enough. Research by the European Association of Conservatoires (AEC) into continuing professional development for musicians and the needs of graduates (Smilde, 2000; Lafourcade & Smilde, 2001) indicates that graduates of music academies encounter a variety of challenges upon entering the music profession, mirroring many of the challenges outlined by Weller in Chapter 4. In sum, more than ever before, the future professional musician is confronted by the question: 'how can I function in a flexible way and exploit opportunities in new and rapidly changing cultural contexts?' To this end it is important to explore with students the concept of lifelong learning, which is a dynamic concept that responds to the needs generated by continuous change. Its key characteristics can be used for the development of new creative and adaptive educational approaches for musicians, enabling them to function in a flexible, responsive and pro-active way akin to the characteristics of the protean career.

Lifelong learning can be defined as a concept spanning an entire lifetime in a process of "transforming experience into knowledge, skills, attitudes, values, emotions, beliefs and the senses" (Jarvis, 2002, p. 60). This learning incorporates the knowledge, skills and attitudes that extend beyond the formal education system. The lifelong learning concept goes further than 'permanent education'; its innovative dimension lies in a new approach to the process and context of learning (Fragoulis, 2002).

In addition to a distinction between formal, non-formal and informal education, characteristics important to the concept of lifelong learning include an emphasis on 'learning' as opposed to 'training'. Different approaches to learning are required according to context as much as the critical interconnection of professional and personal development. Before taking a closer look at lifelong learning for musicians, I will explore in more detail what the music profession in Europe is like at present and what its changes imply for future musicians.

The musical landscape and the professional musician

The European creative sector is blooming (European Commission, 2006). Some 5.8 million people were employed in culture in 2004, equivalent to 3.1% of the total employed population within the European Commission (EU) states. Whereas total employment decreased between 2002 and 2004, employment in the cultural sector increased by 1.85%. In a political sense the creative sector in Europe is widely regarded as beneficial, with the arts increasingly considered important for the economic development of both cities and regions (ibid). International research into labour market requirements for arts graduates (Coenen, 2008) identifies two trends of increasing importance to 'human capital' in the knowledge society: flexibility in a transitional labour market, and internationalisation in a global context. These trends suggest specific requirements in terms of professional expertise, flexibility and innovation.

What is the role of music in this creative sector? It is not possible to give figures on employability for musicians in Europe because statistics created at a European level only address 'cultural employment', which encompasses occupations ranging from architecture to book selling. However, EC trends emerging from quantitative studies of cultural employment (EC, 2007) align with those from qualitative research into musicians' employment in Europe, which are addressed in the following section.

The music industry in Europe paints a complex picture. With European musicians increasingly creating and producing their own performances, there is a corresponding growth in the number of independent producers as well as small enterprises. Although this situation definitely increases employability, often the pay and conditions of such work are below the minimum standards of the countries in question. At the same time, musical niches are being created, providing opportunities for generating new work as well as a new demand for creative musicians who are able to lead creative workshops in the community and in cross-sectoral settings. The British report 'Creating a Land with Music' (Rogers, 2002) details research on the work, education and training of present-day professional musicians in the UK and addresses their changing career patterns. Looking at areas of engagement for the present-day musician, more than 50 roles were identified. From these, four central roles—those of composer, performer, leader and teacher—were identified as relevant to all musical genres and specialisations. To fulfil a particular role, for instance, the composer may be a songwriter, orchestrator or arranger, while displaying the qualities of visionary, innovator, risk-taker or explorer. A performer may sing or play an instrument, and the role may require elements of composition, improvisation or leadership as a bandleader (Rogers, 2002). This approach, common to many of the situations and contexts described in this book, is certainly broadly applicable to the European situation over the past decade.

All in all, it is clear that musicians must take up various interrelated activities (Smilde 2006). One way of approaching this with students is to consider various active roles and to explore how these roles might relate to students' planned lives in music:

- Innovator (explorer, creator and risk taker);
- Identifier (of missing skills, and of means to refresh them);
- Partner/co-operator (within formal partnerships);
- Reflective practitioner (engaged in research and evaluative processes);

- Collaborator (dialoguing with, for instance, professional arts practitioners, students and teachers);
- Connector (in relation to contexts musicians are involved in);
- Entrepreneur (and job creator).

Between 2004 and 2007 a working group within the AEC conducted research on current trends in all sectors of the European music profession. The group visited sites in different countries, investigated examples of innovative practice, and held interviews with individual 'cutting edge' musicians. Qualitative research and analysis into the music 'industry' provided the basis for a thematic description of these trends (Amussen & Smilde, 2007). The main findings of this research will be addressed in the following section, which focuses on European perspectives relating to audiences, the role of technology, teaching in music schools, and community work. It will be shown that these perspectives are manifold, identifying strengths and weaknesses, opportunities and challenges, including the relationships with many areas of policy making. Links to each of the projects are included at the end of this chapter.

Cultural policies

Recent changes in cultural policy and decreases in overall government funding have led institutions and arts organisers to develop many more public-private partnerships, which necessitate a raft of skills in grant writing, promotion and forward planning. Thus, among the trends simultaneously at work in Europe is the shift from a one-sided protection of national or traditional cultures to supporting cultural diversity, with priority given to event programming instead of larger, longstanding cultural institutions. In theory, innovation and creation are at the heart of most current cultural policies and strategies. Thus, key issues for European cultural policies include:

- Prioritisation of culture as a major obligation for governments;
- Encouragement of innovative and varied arts forms;
- Involvement of as many people as possible in cultural activities;
- An accent on economic and social value of the arts and culture;
- The search for new funding sources; and
- Support for diversity and creativity.

Whilst in some countries traditional public funding patterns continue in forms such as subsidies for orchestras, choirs and the like, new efforts are being made to provide 'niche' funding or to broaden audiences in ways that are seen as relevant to society.

Audiences

In line with Beeching's description of the US (Chapter 3), new European audiences have developed partly in response to the multicultural societies of many European countries. Cultural range and diversity have expanded significantly in recent years, playing a distinct role in the changing musical world

(Amussen & Smilde, 2007). In response, a growing number of musicians are exploring the potential of world music, absorbing it into their artistic vocabulary. Encounters with non-Western traditions impact the work of composers and performers in areas ranging from classical music to jazz, and are often integrated into a broad range of pedagogical settings. In addition, new technologies and media present new opportunities and challenges for musicians facing the emergence of 'global audiences' in the virtual world of the Internet.

Technology

As we have seen in earlier chapters, new and evolving technologies have had a considerable impact on music and the professional sector. The production, reception and distribution of music are changing significantly. Music making in home studios provides musicians with the opportunity to create their own music without being directed by producers. As Internet music communities emerge, they offer the independent musician an opportunity to place products directly into a huge network. Record companies commonly find new artists via these Internet music communities. Alongside such new portals are new ways of making a profit from music distributed via the Internet. However, this ease of access also signals a new set of generic skills. Whilst on one hand it is easier than ever to be present in a worldwide market, on the other hand competition is similarly global, and remaining visible within the vast media industries is a complex task. Exploring students' existing expertise and activities often highlights an array of skills that can be shared and expanded as well as opening the eyes of other students to the possibilities of using social networking strategies to build their profiles. Weller (Chapter 4) suggests, for example, encouraging students to post their recitals on Facebook and to develop electronic press kits.

Teaching in music schools

Teaching in music schools—in this context, schools where amateurs take music lessons—has changed considerably in recent years. Goal-oriented music education values have been replaced in many cases by those stressing the importance of the musical experience, which relies in part on establishing a good relationship between children and music. Whilst the master-apprentice approach is still at the core of music education, the importance of other approaches is growing steadily. In this respect, the varied cultural backgrounds present in European society provide valuable cultural perspectives whilst presenting challenges for music education.

Music school infrastructure and governance is very different throughout Europe. Many schools are still funded by government or through city grants, but in some countries music schools are suffering from a lack of public funding and other financial resources, resulting in more private schools. Compared to the recent past, music schools have to be more accountable and connected to society, and they need to produce services that meet the needs and expectations of individual clients. These developments imply new requirements for music teachers as well as for the management of music schools. Competition with pupils' leisure time is not always favourable to hobbies that require time and concentration and in which progress can be slow. In some European countries this has seen the development of art schools that encourage new forms of collaboration and inter-arts learning.

Community work and cross-arts collaboration

In regions such as the UK, the Nordic countries and the Netherlands, the past decade has seen an increase in work available within the wider community. Community musicians and teaching artists such as those described by Beeching (Chapter 3) devise and lead creative workshops in health and social care settings, in prisons and the like. Creative workshops developed by music leaders in very diverse venues are underpinned by the notion that the improvisational nature of collaborative workshop approaches can lead to people expressing themselves creatively, instilling a sense of shared ownership and responsibility both in the process and in the final product of the workshop (Gregory, 2005). The exchange of ideas and skills among the participants in the form of participatory learning is an integral part of the process.

In the UK, the profile of the animateur, engaged in creative workshops, has for some time been strongly developed. An animateur can be defined as "a practicing artist, in any form, who uses her/his skills, talents and personality to enable others to compose, design, devise, create, perform or engage with works of arts of any kind" (Animarts, 2003). Musicians working as animateurs can provide the bridge between performers and audiences, often working with performers and other artists to facilitate workshops in outreach projects, and to devise and lead new formats for concerts and community work. As seen in some of the musician profiles featured in this book, many musicians will function as both animateur and performer.

Interaction with other art forms provides openings for inter-arts and cross-genre collaboration. The growing interest in adding a visual or theatrical component to performance, and the development of new media, has led to numerous interdisciplinary collaborations involving musicians, actors, dancers and visual artists of all sorts (painters, cinematographers, video artists and so on). Thus, there is a steady growth of new types of performance and production.

In sum, it is evident that musicians in Europe need to respond to the changing musical landscape, to the many challenges and opportunities to be found within different cultural contexts and, as a result, to regularly revisit their priorities. Renshaw (2001, p. 3) argues that it is "imperative that musicians and the whole arts community begin to engage in both a local and global debate about who we are and about what we can achieve together". The next part of this chapter investigates how post-secondary European music academies are responding to these developments and how the changes in the music profession relate to new European educational policies.

European music academies responding to change

Systems of training

The systems of professional music training differ substantially across Europe. For example, the Bachelor program can have a duration of three years in one country and four years in another, and curricula can vary considerably. The Master's degree varies from one to two years and music academies in a number of European countries offer Doctoral-level studies. The responsibility for higher music education also differs within European countries. Curricula can be state-directed and controlled, and music academies can be fully or partly funded by the state. In some countries, quality assurance and institutional performance is directly aligned with government funding or accreditation.

Table 7.1 gives an overview of the number of students enrolled in music academies in Europe. When looking at the table it is important to keep a few things in mind. Firstly, the information has been gathered by the AEC (European Association of Conservatoires) and therefore concerns numbers of students enrolled in AEC member institutions. Not all institutions of higher music education in Europe are members. Also, in some countries, the number of students in the table can include junior departments of the music academies. And, lastly, conservatoires in some European countries offer tuition for amateur musicians. This is also the reason I use the term 'music academy' in this chapter to indicate professional training institutions at a post-secondary (higher education) level.

Dealing with graduates' needs

Regardless of the systems of training, change in the music profession has occurred throughout Europe. But how successful are European music academies in preparing their students for a future professional life that is so complex and multi-dimensional? What do graduates need once they enter the profession, and how do music academies respond to these needs? In 2000, the AEC began Promuse, an investigation into professional integration and continuing professional development for musicians as well as the needs of recent graduates from European music academies (Lafourcade & Smilde, 2001).

During the Promuse study, former students of music academies in the EU were asked about their professional lives and needs after graduation. The results revealed a variety of problems for graduates, almost all of which related to finding or generating work. The aspects most often identified as missing from music academy training were health-related knowledge, improvisation, and participation in chamber music and large ensemble performance. The graduates also reported that they had not gained enough experience in the professional world prior to graduation. The top skills that respondents felt should be offered after graduation were those of further instrumental and technical training, teaching and marketing. Other skills regularly highlighted were those required for management and for leading inter-arts workshops. The main thrust in the responses was the strong need for life skills: transferable generic skills.

Table 7.1: Students enrolled in European Music Academies in 2007

Country	Number of music students
Austria*	11 036
Belgium	2 928
Bosnia Herzegowina	720
Bulgaria	1 747
Croatia	674
Cyprus	88
Czech Republic	874
Denmark	1 259
Estonia	1 248
Finland	5 082
France*	22 653
Germany	26 410
Greece	499
Hungary	980
Iceland	278
Ireland*	6 700
Italy*	15 956
Latvia	426
Lithuania	1 150
Luxembourg*	3 188
Netherlands	5 097
Norway	1 496
Poland	5 253
Portugal	829
Rumania	2 987
Serbia	1 450
Slovakia	1 226
Slovenia	360
Spain	6 200
Sweden	3 216
Switzerland*	5 800
United Kingdom	6 310

* The divide between the number of tertiary students and amateur students is not known; hence those countries marked with an asterisk show a much higher number of students.

Furthermore, information was gained regarding what provision for continuing professional development existed and whether there was a match between the needs of graduates and this provision. The outcomes, shown at Table 7.2, were striking: the highest priority identified by the former students, 'life skills', was the lowest priority of the music academies and other providers. 'Information exchange' (the opportunity to receive information on career perspectives and create possibilities for networking, including international orientation) was at the top of the providers' priority list and at the bottom of the graduates' list. Performance skills and pedagogical skills were emphasised equally by both groups.

Table 7.2: Continuing Professional Development (CPD) priorities of graduates and providers (1 = most important, 4 = least important)

Former students ask for:	Providers offer:
1. Life skills	1. Information Exchange
2. Performance skills	2. Performance skills
3. Pedagogical skills	3. Pedagogical skills
4. Information exchange	4. Life skills

One of the explanations for this mismatch might be the low value afforded by institutions to the opinions of former students. The research showed that more priority was given to providers' *own* perception of graduates' needs than to the perceptions of graduates themselves, as can be seen in Table 7.3.

Table 7.3: Providers' decision criteria for the provision of CPD (1 = most important, 5 = least important)

1. Institutional perception of what graduates need
2. Availability of funding
3. Perception of staff and colleagues
4. Availability of staff
5. Opinion of former students

All in all, it is clear that the dialogue with music alumni is important in generating continuous information about the relevance of curricula to changing needs in the profession. Moreover, former students are often eager to stay in contact with their school and appreciate being informed.

What, then, is the current state of alumni policies and programs in Europe? The aforementioned AEC working group on the music profession conducted a study on alumni policies in European music academies, and the outcomes were promising: 33% of participating institutions had constituted alumni policies, mostly within the last five years, with 41% intending to establish an alumni policy in the near future. However, 27% of the institutions had neither an alumni policy nor plans to establish one. The potential benefits to alumni were seen as the development of a professional network, lifelong learning opportunities as well as access to institutional facilities or resources such as a library, career service and instrument loans (AEC, 2007). In turn, initiating dialogue between alumni and students provided students with an immediate network of expertise, opportunities and respected peer opinion. Nonetheless, the increasing potential to move between European music academies is equally important when considering both graduate and faculty needs.

International mobility and opportunities through the Bologna process

Many European music students can spend between three and twelve months on exchange at another European music academy. With a learning agreement between the home institution and the host institution, students can, without risking delays in their studies, spend a period in an institution that perhaps offers courses not offered in the home institution, or study with a highly valued teacher. Spending a period abroad often broadens students' horizons and increases career confidence. In general, these exchanges are well organised and they are supported by the European Erasmus program for student and teacher exchanges.

The international mobility of music students and teachers has been made easier through the Bologna Process, an important educational reform in European Higher Education. The Bologna Process aims to create more transparency in European systems of higher education in order to ease the mobility of students and to make sure that qualifications are recognised in all countries, which is of course a major consideration for musicians' future employability. The 'Bologna Declaration' was undersigned in 1999 by ministers of Education from 29 European countries and is already undersigned by 47 countries. The Declaration also has agreement with several non-European countries such as Australia. In the Declaration it was agreed that, by 2010, a European Area for Higher Education would have been established.

One of the important results of the Bologna process is the establishment of a Europe-wide Bachelor-Master system and the use of common European credits. This means that students can take exchange study or transfer between institutions without loss of credit. An AEC (2007) inquiry into mobility figures showed that each year an average of nine students per European music academy go on exchange to another institution, and that institutions receive approximately nine students per year. More students from Eastern Europe visit schools in Western Europe than vice versa. In terms of teachers' mobility, each year an average of six teachers per institution go on exchange, and institutions host an average of five visiting teachers. By 2007, one-third of the institutions used the European credit point system for student exchanges. However, this did not yet occur in Southern Europe or in France and Germany. Whilst implementation of the Bologna process is still underway, a great deal has already been achieved within higher music education.

Lifelong learning for musicians

When considering the changes, challenges and opportunities in musicians' careers, it is clear that musicians need to be lifelong learners in order to adapt to continuous change. As we saw at the beginning of this chapter, lifelong learning encompasses more than 'just' taking courses in the framework of continuing professional development. It is clearly important to establish how young professional musicians can strengthen their professional role as well as their awareness as entrepreneurial and reflective musicians of today and tomorrow. One of the most powerful ways of illustrating this is with the narratives of young musicians with diverse career paths.

For this illustration I draw on my research on 'musicians as lifelong learners', which employed biographical research to ascertain how musicians learn and how careers develop (Smilde, 2009; 2009a). After writing and analysing 32 learning biographies of European musicians with different roles and from various age categories, three key areas of personal and professional development emerged. These can be described as:

- Musicians' different forms of leadership;
- The interconnection between musicians' varied learning styles; and
- Musicians' need for an adaptive and responsive learning environment.

Musicians' artistic, generic and educational leadership is underpinned by different learning styles and critical reflection. The next section addresses musicians' learning styles and leadership before turning to the biographies of three lifelong learners.

Musicians' learning styles

The narratives clearly show that informal learning—playing together, observing each other and experiencing music—is a very important mode of learning in music, no matter whether this takes place in childhood or later in life, including the period of post-secondary music study. The bedrock of this informal learning is participatory learning such as collaborative music making in, for example, a choir, a wind band, chamber ensemble or orchestra. Peer learning, which takes place in a setting of trust between friends, is a second important aspect of musicians' informal learning. Musicians learn in a reflexive way by playing together, by listening, observing and making conversation. A very important feature of informal and participatory learning was identified as improvisation, which deals with expressing one's inner self and relates to expressivity, communication, musical identity, social learning, ownership and sharing musical ideas, as well as sharing one's vulnerability with other musicians. This was of great importance to nearly all musicians.

In sum, creating space for informal and participatory learning within formal learning settings was shown to lead to personal and artistic growth. This suggests that it is of major importance to the concept of lifelong learning. Opportunities for active learning or experiential learning in formal settings, especially in the music academy, were often created by musician-led educational interventions. For example, musicians often employed improvisation in the prevention and management of performance anxiety. Towards the end of this chapter I address strategies for the incorporation of informal learning into formal settings.

Musicians' leadership

The word 'leadership' can evoke images of a school, business or orchestra. However, leadership can also have meaning on an individual level. Leadership is dependent on the ability to exercise authority. Within musicianship we speak of shared authority through collaborative artistic practice that is underpinned by qualities such as informed decision-making (sometimes in an implicit way, for instance while playing chamber music), adaptability, flexibility and committed values and attitudes. Generic leadership can be described as the ability to lead by example and attitude, while developing and using life skills (which are highly important for entrepreneurship) as well as social skills. Educational leadership refers to the many roles a music teacher can have: an artistic and pedagogical leader, a guide, a mentor and an educator. Most musicians exhibit forms of artistic, generic and educational leadership, which can be brought out with tools such as those proposed in Part II by Beeching and Perkins. The connections between lifelong learning and the characteristics of leadership are revealed in the following biographical accounts, which can be used as a student reading. Guiding questions for this reading are included in Part II (tool 20).

Isaac, Daniel and Wendy: Three lifelong learners

The concept of lifelong learning is best explained here in the words of three young Dutch musicians trained in classical music: Isaac, a guitarist; Daniel, a saxophonist and clarinettist; and Wendy, a trumpet player and conductor. All three musicians enjoy diverse careers and exemplify the changes in the European musical profession. Two of the three musicians have an international career. Isaac is a performer who has found a niche in the market, Daniel is an improvising cross-genre musician working in a range of ensembles, and Wendy is an entrepreneurial musician who teaches, performs and conducts. If we reflect back to the description of musicians' roles within the four main categories of performer, teacher, leader and improviser, these profiles show that all four roles are applicable to these young professional musicians.

Isaac

Isaac, aged 27, studied the classical guitar and earned his Master's degree. By the time he was fourteen he had won a competition that resulted in an agency for chamber music. Playing chamber music became close to his heart and remains an important part of his career. In addition, Isaac became engaged in the performance and research of 19th century music. Both chamber music for guitar and historic performance of 19th century guitar music were niches in the market. Although Isaac is a very talented guitarist, it was not easy for him to realise his performance ambitions. After graduation, he had thought over his career very thoroughly:

> *I realised that I had to put a lot of effort in my further artistic development if I wanted to reach making a living out of performing. So I made use of a special program in the Netherlands, giving me a basic income for two years. It was my challenge to use this program for as short a time as possible, but I would not have succeeded in making a living out of performing if, after graduation, I had been forced to teach a lot of students. I would not have had enough time for practice.*

The two years of basic income gave Isaac the time to practice and to organise concerts. At present Isaac can make a living of performing, partly because he stays abreast of the demand for concerts and addresses the continuous demand for 'different and unusual' programs. The chamber music agency continues to offer him concerts in the Netherlands, which he supplements by organising his own concerts overseas. This, he reflects, "*takes a lot of time and effort, photos, demos, CDs and so on. It also takes a lot of patience*". Although Isaac learned some of these skills at the music academy, at that time the relevance was not evident: "*This is typically a matter of learning by doing. I now learn it by doing it, including screwing it up from time to time*". Isaac's career has developed as he intended, but he feels strongly that this is only possible when one passionately wants it and does the right things to achieve it. Isaac has strong views on these matters:

> *I have discovered that there is not only one path to achieve the same goal. Take the example of competitions: it is nonsense that taking part in competitions is the only way to develop an international career. I find it a waste if people get stuck in that. You must be constantly flexible and be aware of the path that fits you personally.*

Daniel

Daniel, aged 32, graduated at Master's level in both saxophone and clarinet and became an improvising musician. He describes himself as a jack-of-all-trades. He followed an abundance of artistic and creative impulses during his time at the music academy and also during the year he spent in New York after graduation. That was, he recalls, an amazing experience:

> *[I went] from a classical teacher to Andy Statman, a klezmer clarinettist who actually started as a blue grass mandolin player and then got deeply into his Jewish roots, becoming the protégé of Dave Tarras, who was the klezmer immigrant clarinettist, and thus learned his style and subsequently used it as Coltrane played his jazz: very driven and with passion. This resulted in fabulous music with both Coltrane and Andy Statman, and that sound is in my baggage as well.*

For Daniel, musical genres are not considered separately, and Statman and Coltrane influence his classical performance: "*Music is a vibe of the moment, a musical expression of (and in) that particular moment*". He feels that thus far his career has developed organically: "*I have never had to strain myself*". He realises, however, that now, five years after graduation, he has entered a phase of his life in which he will have to make an extra effort in order to maintain his career development:

> *I know that I will not play in a series of 'Young Talents' for the rest of my life. Until now everything was relaxed. I have always been broadly interested and able to get along easily. That may not always be the case. I know now that I'll have to organise a lot in order to get things going.*

Daniel chose to be a freelance musician rather than a regular member of an orchestra: "*It has never been part of my world, so I never had that ambition* [to be a member of an ensemble] *unless something very interesting comes by*". He felt challenged by the many gigs that came along, "*where I could sound my own voice and could determine the programs myself*". Having made this choice, he realises that he will now need to take the initiative to go after subsidies and write to concert halls. Whilst at music academy he did not take any classes on public relations, marketing and organisational issues. Although as a new graduate he received many invitations to perform, he now wishes that entrepreneurship had been included at school "*in a flexible way, adapted to the wishes of the students*". This need for generic skills 'on demand' is similarly noted in Chapters 4 and 5. Daniel thinks that if he had graduated with skills in entrepreneurship, it might already have played a more important role in his career.

Daniel was fortunate to have studied with a teacher who took him to concerts and brought him into contact with the world of ensembles, and for some time Daniel has assisted his former teacher in the music academy. He very much enjoys teaching, especially the aspect of sharing his enthusiasm and encouraging independent learning: "*I will never be a teacher who preaches an absolute truth; rather I'll stimulate my students to engage in their own thing*". He finds that he learns much from teaching:

> *In the first place I learn 'to practice what you preach'. I enjoy the art of teaching: building things up together, having patience, being creative in finding the right words. I want to stimulate students to find their own material and vocabulary and explore the references that contribute to their artistic development as a musician.*

Wendy

Wendy (22) had at the time of the interview just graduated in wind band conducting and trumpet. She was already very active within a protean career in which she combined playing in two wind bands, conducting an orchestra, and teaching groups of young children who were preparing to play in the wind band. In addition, she had started a small business that took on assignments from music publishing houses. Wendy explained that the multiple roles were an active choice:

> *I find it important to do different things. I am not someone who conducts five orchestras: I think my enthusiasm would diminish if I would have to go out every evening to a different orchestra. The same goes for teaching. I couldn't teach the same songs to children four days a week.*

Social learning is of great importance to Wendy's career:

> *First thing is to keep your ears wide open. Listen to people and talk to them. I find it important to be on the same page as the administration of the orchestra, so the last meeting of the year I will be there to talk things through. Having chats in the intervals of the rehearsals with band members and with newcomers is also important. I find it important that people feel at ease and confident. I am open to criticism, but I want other people to be open as well and not talk behind each other's backs. I don't care that I am younger than the average member; I stick to those things.*

Wendy is also clear about her professional identity:

> *In the first place I am a conductor: someone who likes guiding people in their hobby, and stimulating them in a positive way. To make sure that they enjoy what they are doing, but also see to it that there is progress. In the second place I am a teacher. I like to teach children and make them enthusiastic about continuing to make music – see to it that they take it seriously and practise at home as well, and stimulate their parents to help them. And in the third place I am a performing musician, mainly with amateur orchestras, happy to make a wonderful concert with each other. Never against each other, but always together and giving each other something. I am happy in what I am doing. I really think that I went to the music academy with ideals that, right now, I am trying to make come true.*

Wendy's narratives speak for themselves: her career is amazingly varied and she shows strong professional skills even within months of graduation.

Musicians' roles revisited

Isaac, Daniel and Wendy have diverse, changing careers: Isaac works as a performer, leader and entrepreneur; Daniel holds roles as a performer, teacher, leader, composer, improviser and entrepreneur; and Wendy is a performer, teacher, leader, conductor, administrator and manager. All three musicians show that they require generic skills in addition to their performance skills. All three musicians are reflective practitioners, collaborators, connectors and entrepreneurs. And all three were open to 'significant others' (Antikainen *et al.*, 1996) in their learning: people who have guided and mentored them during critical stages of their lives and careers. Many of these significant others have been tertiary educators.

A niche: Educational leadership

Isaac, Daniel and Wendy all show artistic and generic leadership. Daniel's artistic leadership, for instance, is underpinned by his identity as an improviser:

> *I like to step on a stage and to start improvising without having prepared anything. I just hope then to bring something as compelling as can be the case with written music. I'm in pursuit of beautiful moments, searching for the moments that strike a right chord for me.*

Wendy, however, demonstrates a kind of leadership that is often underestimated in the professional music world: educational leadership. Educational leadership addresses learning and teaching activities that interconnect artistic and generic leadership. High-quality teaching is fundamental for high-quality performance and practice in music, hence it is a mystery why good teaching is so often undervalued in a perceived hierarchy of music professions. My research has often showed that musicians find an attitude within the music academy and among colleagues that teaching is a profession for 'failing performers'. Solbu (2007, p. 1) calls this 'pyramid thinking', arguing:

> In most cases the traditional music academy hierarchies imply that those students (and teachers for that matter) of which there are only a few—orchestra conductors, soloists and perhaps composers—are *better musicians* than those of which there are many, e.g. ensemble players, not to mention the classroom music teachers. *Better musicians* meaning that they play the standard repertoire—the canon—better than the rest, or do something that, for the majority, seems very advanced like conducting or composing. In other words, those at the top have really succeeded as professionals. Those further down unfortunately—sorry for them!—did not have the potential to succeed in the ultimate sense. He couldn't make it in the orchestra, therefore he took up teaching! Failures, second hands!

Teachers, of course, need to be much more than good teachers: they need to be knowledgeable, reflective and communicative, and also to be organisers and leaders. This requires high-quality artistic, generic and entrepreneurial skills.

Strategies for preparing future musicians

It is evident that musicians in Europe face many of the same challenges and working patterns in building sustainable careers as their non-European counterparts. As such, the information contained here is useful in demonstrating, in a positive way, the variety of roles within musician careers. The chapter concludes with some thoughts on applying the concept of lifelong learning in the music academy. When considering career-building and lifelong learning strategies that could be employed by educators, perhaps the most important aspect is that this is never a matter of simply giving out ready-made recipes: it starts with considering the mindset and identity of each individual.

To begin with, the learning environment of the music academy can usefully be viewed as an artistic, generic and educational laboratory that not only reflects the workplace, but also encompasses learning in non-formal contexts with a strong commitment to quality and knowledge-ability. This requires a learning culture that is inviting and non-judgemental, leading to increased self-confidence. Training can then take place in a learning environment in which ideas can be transformed entrepreneurially, and where the concept of leadership in a variety of contexts is valued and woven organically into the curriculum.

An example of this is a new joint Master program titled 'For New Audiences and Innovative Practice', which was developed with European funding from 2006 to 2009. The collaborating institutions are the Prince Claus Conservatoire in Groningen and the Royal Conservatoire in The Hague (the Netherlands); Guildhall School of Music & Drama in London; Reykjavik Academy of the Arts, Department of Music (Iceland); and the Royal College of Music in Stockholm. The program aims to enable students to develop and lead creative projects in diverse artistic, community and cross-sectoral settings, thereby creating new audiences and developing their leadership skills in varied artistic and social contexts. Four important characteristics of the concept of lifelong learning are captured in this program:

- The notion of the artistic laboratory;
- Ongoing mentoring and co-mentoring;
- Strong involvement of external professional partners; and
- Reflective practice based on action research.

It is, however, of critical importance that the institutional definition of quality is not narrowly limited to the quality of performance, failing to take into account the contextual variables when making qualitative judgements about various processes, projects, performances and contexts. Critically, if in the music academy we want to prepare students for their future careers, enabling them to be open-minded and acting as reflective practitioners in an ever-more challenging and interesting professional music practice, it is important to capture their interests when they enter the music academy. The questions posed by Perkins (Chapter 2) and Bennett (Chapter 5) are an excellent example of how this conversation can begin.

We are reminded of the narratives from Isaac and Daniel: both acknowledged the fact that life skills (generic transferable skills) are critically important for a successful career in music. However, both musicians mentioned the fact that, although relevant non-performance courses had been offered in the music academy, these did not appeal to them at that time. One of the reasons for this perceived irrelevance is that many music students initially identify themselves as performers (see Perkins's chapter for in-depth information on the development of professional identities during undergraduate training). As performing is the basis of students' intrinsic motivation, taking identity as the point of departure can achieve a great deal when career preparation takes place through action learning in a laboratory setting. If teaching and learning start from here and embed entrepreneurship in an integrated and relevant (experiential) way, informed by artistic values, the relevance becomes clear and the impact far-reaching.

When we approach the education of future musicians in this way, we see increased personal development emerging from an awareness of one's identity as a musician, fostered by self-exploration and self-management and, last but not least, the integration of continuing professional development into all aspects of music academy life.

References

Amussen, G., & Smilde, R. (Eds.). (2007). *Trends and changes in the European music profession*. Thematic report of the working group on the music profession of the European Erasmus Thematic Network 'Polifonia'. www.polifonia-tn.org.

Animarts. (2003). *The art of the animateur: An investigation of the skills and insights required of artists to work effectively in schools and communities*. London: Aminarts. www.animarts.org.uk.

Antikainen, A., Houtsonen, J., Huotelin, H., & Kauppila, J. (1996). *Living in a learning society: Life-histories, identities and education*. London: Falmer Press.

Bennett, D. (2008). *Understanding the classical music profession. The past, the present, and strategies for the future*. Oxon, England: Ashgate Publishing.

Coenen, J. (2008). *De arbeidsmarktsituatie en competenties van afgestudeerden van het Nederlandse kunstvakonderwijs in internationaal perspectief*. Maastricht: Research Centre for Education and the Labour Market.

European Commission. (2006). Culture sector study. Available at http://europa.eu./culture/eac/index_en.html.

European Commission. (2007). Eurostat Cultural Statistics. Available at http://ec.europa.eu/eurostat.

Fragoulis, H. (2002). Innovations to address the challenges of lifelong learning in transition countries. In D. Colardyn (Ed.), *Lifelong learning: Which ways forward?*, pp. 221-238. Utrecht: Lemma.

Gregory, S. (2005). The creative music workshop: A contextual study of its origin and practice. In G. Odam & N. Bannan (Eds.), *The reflective conservatoire*, pp. 19-28. London: Guildhall School of Music & Drama/Aldershot: Ashgate.

Jarvis, P. (2002). Lifelong learning: Which way forward for higher education? In D. Colardyn (Ed.), *Lifelong learning: Which ways forward?* Utrecht: Lemma.

Lafourcade, D., & Smilde, R. (Eds.). (2001). *Promuse: Professional integration of musicians and continuing education in music*. Utrecht: European Association of Conservatoires.

Myers, D. (2007). Initiative, adaptation and growth: The role of lifelong learning in the careers of professional musicians. *Dialogue in Music*. Groningen/The Hague: Lectorate Lifelong Learning in Music.

Prchal, M. (2006). Bologna & music: Harmony or polyphony? The European dimension in professional music training. In E. Froment, J. Kohler, L. Purser & L. Wilson (Eds.), *EUA Bologna handbook—Making Bologna work?* Paragraph B 6.3, pp. 1-18. Berlin: Raabe Verlag.

Renshaw, P. (2001). Globalisation, music and identity. Paper presented to the *International Music Council* in Tokyo, September 2001. www.creativecommunitites.org.uk.

Renshaw, P. (2010). *Engaged Passions: Searches for Quality in Community Engagement*. Delft: Eburon Academic Publishers.

Rogers, R. (2002). *Creating a land with music: The work, education and training of professional musicians in the 21st century*. London: Youth Music.

Smilde, R. (2000). *Lifelong learning: Continuing professional development for musicians*. Final Report of the AEC working group on Continuing Professional Development for Musicians in the framework of the Socrates Thematic Network (TNP) for Music. Paris: European Association of Conservatoires (AEC).

Smilde, R. (2006). Lifelong learning for musicians. Proceedings of the 81st Annual Meeting of the National Association of Schools of Music, Boston, USA in 2005. Reston: NASM.

Smilde, R. (2009a). *Musicians as lifelong learners: Discovery through biography*. Delft: Eburon Academic Publishers.

Smilde, R. (2009b). *Musicians as lifelong learners: 32 biographies*. Delft: Eburon Academic Publishers.

Solbu, E. (2007). Models of excellence. *Dialogue in music*. Groningen/The Hague: Lectorate Lifelong Learning in Music.

Notes

- The working group consisted of Lincoln Abbotts (BBC learning projects), Gretchen Amussen (Conservatoire de Paris, co-chair), Rui Fernandez (International Federation of Musicians), Fiona Harvey (Association of British Orchestras), Timo Klemettinen (European Music School Union), Katja Schaefer (Bayerische Akademie der Schönen Künste), Einar Solbu (European Music Council), Rineke Smilde (Prince Claus Conservatoire Groningen and Royal Conservatoire The Hague, co-chair) and Ester Tomasi (AEC).
- Information on the Bologna process for musicians and music academies can be found at www.aecinfo.org
- Detailed information about the content, work form and curriculum of the program is available to view at www.jointmusicmasters.org

Further reading and information

European organisations

European Association of Conservatoires: www.aecinfo.org
The AEC, having 280 member institutions in 55 countries, has a very informative website. Numerous kinds of information, publications, handbooks and research reports can be downloaded from this site. The website has links to the sites of all member institutions as well as many links to professional organisations.
Thorough research into the various systems of professional music training, including the training of music teachers in European countries, has been carried out by the European Association of Conservatoires and can be found at www.bologna-and-music.org. The country overviews give information on pre-college training in music throughout Europe and on regulated music professions (those requiring a qualification) in European countries.
European Music Council: www.emc-imc.org
European Association of Youth orchestras: www.eayo.org/index.php
International Arts Management Network: www.artsmanagement.net
European Union, Education and Training: www.ec.europa.eu/education/index_en.htm

Music profession and professional musicians

The full research of the working group on the music profession can be downloaded at www.polifonia-tn.org including numerous descriptions and examples as well as a handbook on Alumni Policies in English, French and German.
Dialogue in Music. This is a DVD that contains the outcomes of the work of the AEC working group on the music profession, research of the research group *Lifelong Learning in Music in the Netherlands* (see below), a film, and the proceedings of an international conference, 'Trends and Changes in the European Music Profession; Lifelong Learning and Employability', held in the Netherlands by the AEC and the research centre of Lifelong Learning in Music. The DVD can be obtained for no charge through www.aecinfo.org or through www.lifelonglearninginmusic.org.

Curricula in European music academies

Europe's Caprices (1999). Comparison of violin curricula throughout European music academies. Available at www.aecinfo.org.

Mobility of musicians, music students and teachers

The following website includes everything there is to know about the international mobility of musicians and music students, including transatlantic cooperation: www.doremifasocrates.org
Vrijland, J. (2005). *Free movement and recognition of qualifications in the European Union: The case of music professionals*. www.polifonia-tn.org
A comprehensive website about the development of the European joint master program 'For New Audiences and Innovative Practice', including the handbook 'How to Develop a Joint Master Programme in Music', can be found at www.jointmusicmasters.org

Qualifications and regulations of the music professions

This highly comprehensive website also gives insight into systems of training in each country: www.bologna-and-music.org
The very informative 'Handbook on the International Recognition of Studies and Qualification in Music' can be downloaded from this site.

Lifelong learning for musicians

The website of the international research group on Lifelong Learning in Music, based in the Netherlands, is www.lifelonglearninginmusic.org. The website incorporates research and descriptions of lifelong learning projects for students and graduates, and research on competences of teachers in the music academy. The site includes a continuously updated online handbook on marketing and communication for starting musicians.

European networks and agencies

Articles and advice for young music professionals: www.musiccareers.net
Arts partnerships throughout Europe: www.cecartslink.org
Dutch network with info for different professional art sectors: www.beroepkunstenaar.nl
French cultural network: www.cortex-culturemploi.com

French network for cultural vacancies: www.profilculture.com
General support for musicians (jobs, competitions, instruments, etc.): www.musicalchairs.info
German Network for Cultural Management: www.kulturmanagement.net
Incorporated Society of Musicians: www.ism.org
Online Art Agency: www.artjob.org
Online job agency for musicians and employers with membership fee: www.mymusicjob.com
Performing arts vacancies: www.cultgrid.com
Theater Institute (with vacancies for musicians and cultural administrators): www.theaterinstituut.nl/nl/theater_instituut_nederland/vacatures
The Contemporary Music Centre of Ireland (including competitions and other opportunities): www.cmc.ie
The Musicians' Union (professional advice for musicians): www.musiciansunion.org.uk
UK Art vacancies: www.artshub.co.uk
UK Music Network with job advice and competitions: www.scottishmusic-centre.com

Orchestral organisations

Association Françoise des Orchestres: www.france-orchestres.com
Association of British orchestras: www.abo.org.uk
Association of the symphonic Danish regional orchestras (with vacancies): www.symphony.dk
Deutscher Bühnenverein/Bundesverband Deutscher Theater (with vacancies): www.buehnenverein.de
Finnish orchestras (with vacancies): www.sinfoniaorkesterit.fi
Norwegian association of theatres and orchestras: www.nto.no
Spanish Symphonic Orchestras Association: www.aeos.es

Table 7.4: Overview of research into music careers in Europe

Research project	Aims/objectives	Outcomes
Lifelong learning; Continuing professional development for musicians (2000) www.aecinfo.org	Small-scale research into the (perceived) need for CPD for graduates. Target group: violinists (heads of string departments, recent graduates, final year students). Matching outcomes with survey data from conservatoire directors.	Four areas of skills emerged: performance, pedagogy, life skills, information exchange. Conservatoire directors: life skills least priority.

Promuse: Professional integration and continuing education in music (2001) www.aecinfo.org	Development of tools and policies for CPD in music at a European level. Comparison of information from providers of CPD (including conservatoires) and former students. Orchestral audition practices; keeping track of former students; Outline European Observatoire for Music Professions.	Mismatch between provision of CPD by conservatoires and former students' needs: life skills the top priority of graduates and lowest priority of conservatoires. Within performance skills high demand for skills for new repertoire and improvisation. Decision-making on provision through conservatoires' own perception and by asking graduates.
European forum for music education and training (2004) www.emc-imc.org/efmet	Mapping systems of music teacher training in HE in Europe, including professional partnerships.	Overviews of national systems and qualifications.
European thematic network: Polifonia (2007) working group on the European music profession www.polofonia-tn.org	Research into the trends and changes in musical life in Europe. Implications for the music profession and competences required for musicians.	Rapid change in musical life. Emergence of required new competences. Need for dialogue with conservatoires. Need for more partnerships between conservatoires and professional organisations. Consultation with stakeholders suggests significant more attention should be given to generic learning outcomes in conservatoire curricula.

Research Group *Lifelong Learning in Music* (since 2004) www.lifelonglearninginmusic.org	Examining the concept of lifelong learning for musicians and its consequences for adaptive learning environments, its piloting and implementation.	Establishing learning environments based on the concept of lifelong learning.

Chapter 8
Reflections on the Protean Music Career

Michael Hannan

Once upon a time a princess was wandering in the forest when she encountered a frog. The frog said to her: 'Excuse me princess, if you kiss me I'll turn into a fabulous jazz bass player'. Being unfamiliar with jazz and brought up to be cautious, the princess took the frog back to the castle to ask the king's advice. 'Dad, I just found this frog who told me if I kissed him he would turn into a fabulous jazz bass player. What should I do?' The king said: 'What ever you do don't kiss him. In the entertainment industry he's far more marketable as a talking frog'. (author unknown)

In Greek mythology, Proteus was a sea-god who could see into the future but would radically change his appearance to avoid being asked to do so. Homer (1946, p. 75) gives the following account of the story in *The Odyssey*:

> Directly you see him settled, summon all your strength and courage and hold him down however hard he strains and struggles to escape. He will try all kinds of transformations, and change himself into every sort of beast on earth, but into water too and blazing fire. But hold him fast and grip him all the tighter. And when he speaks at last and asks you questions in his natural shape, just as he was when you saw him lie down to rest, then, sir, you may relax your pressure, let the old man go, and ask him which god is your enemy, and how to get home along the highways of the fish.

* * *

This book clearly illustrates that there are thousands of aspiring musicians for every one who has a mono-cultural, full-time appointment in an orchestra, ensemble or music theatre company; and that most professional musicians can expect to undertake a broad range of activities in order to survive.

Music, like all freelance activities in the arts, is a business, and the protean creation of professional networks provides many opportunities to expand into fulfilling areas beyond traditional expectations of a music career.

The Wikipedia entry for Proteus defines the adjectival form of Proteus, 'protean', as having "the general meaning of versatile, mutable, capable of assuming many forms", with "positive connotations of flexibility, versatility and adaptability". Similarly, *Brewer's Dictionary of Phrase and Fable* (Evans, 1971, p. 868) defines the phrase "as many shapes as Proteus" to mean "full of shifts, aliases, disguises, etc., and the adjective protean, readily taking on different aspects, ever changing, versatile". Chetwynd (1982, p. 339) suggests that Proteus "represents the underlying truth beneath the changing appearances, in the depths of the mind". In the story of my own protean career, everything seems connected: each new opportunity seems to be made possible by those that preceded it. The opportunities for getting new work are the result of expansions of professional networks and the broadening of skills through formal and informal learning along the way. I will begin my story with an event that stimulated the reflections on my own protean career.

Many years ago, when I was lounging in the green room of the Sydney Opera House between rehearsals, I overheard a conversation between David Ahern, the *enfant terrible* of Australian music at the time, and Dave Ellis, a seasoned professional bass player. Ahern had a teenage protégé, John Somebody, in tow. 'Dave', he said. 'Young John here would like your advice on how to become a professional musician'. Dave paused a moment and then quipped: 'That's easy. Start playing for money!' Ellis was a greatly admired protean musician. He played double bass in the Sydney Symphony Orchestra, he was an excellent jazz bassist and he played a mean rock and funk electric bass. He was a highly sought-after session musician who supported new music by playing and promoting his own concerts. I remember he once organised a performance of a complex work by Colin Bright for eight double basses. That's dedication.

The green room incident set me to thinking about how this sensitive young man, John Somebody, was going to have to transform himself into a hardnosed small businessman in order to survive as a freelance professional musician. He was going to have to diversify his activities, not just confine himself to his beloved jazz. He would probably make most of his performance income as a backing musician for country music recording artists. He would write his own compositions to exploit his copyrights. He would become a clinician for a bass guitar manufacturer and sign an endorsement agreement with them. And to pass on his considerable range of skills, he would establish a private teaching practice and teach in a tertiary music school.

Dave was being ironic about becoming a professional musician: it isn't so easy.

This protean vision of John Somebody's future made me reflect upon the development of my own protean career as a musician, upon some of the protean musicians I have encountered, and upon how, as we suggest in Chapter 1, the protean musician is not really a new phenomenon. In this reflection I use auto-ethnography, a qualitative research method designed to make sense of personal experience through storytelling. With a view to generating useful insights for the reader, a strong element of this technique is the formation of understandings of the culture or cultures with which the author is engaged (Ellis 2004; Chang 2008). Thus the narrative approach used in the following section results in writing that can be readily shared and discussed with students.

My background

I come from a family obsessed with education. My father was a high-school mathematics teacher who covered the walls of our toilet with blackboard paint so we could study equations while we sat there. His heroes were Pythagoras, Euclid and Descartes. Thus, it is no accident that from an early age I aspired to be an academic. As my best subject was music, I chose to study musicology at university. But as an impoverished undergraduate student I looked for paid employment in the music industry to help keep the wolf from the door. Initially, my skills as a classical music piano performer were the only wares I had to peddle. My first gig was as a rehearsal accompanist for the St Andrews Cathedral Choral Society. Eric Gross, one of the lecturers at the University of Sydney, was its conductor, and he had luckily spotted me performing in the Music Department. I did not realise it at the time but I was starting to develop my professional music network.

Looking back now, it is impossible to overstress the importance of making contacts and communicating with others in your field of work to facilitate creative and/or business opportunities. Where you study music provides your first big chance to network. Where else in the music industry does one have immediate and constant contact with hundreds of other like-minded people - all potential collaborators, students and teachers alike? A lot of networking happens by accident, but the protean musician transformed into music-industry networker will be proactive in making contacts and will know how to behave in order to achieve the best results (Kimpel, 1993; Beeching, 2005). To create a network, one needs the respect of one's peers, a personal style that is attractive to others in the field, and, above all, the initiative and persistence to make and maintain the contacts. Joining professional associations, attending music seminars and conventions (which often include 'schmoozing' sessions) and just hanging out at gigs and in music shops, are the best ways to begin to create a network.

Accompanying the St Andrews Cathedral Choral Society rehearsals for Bach's *St. John Passion* was an excellent learning experience for me, as well as being paid work. It led, over the years, to many other similar and often more challenging employment opportunities as my range of accompanying skills improved. For instance, learning to realise figured bass parts at university came in handy for accompanying rehearsals of early music operas that had no keyboard reductions; and the ability to play from chord charts assisted in gigs as an audition pianist for commercial theatre productions. I began to see that adaptability and versatility were essential for survival as a freelancer.

During my second year at university, one of my tutors recommended me for paid work as the assistant to Peter Sculthorpe, now regarded as Australia's most successful concert composer. This time it was my musical handwriting that had been noticed. Initially the work involved inking in Sculthorpe's very neatly pencilled scores. I worked at his kitchen table as he composed at the piano in the next room. At that stage I had no ambitions to be a composer. I was drawn into the world of composing by experiencing a composer at work, by being constantly asked my opinion about various creative options, by looking for possible errors in the pencilled score before applying the ink and, occasionally, by being asked to make creative contributions when deadlines loomed.

I did not realise at the time that I was receiving an apprenticeship as a composer, learning not only about the technique of writing and editing music, but also about the business of being a composer. I was privy to how Sculthorpe dealt with his British publisher (Faber Music Limited), how he negotiated commissions, how he organised performances of his works, how he attracted publicity as well as how he communicated brilliantly with all the people essential for the successful operation of his business (particularly with the musicians playing his music). I realised that none of this business knowledge was part of any music course, but that one really had to know about it in order to forge a successful career. This form of 'situated learning' through 'legitimate peripheral participation' is, of course, considered one of the most effective ways to achieve expertise in craft-based activities such as music (Lave & Wenger, 1991; McLellan, 1996).

Although an accomplished pianist, Sculthorpe chose to focus on composing. He rarely gave public performances or made recordings, but he did maintain a career as a composition professor for nearly 40 years before retiring from academia to concentrate on composing. Whilst I was observing Sculthorpe's career, what impressed me most was that he never let an opportunity go by. Although a composer's income depends mainly on commissions and performance royalties, Sculthorpe would respond to almost all requests by performers (amateurs, students and professionals alike) to provide music they could play. To satisfy the needs of individual musicians who wanted him to provide new works for them, he would, without a commission fee, regularly re-arrange works he had already composed. In this context the Sculthorpe *oeuvre* is protean: the same tunes turn up in different instrumental settings. The extent of the practice of arranging and re-arranging existing works to create new works is evident from the titles of Sculthorpe's works, but the recycling of previously composed sections of music is also often practiced in differently titled works (Hayes, 1993).

Sculthorpe also constructed a compelling public image for himself and his music. There is a consistent narrative running through all the program notes for his pieces, many of which are reprinted in Hayes (1993). Through his word-writing practice and interviews with journalists, also documented in Hayes, he carefully constructed the meaning of his music for his audience, promoting visual and cultural notions such as a flat landscape, wilderness, loneliness, Aboriginal stories as well as specific geographic and historical references. It is no accident that his music has come to be associated with outback Australia, so much so that whenever there is a new film that includes outback locations, the filmmakers are invariably keen to secure his services to compose the score (McGee, 1995). As Beeching (2005) reminds us, musicians of all kinds must be able to transform themselves into writers of press releases, program notes, grant applications and opinion pieces in order to promote their music, and they must find the best way of articulating what is interesting about the music for the listener.

One of the works with which I assisted Sculthorpe was *Love 200* for rock band and orchestra. Apart from copying the score, my roles in this were advising the composer on all matters 'rock', rehearsing the band (none of whom could read music at all), and assisting the lighting designer with lighting cues during the performances. By this time I had made the transition from being a European classical music performer to that of a contemporary rock performer: I had become bi-musical (Nettl, 1995).

Many people who study classical music performance from a young age are drawn to contemporary popular music, especially in their rebellious teenage years when music is tied up with identity formation (Shuker, 1998). I was obsessed with The Beatles. I purchased some of their sheet music and learned to play other songs by ear. I secured gigs playing pop music (especially Beatles songs) as background music in restaurants and piano bars. This work helped develop additional skills such as turning a lead sheet (melody and chord symbols) into a coherent performance, as well as playing from memory songs the diners requested. The most important activities in my rock music education, however, were jamming with friends, learning collectively to improvise and groove, sharing repertoire, sharing knowledge about musical genres, techniques and technologies and eventually feeling confident enough to form a band (or audition for a band). I also learned to sing in contemporary styles. It made me instantly more employable. The process of collaborative popular music learning with peers is well documented in Baynton (1997), Bennett (1980), Cohen (1991) and Green (2001). Collaborative learning among classical music students is attracting increasing attention, as emphasised by Smilde in this volume (Chapter 7).

Going into business

Continuing my protean journey, I was approached by Wayne Findlay to go into partnership writing advertising music. It was unknown territory, but nothing seemed impossible since I had received my accidental apprenticeship working for Peter Sculthorpe. Wayne had dropped out of university to join a rock band. Because he was musically literate he soon found additional work as an arranger, mostly for performing and recording artists who did not have their own regular bands. When we started the business, Wayne already had a good network of session musicians, songwriters, arrangers and audio engineers, some of whom were making good money in advertising music.

Our first task was to create a demo tape to market our music. We had no capital other than musical talent, intelligence and cunning, so we called on favours from musicians we knew and persuaded others to contribute 'just for the experience'. These included three talented senior high school students who later became prominent in the music industry: Kim Ryrie, one of the inventors of the world's first dedicated music computer, the Fairlight, who owned a four-track reel-to-reel tape recorder and agreed to engineer the project for us; Geoff Collins, later to become one of Australia's most celebrated flautists, who played on a few tracks; and Cameron Allen, later to become a screen composer and record producer, who played some trombone parts.

To write successful advertising music requires stylistic versatility. Certain styles of music are associated with certain types of products; therefore it is important to be able to parody music styles for humorous effect. Being in touch with the latest styles is important because the trendiest sounds sell youth-oriented products (Hannan, 2003). Having never done any advertising music before, we had to come up with simulations for our demo reel. We wrote a pretend jingle for Wrangler jeans using a fast country music style, and another for a toothpaste brand using a sparkling calypso idiom; and we recorded a lot of instrumental and vocal music in different styles and moods, mostly in contemporary genres but also including some mock baroque pieces (*Switched on Bach* was popular at the time). To achieve all this we took on the multiple roles of copywriter, songwriter, composer, arranger, musical director and producer. And we had to be extremely nice to our army of volunteers.

Having got our demo reel 'in the can' it was time to look for work. Although our music industry network was growing, we had no contacts in the advertising agency world. Turning to the *Yellow Pages*, Wayne and I discovered the existence of about 100 agencies in Sydney. As in all large cities, these ranged from multinational companies like McCann Erickson and J. Walter Thompson (now JWT) down to two- or three-person operations. Starting at the top of the alphabetical list, we made appointments with the creative directors of each of these companies. Generally, they were prepared to listen to our spiel and to a few tracks from our tape. We discovered that they all had one or more composers with whom they worked regularly, and it was virtually impossible to get a foot in the door. It was soul-destroying. Eventually, once we had been right through the list of agencies and started again at the top, our persistence started to pay off. A few small companies employed people with whom we had built a strong personal rapport, and the work started to trickle in. Once we had recorded some real ads to add to our reel, things got better.

Our success in getting work also depended on learning about the less interesting bits of being in business: about business structures, business name registration, taxation, insurance, contracts, preparing budgets, book-keeping, cash flow and profit forecasts. A considerable industry of music business self-help books has recently developed (Cann, 2007; Dann, 2003; Passmore, 2004; Simpson, 2002), but back then Wayne and I had to do it the hard way by talking to experienced freelance musicians, as well as by trial and error.

One of the recording facilities we often used for our advertising work was Albert Studios, which was part of the music publishing company J. Albert & Son, based in Sydney (and now also in London). It was an exciting time, with AC/DC recording there with producers Harry Vanda and George Young. And we were honoured to be working with a host of brilliant session musicians such as guitarist Jim Kelly and bassist Greg Lyon (who later became my colleagues for many years in a university music department), and slide guitarist Kirk Lorange (who is one of the Protean musicians I will discuss later in this narrative).

Hanging out in the Albert Productions building, I talked with people in the print music division who were looking for someone to transcribe rock music recordings. That sounded like an easy way to earn some money. I soon found out, however, that my aural training classes at university had not really prepared me for the syncopated rhythmic complexities of a lot of the music I was working on. Over the next decade I completed about 400 lead chart transcriptions of songs by all the artists on the publishing roster. This wasn't too taxing and was good pocket money to bolster my postgraduate scholarship. It was an excellent example of applying musicianship skills learned in the academy to routine jobs in the music industry. And, of course, it had spin-offs. In doing the work, I improved my listening skills immensely and also learned a lot about pop song structures and chart writing.

Towards academia

My career now turned towards that of music academic. I was very interested in the music of the French composer Olivier Messiaen (1908-1992), particularly his harmonic techniques, and decided to do my research thesis on this subject. Messiaen is himself a role model of the protean musician. Although known best for his monumental compositions, he was the organist at the Parisian church La Trinité from 1931 until his death. That's more than 60 years of masses, benedictions, weddings and funerals, not to mention repertoire recitals and improvisations. It must be one of the longest continuous musical appointments in the history of music.

Messiaen was also a professional pianist and toured a lot in the early part of his career. He was the Professor of Harmony at the Paris Conservatoire from 1941, and Professor of Composition from 1966 to 1978. Amongst his many students were Boulez, Stockhausen, Xenakis, Goehr, Davies, Theodorakis and Barraqué. Not content to be 'just a musician' he was also an ornithologist, making extended fieldtrips initially in France and then later throughout the world to record and transcribe birdcalls. Messiaen is one of the few composers ever to write an extensive account of his own compositional technique (Messiaen, 1947). In addition he wrote numerous analytical works, some published during his lifetime and many published posthumously in eight volumes (Messiaen, 1994-2002). He even wrote the poetic texts for some of his vocal works, including the song cycle *Harawi* (1945) and the opera *Saint-François d'Assise* (1975-1983).

Messiaen's music was, and still is, a great inspiration to me. Despite my love of it, I could not continue with the research because of a lack of academic supervision and problems I had reading the academic literature on Messiaen, most of which was in French. The ability to read journal articles in the major European languages was expected of musicology students, but sadly that was a skill I had not acquired. So I turned my attention to a thesis on the music of Peter Sculthorpe. It was an obvious alternative project since I had worked closely with him, had access to all his scores, sketches and other relevant documents, and was able to interview him about his life and music. In a sense I had been doing fieldwork on this project for about five years. Interrupted by many more protean career excursions, over the ensuing years I eventually completed the thesis (Hannan, 1978).

Putting music into words

One of these excursions was into music journalism. A friend, Susan Dermody, was editor of a fortnightly trade magazine titled *Showbusiness*. The focus of this publication was on theatre, television and film. Realising there was a large gap in the range of entertainment it covered, Susan asked me if I would write a regular music column and also do reviews of concerts. The job forced me to find out what was happening in the music scene (more networking), to increase my knowledge of different genres of music, and to hone skills such as working to a brief, keeping strictly to word limits, and writing in an entertaining way. I have maintained my practice as a music journalist since that time, particularly as a reviewer of contemporary music recordings.

Another friend, Sue Butler, had majored in both music and linguistics and had a job working on a new general dictionary research project. Her boss was looking for consultants for specialist groups of words, and she suggested me as suitable for dealing with the music words because of my range of musical genre interests. As it turned out, the dictionary they were using as a starting point included only European classical music terms, so I was able to introduce thousands of words relating to popular music, jazz and world music. I worked on *The Macquarie Dictionary* (first published in 1981) over the next three decades, and Sue Butler is now its publisher. The experience with Macquarie illustrates that even people working outside the music sector can be part of the protean musician's professional network.

Teaching

Postgraduate research students are usually offered casual teaching employment as professional development towards their possible future careers as academics. I started my tutoring career, as many do, with aural training, and eventually took over the teaching of keyboard harmony and improvisation. My music industry employment experiences served me well in these areas, but it is amazing how much one's skills and knowledge develop in something when teaching it (Winn, 1996). With keyboard musicianship, for example, one has to be able to demonstrate all the things the students are expected to do:

- Sight-reading music in different clefs;
- Making a piano reduction at sight from a full orchestral score involving transposing instruments;
- Harmonising melodies at sight;
- Realising figured basses at sight; and
- Improvising pieces such as two-part inventions in the style of Bach from a given motif.

Looking back, I believe I learned more about the inner workings of music from teaching this subject than from any other learning or teaching experience I have ever had.

Keyboard musicianship was a difficult discipline to teach because many of the students required to study it were majoring in solo instruments (not piano, harpsichord or organ) and some of them had no prior keyboard experience. This was just one of the curriculum anomalies typical of traditional university and conservatoire music training (Nettl, 1995). My interest in curriculum development stems from this early period of my teaching career. Realising the frustration and sometimes anger felt by non-keyboardists towards this subject, I started to develop alternatives to enable them to do the traditional exercises, and also to expand the range of tasks into more contemporary styles such as blues improvisation and improvisation on pitch sets, including the 'modes of limited transposition' that Messiaen had developed (Messiaen, 1947). It was a case of asking: "what learning activities are most suitable for meeting the needs of our learners?" (Ornstein & Hunkins, 2004, p. 14).

Eager for more varied teaching experiences, my casual teaching eventually extended beyond my alma mater to the University of New South Wales and the Sydney Conservatorium. The music department at the former had no music majors at the time, but rather provided mandatory 'general studies' electives for students in professional programs such as law, medicine, architecture and engineering. As such, the focus of the lectures and tutorials was sociological and anthropological rather than musicological. It was a chance to engage with big ideas rather than the nitty gritty of practical musicianship skills. In contrast, at the Conservatorium I was teaching students who were training to be music teachers in high schools. In a radical educational move for the time, I was contracted to teach these students some practical rock music skills. We based ourselves in the Wurlitzer electric piano lab and worked on song writing techniques, 12-bar blues improvisation skills, and developing groove ideas from riffs. Some of my contacts from bands and recording sessions occasionally volunteered to give the students some experience of rhythm section concepts. Little did I know that my career as a music educator was heading in this very direction. But not before a few more twists and turns.

More study

When I graduated with my PhD it was time to look for a full-time appointment. The only problem was that I was now something of an expert in contemporary Australian concert music, and most of the jobs in musicology still involved teaching the history and theory of European music from medieval times to the mid-20th century. Looking around the country I discovered that courses on Australian music were taught exclusively by composers as part of their composition teaching duties. I realised that if I was ever going to get a job in this area it was going to have to be a composition appointment. Although I was a composer of sorts, I had no qualifications in this discipline. I felt, in any case, that it would be stimulating to study composition formally, and so enrolled in a Graduate Diploma of Musical Composition. Whereas I had previously specialised in writing miniatures (28.5 sec. and 58.5 sec. advertising jingles) played by brilliant session musicians, I was now wrestling with long, virtuosic modernistic works and going through the often-humiliating process of trying to persuade competent-enough musicians to perform them.

The composition diploma secured, my search for the elusive full-time job continued, but was interrupted by winning a postdoctoral scholarship to conduct research for a year in the US. I chose the Program in Ethnomusicology at the University of California, Los Angeles (UCLA) to continue the work on popular music lexicography that had arisen from *The Macquarie Dictionary* consultancy. My visa didn't allow me to accept paid work, but I had many opportunities to increase my knowledge and skills as a protean musician. The UCLA School of Music had about fifteen world music ensembles. I joined the *gagaku* (Japanese court music) orchestra playing *ryuteki* (a transverse flute), took one-on-one lessons in the *honkyoku* repertoire of Japanese *shakuhachi* music, and also played with the Ghanaian drumming ensemble and the Balinese gamelan. The *gagaku* experience was particularly wonderful because the orchestra played public concerts as well as at Buddhist ceremonies (Los Angeles has a large Japanese community). Along with these experiences, attendance at ethnomusicological methods seminars extended my understandings of music as a global cultural phenomenon and I became, in the process, polymusical (Nettl, 1995).

My music lexicographical research brought me into the orbit of Nicolas Slonimsky (1894-1995) who, when I met him, was still writing music dictionaries at the age of 89. When asked about his secret for longevity he would reply: "I can't afford to die, I've got too many deadlines". Another Protean musician, Slonimsky had been a concert pianist, orchestral conductor, musicologist, lexicographer, teacher, music critic and composer, as well as a prolific writer of books on music. Among these were the famous *Lexicon of Musical Invective*, a collection of bad reviews received by the great composers from Beethoven onwards (Slonimsky, 2000), and the *Thesaurus of Scales and Melodic Patterns* (Slonimsky, 1947), which influenced musicians as diverse as John Coltrane, Frank Zappa and John Adams.

While I was living in LA, Nicolas was asked to compose a chamber work to be premiered at one of the 'Monday Evening Concerts' (a series initiated in 1939 and still going). He was too frail to write the score, so I volunteered to be his amanuensis, and in due course the work was completed in time for the concert. In LA, I also shared an apartment with the Fairlight Computer Musical Instrument inventor Kim Ryrie. Fairlight had opened a distribution company in LA because the American market was its biggest opportunity for global success. We had a Fairlight in the apartment so I learned to program it and wrote six pieces on it. Through this experience I also got to network with other Fairlight users and to learn their tricks.

At last, a full-time job

Arriving back in Australia on a Saturday morning, I bought the weekend newspapers. There was an advertisement for a Lecturer in Composition and Writing Techniques at the Queensland Conservatorium of Music. Because of the timing, I had a feeling this was the full-time job I was destined to get. I was duly appointed, but largely because they were looking not only for a person who could teach composition and writing techniques (including the arcane discipline of species counterpoint), but also for someone who could teach a course on Asian musical traditions. This had not been mentioned in the advertisement. Versatility had won the day. I was with the Queensland Conservatorium for only a year before leaving to establish a degree course in contemporary popular music at a small college in the country town of Lismore (the institution is now called Southern Cross University). They were looking for someone who combined academic credibility (meaning someone who had a PhD) with music industry experience in contemporary popular styles of music. This was certainly not a typical combination for its time.

I was appointed Head of Music and charged with the responsibility of transforming a classical music degree course into a dedicated contemporary music course, which would be the first of its kind in Australia. This was no easy task because there were virtually no resources, human or physical, to do it. One resource we did have, however, was the strong support of the Australian music industry, which at the time saw education and training as an important way forward. An industry advisory board, the Australian Contemporary Music Institute (ACMI), was convened. This pulled together organisations and influential people from across the music sector. Representatives from record companies, publishers, copyright collection agencies, intellectual property law firms, entertainment unions, management companies, booking agencies, promotion and touring companies, and music radio joined a group of prominent musicians. In particular, Rob Hirst, the drummer/songwriter from Midnight Oil, gave many years of support.

What became clear from the course development advice received from industry, and from other sources such as Sly (1993), was that the education of contemporary musicians should involve a heavy emphasis on business and management skills. But there were other considerations for the training of the contemporary musician. Most contemporary performers write their own songs, and most songwriters need to perform their songs in order to establish an audience, thus making it necessary for students to study both performance and composition, ideally to equal degrees. Add to that mix the fact that contemporary music is electric/electronic and amplified, then already there is a very wide range of things to consider in designing a curriculum that will prepare student musicians for the industry. At degree level, there is also an expectation that courses will include generic skills and attributes such as intellectual rigour, creative thinking, critical thinking, cultural awareness, social justice, professional ethics and community responsibility (Barrie, 2006).

In retrospect it is clear that we were designing a protean music curriculum. This included, in no particular order:

- Occupational Health and Safety: mains power, noise levels, lifting, climbing, overuse injuries, posture, fitness, vocal health, performance anxiety, work stress, crowd control, road safety, work/life balance, substance abuse;
- Composition: song-writing, lyric-writing, music theory, music analysis, arranging, programming, synthesis, record production, screen composition;
- Performance: instrumental and vocal technique, musicianship skills, work discipline, performance practice in diverse genres, improvisation theory and practice, instrumental and vocal technologies, stage planning,

stage etiquette, stage movement, communication with the audience, visual image, memorisation, repertoire knowledge, ensemble skills, musical direction, chart-reading, chart-writing, transcription;

- Technology: live sound reinforcement, lighting and projection, sound design, stage management, stagecraft, recording, editing, signal processing, mixing, mastering, systems design, composition technologies, multimedia technologies, technology troubleshooting, crisis management;
- Business: industry structures, career planning, intellectual property, standard contracts (for performance, recording, publishing, agency, management, merchandising), image creation, negotiation, self-promotion, public relations, entrepreneurship, networking, audience development, small business management (business structures, financing, market analysis, marketing, marketing technologies, business planning, insurance, business communications, office management, office technologies. etc.), project management (planning, team building, quality control, budgeting, sponsorships, grant applications, conflict management, project evaluation) and time management;
- Contextual Studies: popular music history (styles, technology, legislation, business practices, cultural movements], music cultures [world music traditions and the global music industry), industry critique (of genre, production, commodification, consumption, demography, mediation, technologisation, appropriation, copyright, authenticity, identity, censorship, cultural policy, globalisation, localisation, taste, fashion, gender, ethnicity and so on); and
- Embedded generic skills including reflective practice relating to all aspects of music making and music business.

A staggering range of skills and knowledge had been identified as crucial elements in the training of contemporary musicians. But is it really any different for the classical musician, or any other kind of professional musician? Reflective practice, for example, is a self-critical tool that is essential for further development beyond the years of formal study. In discussing 'music as social action', Martin (1995) suggests that successful musicians are continually modifying their practices through self-critical reflection in order to improve their acceptance by peers, employers and audiences. Being able to accurately gauge the musical and personal abilities of fellow musicians is also an important skill in the intensely collaborative and competitive environment of professional music making, for instance, in the practice of deputising (Cottrell, 2004). Similar occupational health and safety issues exist for all musicians: instrumentalists are small-muscle athletes, but to maintain their fitness to perform they need to work on their large muscles as well.

Unlike in the Baroque, Classical and Romantic eras, few of today's classical music performers write music, but being able to compose and arrange music is a useful addition to the repertoire of skills as well as providing another level of artistic satisfaction and source of income. Many of the most prominent and successful contemporary classical composers play or conduct their own music, or have ensembles devoted to playing their music. In order to maintain their market edge, many classical music companies and individual musicians are looking for different ways to present their music using amplification, lighting and projection. And all freelance musicians (contemporary, jazz, classical, world) are in small business and need to treat their careers as businesses using the most up-to-date marketing tools. Even classical music performers with full-time jobs in orchestras or music theatre companies will invariably be involved in freelance performing and teaching.

The academic career

Although getting a full-time job in a school of music was what I was always aiming for, to a great extent it removed me from the hurly burly of the freelance musician's lifestyle. This is not to say that my new job was no less protean than my career had been up to that point. In actual fact, a musician working in a conservatoire or university music school or department is expected to maintain his or her profile as a performer, composer, technologist or researcher, as well as do many other things. At the core of the job is teaching, but one is likely to be required to teach in areas other than one's specialisation, and that demands a lot of preparation time and stress if one is not on top of new topics. The job comes with the expectation of administrative work, and that is not only for academics appointed in designated administration roles. One is expected to participate on committees concerned with academic governance and planning advice as well as to make contributions to relevant community organisations. Musicians without teaching qualifications are likely to be forced to undertake in-house postgraduate qualifications in teaching and learning as a condition of employment. Similarly, postgraduate qualifications are needed to maximise the chances of promotion to higher academic levels. Even high-profile performers or composers feel the pressure to develop a written research practice, because written research publication is, in many contexts, valued above artistic achievements (Biggs, 2009).

Academia is perhaps not the ideal situation for the artist unable to adapt to the bureaucratic culture and the time-consuming nature of its core activities. But it does have many benefits for those who can somehow maintain the momentum of their creative or performance practice and reap the rewards of an academic appointment, the greatest of which is what one can learn from talented students. Clearly, having a full-time job is going to put a dampener on any national or global performance career expansion, but the job might provide the space to develop a launching pad for such an ambition in a later career phase. (Some of the issues involved in this duel career combination are discussed in an interview-based article on composer/performer academics; Hannan, 2006.)

My own composition and research activities in the academy have tended to be protean, though some might call them unfocused. Because of the politics of research production, my composition activities have tended towards the experimental: it is easier to get funding if you can make a case for your work being innovative. But, perhaps in homage to Messiaen, I also write and play a lot of piano music that uses my transcriptions of pied butcherbird songs. As for written research, I had spent so much time researching the competencies of contemporary musicians and other music industry operatives to inform curriculum development that I wrote a number of articles on this subject, as well as a book on careers in music that details what is involved in 150 different jobs (Hannan, 2003). A decade ago I took up the unexpected opportunity to write an article on an aspect of Australian film music. This led to similar opportunities and, ultimately, to this subject becoming my main field of research activity. Since most of my postgraduate students are composers whose projects are practice-based artistic research (consisting of a folio of works and a contextualising paper, sometimes known as an 'exegesis'), I started writing papers about my own creative and performance practices, engaging with the issues of practice-based research in the arts. And the chance to go to the *Beatles 2000* conference in Finland has led to The Beatles' music being another of my growing research interests.

The landscape is changing so rapidly for the production and consumption of music of all kinds that the details of curriculum such as that given earlier, particularly under the headings of technology and business, are constantly transforming. Today's musicians are, for instance, finding their audiences through Web 2.0 social networks such as MySpace and Facebook, creating interest in their work by showing their clips on a video-sharing website such as YouTube as well as using blogging and podcasting to promote themselves and their businesses.

Nonetheless, whilst joining an existing social network such as Facebook has the advantage that there are already millions of participants, as an online community, it may not have the kinds of members that are relevant to the business enterprise being promoted. In circumstances like this it is advisable to start a customer-specific social networking site (Weber, 2007). A case in point is the site 'Guitar for Beginners and Beyond', which was set up by my old friend Kirk Lorange to promote, among other products, his book *Plane talk—The truly totally different guitar instruction book*.

Kirk developed this book in the 1990s, sensing a gap in the market for guitar instruction that did not rely on the learning of conventional music notation, but rather used a combination of text and comic book drawings to get the message across. With the advent of online social networking, Kirk took the bold step of creating a website that offers more than 100 free lessons and provides a forum for its astonishing 121,000 online community members (currently growing by 100 per day). Members can respond to the content of the site, air their own compositions, communicate and collaborate with other members and seek feedback on their playing. Through this site (and others such as YouTube), Kirk has been successful in marketing his book and many other music products. In particular, if members like any of the online free lessons they can buy downloadable expanded versions that include extras such as half-speed movies and Guitar Pro files, all of which enhance the learning process. Because the site has a lot of traffic (the record is 1,630 members online at any one time) it also generates a sizable income from Google AdSense. Guitar for Beginners and Beyond is an excellent example of 'new marketing' principles that "combine professional and user-generated content" (Weber, 2007, p. 38).

Kirk Lorange is a classic protean musician: a highly sought-after session guitarist for more than a decade, a singer/songwriter recording artist, a touring musician working with big names in the music industry, an influential teacher and clinician, a textbook author and illustrator and, finally, a website designer and online marketing expert. This is how business-savvy musicians now operate, and who knows what tomorrow's musicians will be doing. Well, Proteus would know of course, if we could pin him down for long enough to tell us.

Concluding reflections

A talking frog has no need to be protean in order to survive, but very few classical musicians can make the same claim. For every musician with a mono-cultural full-time appointment in an orchestra, ensemble or music theatre company, there are thousands of others for whom change is both constant and expected.

The creation of professional networks provides many opportunities to expand into fulfilling areas beyond traditional expectations of a music career. In my own protean career, everything seems connected: the opportunities for getting new work are the result of expanding professional networks and the broadening of skills through formal and informal learning along the way. Each new opportunity seems to have been made possible by those that preceded it.

Music, like all freelance activities in the arts, is a business. Musicians who do not learn what's involved in small business management, and who do not put effort into finding out how to develop audiences for their work, are selling themselves short. Whilst most professional musicians undertake a broad range of activities in order to survive, these activities are not driven solely by survival. It is exciting to be involved in the many facets of being a musician through performing, composing, arranging, producing, organising, directing, teaching, researching, critiquing, philosophising, promoting, advocating and facilitating. There are many ways for musicians to utilise the skills they have acquired through their education and experience, and most musicians feel honoured and satisfied to be participating in these ways.

References

Barrie, S. (2006). Understanding what we mean by generic attributes of graduates. *Higher Education, 51*, 316-341.

Baynton, M. (1997). *Frock rock: Women performing popular music*. Oxford: Oxford University Press.

Bennett, H. (1980). *On becoming a rock musician*. Amhurst: The University of Massachusetts Press.

Beeching, A. (2005). *Beyond talent: Creating a successful career in music*. Oxford: Oxford University Press.

Biggs, Iain. (2009). *Art as research: Creative practice and academic authority*. Saarbrücken: Verlag Dr. Müller.

Cann, S. (2007). *Building a successful 21st century music career*. Boston, MA: Thomson Course Technology.

Chang, H. (2008). *Autoethnography as method*. Walnut Creek, CA: Left Coast Press.

Chetwynd, T. (1982). *A dictionary of symbols*. London: Paladin.

Cohen, S. (1991). *Rock culture in Liverpool: Popular music in the making*. Oxford: Clarendon Press.

Cottrell, S. (2004). *Professional music-making in London: Ethnography and experience*. Aldershott (Herts): Ashgate.

Dann, A. (2003). *How to succeed in the music business*. London: Omnibus Press.

Ellis, C. (2004). *The ethnographic I: A methodological novel about autoethnography*. Walnut Creek, CA: AltaMira Press.

Evans, I. (1971). *Brewer's dictionary of phrase and fable*. Revised edition. London: Cassell.

Green, L. (2001). *How popular musicians learn: A way ahead for music education*. Aldershot: Ashgate.

Hannan, M. (1978). 'The music of Peter Sculthorpe: An analytical appraisal with special reference to those social and cultural forces which have influenced the formulation of an Australian vision.' PhD thesis, The University of Sydney.

Hannan, M. (2003). *The Australian guide to careers in music*. Sydney: UNSW Press.

Hannan, M. (2006). Making music: Inside/outside. *Realtime, Issue 74*, August-September. Retrieved September 13, 2009, from http://rt.airstrip.com.au/article/issue74/8157.

Hayes, D. (1993). *Peter Sculthorpe: A bio-bibliography*. Westport, CT: Greenwood Press.

Homer. (1946). (trans. Rieu, E.). *The Odyssey*. Harmmondsworth, UK: Penguin Books.

Kimpel, D. (1993). *Networking in the music business*. Cincinnati, OH: Writer's Digest Books.

Lave, J. & Wenger, E. (1991). *Situated learning: Legitimate peripheral participation*. Cambridge: Cambridge University Press.

McLellan, H. (Ed.). (1996). *Situated learning perspectives*. Englewood Cliffs, NJ: Educational Technology Publications.

Magee, J. (1996). 'From fine cut to mix: An exploration of processes and issues in Australian film score composition.' BA Honours thesis, Southern Cross University.

Martin, P. (1995). *Sounds and Society: Themes in the sociology of music*. Manchester: Manchester University Press.

Messiaen, O. (1944). *Technique de mon langage musical*. Paris: Leduc.

Messiaen, O. (1994). *Traité de rythme, de couleur, et d'ornithologie*. Paris: Leduc.

Nettl, B. (1995). *Heartland excursions: Ethnomusicological reflections on schools of music*. Urbana, IL: University of Illinois Press.

Ornstein, A., & Hunkins, F. (2004). *Curriculum foundations, principals and issues* (4th ed.). Boston: Pearson/Allyn & Bacon.

Passmore, D. (2004). *All you need to know about the music business*. London: Penguin.

'Proteus'. In *Wikipedia*, http://en.wikipedia.org/wiki/Proteus. Retrieved 29 November, 2007.

Shuker, R. (1998). *Key concepts in popular music*. London: Routledge.

Simpson, S. (2006). *Music business* (3rd ed.). London: Omnibus Press.

Slonimsky, N. (1947). *Thesaurus of scales and melodic patterns*. New York: C. Scribner.

Slonimsky, N. (2000). *Lexicon of musical invective*. New York: W.W. Norton.

Sly, L. (1993). *The power and the passion*. Sydney: Warner Chappell.

Weber, L. (2007). *Marketing to the social web: How digital customer communities build your business*. Hoboken, NJ: John Wiley & Sons.

Winn, W. (1996). Why I don't want to be an expert sitar player. In H. McLellan, (Ed.), *Situated learning perspectives* (pp. 175-187). Englewood Cliffs, NJ: Educational Technology Publications.

Further reading and information

Networking tools

www.isound.com/artist_blog/11_social_networking_steps_to_promote_your_music_0

General overview of social networking: http://en.wikipedia.org/wiki/Online_Social_networking

Further readings

Anderson, C. (2006). *The long tail: Why the future of business is selling less of more*. New York: Hyperion.

Beeching, A. (2005). *Beyond talent: Creating a successful career in music*. Oxford & New York: Oxford University Press.

Cottrell, S. (2004). *Professional music-making in London: Ethnography and experience*. Aldershot: Ashgate.

Draper, P. (2009). How online social networks are redefining knowledge, power, twenty-first century music making and higher education, in *Journal of Music Research Online*. Available at: http://journal.mca.org.au/ojs/index.php?journal=mca2&page=index

Duckworth, W. (2005). *Virtual music: How the web got wired for sound*. New York: Routledge.

Hutchison, T. (2008). *Web marketing for the music business*. Boston: Focal Press.

Kimpel, D. (2003). *Networking in the music business*. Cincinnati: Writers Digest Books.

Lorange, K. Guitar for beginners and beyond: www.guitarforbeginners.com [website].

Vincent, F. (2010). *MySpace for musicians*. Boston: Thomson Course Technology PTR.

Weber, L. (2007). *Marketing to the social web: How digital customer communities build your business*. Hoboken (NJ): John Wiley and Sons. Inc.

Part II
Resources

Introduction

This is an exciting time to enter the professional world of music. However, careers unfold in dramatically different ways from those of the past and they can be difficult, if not impossible, to imagine during training. And there lie both the challenges and the opportunities.

In Part II we highlight the importance of awareness, attitude and professional relationships. We do this with activities that encourage reflection on individual temperament, personality and style, skills and attributes, strengths, weaknesses, likes and dislikes. The activities contribute to the development of a clear-headed self-awareness, a flexible and adaptable outlook, a developing savvy for the music world as a whole, and the interpersonal skills to put it all together.

The materials can be used in a variety of ways such as panel discussions, group work, journaling, online chat, blogs, interviews, and as assignment questions, personal reflections, research, guided readings, group challenges and debate topics. Organised into three sections and 35 resources, many of the resources can be positioned in different ways. The first twelve resources focus largely on self, encouraging reflection and future-oriented planning in line with personal strengths, interests and goals. Resources thirteen through to twenty adopt a more outward-looking focus on career; and the final fifteen resources concern development of the attitudes, skills and mindset that will help to build and sustain a career in music.

INTRODUCTION

Whilst the resources are organised into sections as described above, they are not designed to be undertaken sequentially; rather, students and educators can dip in and out according to interest, time and curricular focus. Many of the resources can be used in a number of formats with classes, groups and individuals, and we include in the following table of contents an 'activity type' to indicate how the resource might be used. Electronic copies of all 35 resources are available from www.thetileapproach.ning.com

Part II Contents

Section 1: From self to career

	Title	Activity type	Page
1	Conceptualising music careers I	*Activity*	157
2	Conceptualising music careers II	*Self-reflection*	161
3	Musician profile I: Trying things out	*Reading*	167
4	Plotting your preferences	*Self-reflection*	171
5	Turning on the career light	*Workshop*	173
6	Discussion: Embracing the 'e' word (entrepreneurship)	*Discussion*	177
7	The musician's lifestyle quiz	*Activity*	179
8	Getting what you want I: Deciding *what* you want	*Self-reflection*	183
9	Getting what you want II: Following your passion	*Self-reflection*	185
10	Musician profile II: Following your passion	*Reading*	187
11	Getting what you want III: Likes and dislikes, strengths and weaknesses	*Group work*	191
12	Musician profile III: Filling in the gaps	*Reading*	193

Section 2: From career to community

13	Community I: Teaching artists at work	*Self-reflection and essay topics*	197
14	Getting to know your dream job	*Research task*	199
15	Community II: Finding your mission	*Self-reflection*	201
16	Transitioning to professional life – introduction	*Reading and self-reflection*	203
17	Transitioning I: From professional student to professional musician	*Reading*	205
18	Careers panel: How did you get here?	*Activity*	211
19	Getting inspiration from others	*Self-reflection*	213
20	Reading and reflecting on musician biographies and profiles	*Guided reading*	215

Section 3: Survival skills

21	Musician profile IV: Orchestral life	*Reading*	219
22	Getting a head start	*Discussion*	223
23	Challenge: Action plans	*Discussion*	225
24	Musician profile V: Finding the sparkle	*Reading*	227
25	Transitioning II: From awareness to innovation	*Reading and activity*	231

26	Transitioning III: Know thyself - Temperament and personality	*Reading and activity*	233
27	Skills and attributes I: Professionalism	*Activity and reflection*	235
28	Skills and attributes II: The team approach	*Activity*	237
29	Skills and attributes III: Skills audit	*Activity*	239
30	Expanding the skill set	*Reflection*	241
31	Challenge: Volunteering	*Activity*	247
32	Transitioning IV: Practical strategies for transitioning into professional life	*Reading*	249
33	Networking I: Building circles	*Activity*	253
34	Networking II: Who else do you know?	*Activity*	261
35	Networking III: Reflections	*Reflection*	265

Foreword

If I had the power to grant the best possible life to music students today, I would grant them a musical life just like mine. I have been lucky enough to play in a great American orchestra for forty years, during which time the level of music making as well as the level of compensation have risen steadily. Nothing in my early life pointed to such an outcome. In fact my trajectory resembled many described in this book: it unfolded catch-as-catch-can, without the benefit of the wisdom, skills, and foresight that can be found in these pages.

My father was a music educator in a working-class New Jersey town. When my piano lessons with him threatened to ruin our relationship, he chose the cello for me, and I began lessons at the relatively late age of eight. From the first, I had excellent training with teachers I adored, but never did it include what we now think of as career counselling. I entered the Curtis Institute of Music with only a vague sense that I wanted to be the best cellist I could be, and I graduated without having revisited that goal. I did further study in Europe, went to competitions and finally sought an orchestra position feeling like a failure because I had not succeeded in establishing an international solo career. A double failure, because when I did win an orchestra audition, it was for a section position. Not even principal chair.

When I began what many said was the perfect job, I was terribly lonely. I had no preparation for the transition from conservatory to a professional life with colleagues twice or three times my age. And I had given scant thought to the fact that few orchestras paid a living wage.

Little did I know at the time that the symphonic world was beginning to undergo a transformation that would place American orchestras among the very best in the world. Medium-sized cities that wanted to be taken seriously now began to establish or expand their orchestras. Major orchestras went to fifty two-week seasons. The formation of the International Conference of Symphony and Opera Musicians (ICSOM) helped musicians to obtain increasingly decent collective bargaining agreements, which in turn attracted finer and finer musicians. My colleagues all over the country worked hard to secure effective and meaningful roles in all artistic matters, including hiring, programming and the evaluation of conductors. They served on committees, helped with fund-raising, and safeguarded their own musical development by teaching, organizing chamber music societies, commissioning new works, and continuing to musically challenge themselves and each other.

But we have had to grope our way, often improvising, stumbling, or taking the least direct route. No one anticipated that this was to be part of the job. No one had spoken to us about self-authorship, entrepreneurialism, or interpersonal skills. Quite the contrary. As students, we had been discouraged from letting anything distract us from our central goal – mastering our instruments.

I am truly grateful that my career has coincided with a golden age of American orchestras, an age which musicians themselves have had such a hand in creating. Yet in spite of our best efforts and considerable success, this model that has served our cities so well seems less and less likely to thrive in the twenty-first century. Threats come from many corners, not least of which is the increased marginalization of classical music in general.

The challenge today is no different from when I was starting out: how to define and create authentic musical lives in the real world. No one is more invested in the success — financial as well as artistic — of our profession than musicians themselves. I believe the continued health of classical music depends largely on the energy of young musicians, both helping to shape the musical world in which we live and work, and forging their own vision of music's role in the world.

Life in the Real World comes along at just the right time, an essential and comprehensive guide, outlining the skills needed to help students, indeed all of us, to find effective paths toward satisfying professional lives immersed in the music we love.

Marcia Peck, Cellist, Minnesota Orchestra

Cellist **Marcia Peck** earned her Bachelor of Music Degree from The Curtis Institute of Music, after which she spent two years studying at the Schumann Konservatorium in Düsseldorf. Her teachers—to whom she is enormously grateful for her full and wonderful career—include Orlando Cole, Antonio Janigro, Bernard Greenhouse, Zara Nelsova, and Mstislav Rostropovitch.

Before joining the Minnesota Orchestra in 1971, Marcia toured South America with the Argentine chamber group, *La Camarata di Bariloche*. She was a finalist in the Gaspar Cassado Competition in Florence, Italy and took First Prize in Mainz, Germany. In Minnesota, she was a founding member of the Bakken Quartet, performing the complete quartet cycles of Beethoven and Shostakovitch (US premiere.) She has been fortunate to perform chamber music with such luminaries as Joshua Bell, Pam Frank, Gil Shaham, YoYo Ma, Garrick Olssohn, Stephen Hough and Chris O'Reilly. She soloed with the Minnesota Orchestra, Neville Marriner conducting, in Bartok's Second Rhapsody. Summers, she plays in the Grand Teton Music Festival.

Marcia's essays have appeared in Showcase: the Magazine of the Minnesota Orchestra. Her novel-in-progress, *The Unattended Moment,* was awarded a Minnesota State Arts Board Artist Fellowship. A short story, "An

Unexpected Cadence," will appear later this year in the anthology *A Tribute to Orpheus 2*. Her short-short story "Long Distance" was nominated for a Pushcart Prize.

Marcia lives with her horn-player husband Dave Kamminga. Her daughter Hadley is a Shakespeare scholar.

Section 1
From Self to Career

Chapter 1
Conceptualising Music Careers I

Contributed by Rosie Perkins

ACTIVITY

Part 1 reference: Chapter 2

Figure 1 encourages us to think about *career* as a multifaceted concept, rather than simply a '9-till-5' job. What we term 'objective facets' of career include: (1) the *time* spent on different activities; and (2) the *proportion of income* generated from these activities (recognising that these may well be different). What we term 'subjective facets' include: (3) how people *identify themselves* (how they see themselves), and (4) their *vision* for the future. You can find out more about this in Chapter 1.

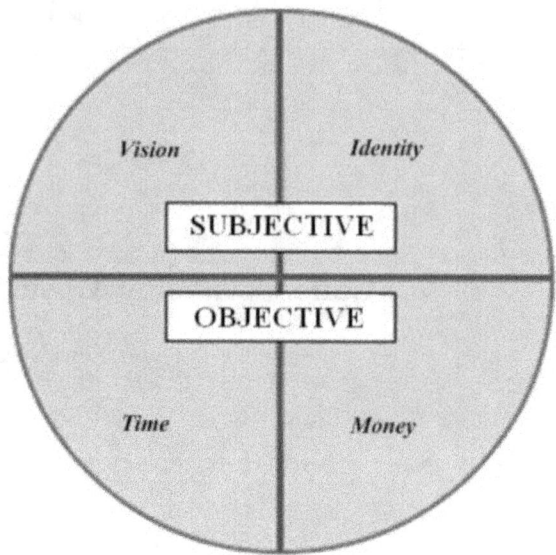

Figure 1: Conceptualising 'career' for musicians (Mills, 2004)

Take a moment to consider these four elements in relation to your career. You may like to use the following questions as a guide, or to pose to peers:

VISION:

- What are your aims for the future?
- Where would you like to be in five years' time? In ten years' time?
- Why do you want to achieve these things?
- How long have you wanted to achieve these things?

IDENTITY:

- How would you describe yourself? Why would you describe yourself like this?
- How do you think others see you as a musician? How would you like to be seen?
- Where do you see yourself fitting in the music profession?
- What makes you happy?

TIME:
- How do you spend most of your time?
- What different (musical or non-musical) activities do you do?
- How is your time divided across the week? Are you satisfied with this?
- How do you imagine spending your time when you graduate?

MONEY:
- Are you taking paid gigs, or earning money from teaching or other activities? If so, how does this reflect the time you spend doing the activity? Why do you do this?
- Do you feel that your time is well rewarded?
- How do you imagine earning your living when you graduate?

Thinking about the answers to these questions may help you to see your career in a new light, and make you more equipped to bring together *what you do* (your objective career) with *what you want to do and identify with* (your subjective career). It doesn't matter if you struggle to answer some of the questions; just thinking about them, and your responses to them, can be useful. Try to return to these questions regularly, taking note of (or recording) your answers so that you can see if and how they change over time. This will support you in understanding your professional aims and aspirations and how they fit with you as a person and as a musician.

Chapter 2
Conceptualising Music Careers II

Contributed by Rosie Perkins

Part I Reference: Chapter 2

The following snapshots come from interviews conducted with a student—Jack—during his three years at the Royal College of Music in London. As you read through them, consider Jack's journey. What changes can you see? What might have influenced these changes? In each snapshot, some of Jack's words have been highlighted as prompts for discussion.

Snapshot 1: End of first undergraduate year

> What does being realistic mean to you?

VISION

'My dream thing would be being a piano soloist but **I think I have to be realistic** and while the piano is really tough, it becomes really hard so I don't know ... I would love to teach. I would really love to teach'.

IDENTITY

'I don't know if the word exists—eclectic. I love contemporary music and chamber music and solo playing and academia and not only music academia. I don't throw myself in one direction, ignoring the others ... **I don't consider myself as a pianist. I think as a person I am a pianist but it is more a job thing. You are a pianist if you earn a living out of it and I don't do that so music student would describe me more correctly**'.

> What do you think? Should or does 'earning a living' determine how you describe yourself?

Snapshot 2: Beginning of second undergraduate year

> Is 'musical scale'—or where you fit among others—important to you?

VISION

'Hopefully I will have found my way into competitions so I can kind of be kind of recognised on the **musical scale**. If I haven't done well in any competitions, I haven't got much hope'.

IDENTITY

'I feel like a music student and even though I have got this big thing which makes me the soloist with the orchestra, I still don't feel like I'm this [amazing] pianist! **I just feel like myself, just a music student, in London. That's it**'.

> How does music fit in to how you see yourself?

Snapshot 3: Midway through second undergraduate year

How important do you think it is to *think* or *ponder* or *write* about music?

VISION

'Happiness. Whatever I do I want to be happy—not rich. [Interviewer: Do you see music as being part of that?] Yes. I can't live without it—whether it is for me or sharing with pupils or an audience. I can't live without making music. [Interviewer: So do you think it will be the only thing you do professionally?] No. I know that I will also need something more intellectual. Music is very intellectual. **I like making music but I also like pondering music and writing about it because they explain the feelings and what you feel when you listen to music**'.

IDENTITY

'I would say musician rather than pianist but at the same time **I would describe myself as open to broader horizons**. I would not like to limit myself to musician'.

Do you undertake activities outside of music? How do different things that you do connect together?

163

CHAPTER 2: CONCEPTUALISING MUSIC CAREERS II

Snapshot 4: Beginning of third undergraduate year

What do you *want* to do with your time? How can you try to make this happen?

VISION

'I want to try to be a better musician all the time. I want to never lose momentum—never lose motivation and I want to always strive never to become bitter because I have now worked hard enough to get where I want to get and I don't want to be in this two square meter little room all day and be thinking 'This isn't what I want to do'. I don't want to do that. **If I am teaching, it is because I want to do that. If I am performing, it is because I want to**'.

IDENTITY

'[I think you need to] bring everything together because **music isn't one island**. It is one piece and you have to know everything... the world of culture is fascinating and it is one thing that makes you think that I don't have to be wealthy. It is the one thing that makes me realise that I don't need that much money and [to] have a wonderful home in Kensington. It is the one thing that makes me feel that I am really rich'.

How many different 'islands' can you think of to describe your musical activities? How do these all link together?

Snapshot 5: After graduation

> *I sometimes think that being versatile is not a strength at all. Perhaps people would like someone who is excellent at doing one thing and who devotes heart, soul and body to doing that one particular thing, which is not my conception of music for life. I am not the most gifted pianist. I haven't got the best technique in the world and I am not the best musician in the world either, but at least I am willing to improve, but I do realise how limited I can be. [Interviewer: And when you say your conception of a musician, what is that conception?] I don't know. It is just, I think ... I think that 90% of the people who audition for here, within the four years they are all hoping to be the world's most recognised musician and that flakes off as we go along and at the end of the time that we are leaving the RCM or we are about to leave it, it has completely crumbled and you realise what you can do around that and that can make you happy. In my case, it is doing different things. It is just about sharing for me. I have realised that piano solos are just not for me and I just don't enjoy that any more. I just like sharing and making people know and learn what music is about. That is what matters to me..*

↓

Finally, what really matters to you? In many ways, this should be at the heart of all of the decisions you take about your career.

Chapter 3
Musician Profile I

Trying things out

Contributed by Dawn Bennett

This is the story of Danish freelance trumpeter Jeppe Uggerhoej, who graduated from his Bachelor degree one year prior to the interview. He talks about how he is building a career in music, the need to be able to perform in different genres, and trying different things to work out what he might want to do in the longer term.

I filled in the university forms for biology and filled in the forms for music, just to make sure I had something to do. When I got in here at the conservatoire, it was great. I knew many people who would like to come in. So I thought I'd do the conservatoire for one year, to see what it's like, and I never got out again. It was quite fun when I started to do it, and luckily it is still fun to play.

There was no system of Bachelor degrees at the conservatoire and I thought I should have a degree, so in my last year I started doing university music studies as well. Then when I finished at the conservatoire I started doing economics. I'm supposed to be doing that now, but I haven't got time! Eventually I will get a Masters in economics, which will go along with my administrative stuff. It's a new area, the same as music was about ten years ago, a new area, exciting. You've loads of possibilities when you've done economics, compared to music on its own. When you finish at the conservatoire you really have to see what possibilities you've got. But if you've got music and economics there's a wider range. I hope so.

Right now I play the trumpet and I try to do as many different things as possible. That's why I freelance: I get to play in bands, symphony orchestras, musicals and small ensembles. That's mainly it, playing-wise. I had concerts all year in a military band when I was studying, and for another year after that. I've been lucky so far: I haven't had any gaps in performance work yet. So it's pure luck, and reputation.

I thought I would try to do some more administrative work. Three months ago I became a leader of a talent school on a small island in Denmark. There are maybe a million people there. The talent school is for people from about eleven years up to approximately 20 years. You take all the best students you have on that island, and they get teaching six times a year on a Saturday from teachers who are principal players in Danish symphony orchestras. Besides the teaching on Saturdays, the students get to play with a professional symphony orchestra, so they get some kind of idea what it is to be a musician.

The talent school has existed for four years, and at the moment I am trying to profile the school a lot more because I think it needs to expand to secure the ongoing work. So by 2010 or 2011 I hope the school will not just be the island, but the whole of the south of Denmark. That would be great. I'll try in the next year to build up some samples from the talent school so they've got some PR materials.

It's quite interesting work because you've got the teachers of the school, who as I said before are solo players in the orchestras, and at the same time the students have a usual teacher at their music school. The music school teachers have to follow the student to the talent school to observe the tuition, so the teachers see the tuition by the talent school teachers. And that's great, because it's more education for the music teachers. Hopefully there is an exchange both ways, and talent school teachers also learn from the other teachers.

Besides the talent school, I'm chairman of an organisation called DAO, which stands for Danish Amateur Orchestral Association. DAO consists of brass bands and wind bands, and quite recently we took in big bands as well. The work in DAO is mainly about arranging national contests and courses, taking care of national agreements concerning copyrights etc., and securing the ongoing work in the national youth bands.

I play purely classical, although in the military band we play some jazz as well, mostly big band style. My improvisation and so on is not very good. It's quite crappy in fact, when I play it. It's a shame really. It's the same when you play musicals, because there's a lot of jazz or rock style in that. And it takes time to get used to. So the first jobs where I played musicals were really, really awkward. It's better now. If you see a lot of the new music written, there's quite a lot of improvisation in that, too. It's really hard.

More and more musicians in Denmark are able to do both classical and jazz. In some places you've got the possibility to take lessons with jazz musicians or classical musicians, or to study folk music. I studied in the US three years ago, at the Eastman School of Music, and the students there, the trumpet students, could do both. Mostly the students there started playing jazz, and later on they started doing classical. I think it would be really fun to do improvisation: it would evolve you as a musician.

I had conducting lessons at the conservatoire as part of my course. I'm now doing a bit of conducting for a wind band, and at the moment I've got a brass band. Actually, my wind band just won the Danish title, last weekend, so that's great. The wind band is called the APO and it's sponsored by the mail in Denmark. I quite enjoy conducting because you meet a lot of different people, and the people you meet in the band are doctors, factory workers, whatever. I've conducted since I was in my second year, so right now I'm conducting two bands and playing full-time, and doing DAO and doing the talent school. Too much, way too much!

About two weeks ago I was playing a concert with a really shit band. All amateurs. Sounded horrible, but they loved it, and the audience loved it because they knew the people playing it. And when the job was done, I was on my way back home in the car and I rang up my friend in the symphony orchestra, and they'd just been playing Rite of Spring, or something really great. And I said, 'how was your evening?' He said it was okay, played Rite of Spring and the audience clapped, and that's it. And I said, after playing with a shit band, turns out it was an amazing evening. Really funny! When you go into the conservatoire, the only thing that really has the high standing, or the high esteem, is a place in an orchestra. But we need to see the other possibilities we've got, and you need to lift these possibilities up so they're at the same level—so a job other than an orchestra position is not less worthy.

I'm just at the moment seeing what it's like to do organisational work because I'm not quite certain that I want to be a trumpet player full-time, which I am now, or if I'd like to do more organisation. So if I do both playing and organisational work for two or three years, I think I'll be able to make up my mind. Doing both means a lot of work at the moment though. I sometimes play in the local symphony, and in other symphony. I also play in a military band, and I play in some musicals. It is a lot, but it fits well with my organisational job so that's nice. I also have two children aged three and two months. I will find performing harder when my children go to school because when I am not working, in the day, they will be at school. That will be harder. So then I have to find ways around that, but that's the benefits of freelancing: you do what you want to do.

The most fun thing I do is playing with groups where the passion is really strong. I really don't care if it's a professional group or an amateur group. I've sometimes been out playing with an amateur band just for one concert, but being in that band you can feel the enthusiasm for music, and the enthusiasm for getting this right. That's great. At the same time, the thing I hate the most in the music business is when you see the passion die—you see this 'factory work' instead of just making music. So I really don't care if it's playing or conducting, or organising. As long as there's passion, as long as there is a will to keep performing, it keeps getting better and better.

Amatørmusikkonsulenten: The National Adviser for Amateur Music: http://www.daos.dk

Chapter 4
Plotting your Preferences

Contributed by Janis Weller

Things I like and do well	Things I don't like but do well
Things I like but find difficult to do	Things I don't like and struggle to do

Instructions

'Plotting Your Preferences' is a simple activity to help you pinpoint some strengths, identify possible future directions, and perhaps learn a bit more about yourself. The activities you list in each square may be music-related or more general in nature. For the lower right square, 'Things I struggle to do and don't like,' consider things you must do, even if they are not an especially good fit for you (not just things you could avoid entirely). Fill in several examples in all four squares before you read the analysis process below.

Analysing the results

The upper left quadrant, 'Things I like and do well', obviously identifies activities in your life that are a very good fit for you, and ideally could be the focus of your career activities. Can these activities generate sufficient income to sustain you? How can you move in that direction and how will you fill in the gaps in the meantime?

The upper right, 'Things I don't like but do well', is one of life's interesting conundrums. Perhaps you are very good at organising events, just not that interested in doing so. Or perhaps you got excellent grades in maths, but are just not that intrigued by the subject. You could, however, consider items in this square when thinking about a possible 'day-job' to make money. Activities you are adept at tend not to be energy drains and may be tasks that others are willing to pay you to do. Bingo! Ideal day-job. You can work, make some money, and still have energy left to pursue your true passions.

The lower left box can be more problematic. 'Things I like, but find difficult to do' can present real challenges in our lives—something to strive toward and improve on, or perhaps something you just find frustrating. What will you do with the items in that box? Finally, the lower right, 'Things I don't like and don't do well'. The activities in this box can take up considerable time and energy in our lives. One solution? There may be tasks on this list that you can hire others to do for you. It could be worthwhile to hire someone to clean your apartment, do your taxes, or shovel snow off your sidewalk. Some of those skills may land in that person's upper right square, after all. You may even be able to trade or barter services, using your skills to help someone else. File away and revisit these answers regularly, or expand them straight away by going to activities 8, 9 and 11: Getting what you want.

Chapter 5
Workshop

Turning on the career light

Contributed by Dawn Bennett

Part I reference: Chapter 5

Objective: To open the conversation about careers in music and to think outside of the square.

Time required: Ideally, two to three hours.

Materials: Archive box or similar containing bags or boxes. I use gift bags, paper shopping bags, shoe boxes etc. It is more interesting for each group if they get to open packages, and it also helps to keep everything together. The boxes and bags should contain a selection of the following:

Feather boa
Viking helmet
Sample contract
First aid kit
Blank business plan, business card, calculator, organiser
Passport application
Grant application
Marketing materials
Telephone
Teddy bear
Apple

Beginner book or teaching schedule
Blank Diploma/certificate
Crystal ball
Some music notes
Toy trumpet

List of personal attributes (for example, the terrific resource at http://www.westone.wa.gov.au/lifeskills/index.asp)

You can use just about anything for the packages. I always throw in something new and it's great to see what students make of it. However, some things are always there and have a particular purpose. For example, the feather boa represents the passion that drives a career; the Viking helmet represents strength; and the first aid kit represents the need to stay physically and mentally well, and also the need to plan one's work to ensure that workload is manageable at all times. This can prompt discussion about time management and budgeting.

Each group will need a sheet divided into three columns titled as follows: 1) Role/activity (what you might be doing); 2) skills; and 3) attributes. Each group should appoint a scribe.

Hint: Groups of three students work best

A week or so before the workshop, ask the students to look up the word musician in the *Grove Dictionary of Music and Musicians*. The students will find that it isn't included. Open the workshop by suggesting that students need to define for themselves what it is to be a musician.

Suggested format:

1. Begin by asking the students what they love to do. Give examples of your own likes and dislikes both within and outside of music, and students will join in.

    I use this as both class discussion and (later) as personal reflection. Questions posed for reflection can include:

    > What is a successful musician?
    > What skills are required to build and sustain this career?
    > What *is* a musician?

    Part II includes several tools for developing this aspect of career development before or after the workshop.

2. Activity to get everyone loosened up and thinking:

    Give the students a sheet of paper divided into four boxes titled strengths, weaknesses, likes and dislikes (see tool 11). Ask them to write three things in each of the boxes and then set the paper aside. No one else needs to see it.

    Hint: Whilst the students are doing this, do it yourself.

3. Give one of the packages to each group, and give them three minutes to consider how each item might relate to them as musicians. They need to write at least one word in each column. Some packages relate most to skills, some to attributes and some to activities or roles. Some are obvious and some less so.

   The scribes have three columns to complete: role/activity; skills; and attributes

   After three minutes, the groups pass their package to the right.

   Hint: suggest that students think about planning lives in music, rather than careers in music. It's a good idea to have a break at this point

4. Workshop each package in turn. I ask the groups to write their responses on a flip chart/white board. They can come up to the flip chart whenever they like. Everyone contributes to and discusses what's there, often with much hilarity. The workshop works best if you have numerous pieces of butcher's paper on the walls, and students can move between them adding words as they wish. Once the writing slows down, start the conversation about each package.

   Here are some real examples of students' responses:

   Viking helmet Being a good actor; commitment; costume/set design; strength; dedication; resilience; vibrant personality.

   Teaching schedule The need for an education; working well with others; confidence; patience; being loud; being able to explain what you know; making a living.

   Toy trumpet Focus; the Salvation Army; healthy lungs; marketing yourself (blowing your own trumpet).

5. After the workshop, the results are sent to students individually by email. They are asked to consider each of the packages and the words put against them, and to compare these to the words they wrote in the boxes at step 2. The reflective task, which doesn't have to be shown to anyone else, is to further develop this thinking in light of the workshop and activities. Most students will swap words around and add more. This is a useful moment to explain that they will be swapping and changing them throughout their careers. They can also mark areas that need development, those at which they are strongest, and so on.

This activity can lead to career action plans and study plans. The main message is to think outside of the square, to recognise that success means to be intrinsically satisfied with what you do, and to open every possible door by engaging with non-performance courses, career counselling sessions and other activities.

I try to always get across that perhaps the most important attribute for graduates is a willingness and ability to keep learning. That attitude takes time to develop.

Chapter 6
Discussion Topic

Embracing the 'e' word

Contributed by Janis Weller

What is the 'e' word?

Many artists avoid the term entrepreneur, deeming it too business-like, but as Bennett mentions in Chapter 5, the root of the word 'entrepreneur' is simply 'to take action', and the ability to take decisive, appropriate action is critical to launching your career (lots more on that below). The classic entrepreneur employs high levels of creativity, innovation, energy, and willingness to take risks: all attributes frequently common to musicians. The core values and attributes of an entrepreneur frame vital skills and attitudes for 21st century musicians.

The mere act of creating a musical product and distributing it through live or recorded performance makes you a small business with numerous rights and responsibilities. The massive changes in music distribution and promotion caused by advances in the Internet and technology have drastically complicated both the opportunities and the challenges of running your musical life. As a result, you will need to learn the basics of managing a small business in order to make knowledgeable decisions about your musical 'product' and to avoid unsavoury managers, distributors or bookers who have only their own best interests in mind. The ability to take personal responsibility for your musical career is in itself an entrepreneurial mindset.

Entrepreneurial and business skills combined with personal awareness can help prepare you for successful transition from student to professional. What motivates you to study and perform music? Can you motivate yourself to create and implement a career plan? How do you respond when you don't win an audition? Do you prefer variety or routine in your daily schedule? Do you like practicing better than performing, or vice versa? Reflecting on your personal goals and motivations in relation to the world around you is a critical step in the process. To delve into this issue in greater detail, jump straight to the Musician's Lifestyle Quiz (next).

Chapter 7
The Musician's Lifestyle Quiz

Contributed by Janis Weller

Career decisions have an enormous impact on musicians' daily lives. Here are some multiple-choice questions to get you thinking about the lifestyle choices that could make you happy and productive. There are no *right* answers. Any answer could be right for you, but some choices might work better than others in certain jobs and careers. Some of your expectations and requirements may change as the years go by, and others will be more consistent. So take the quiz to learn a little more about yourself. You may be surprised.

CHAPTER 7: THE MUSICIAN'S LIFESTYLE QUIZ

Lifestyle quiz

1. My ideal workday would:
   a. Start at 9:00 a.m. and end at 5:00 p.m.
   b. Start at noon and end at midnight
   c. Be different every day

2. My ideal schedule would include:
   a. Travel as much as possible
   b. Occasional travel, but mostly working in one town
   c. Work that gets me home to my own bed every night

3. I would be willing to take the following number of auditions before I landed a performing job:
   a. 1 - 3
   b. 4 - 10
   c. As many as it took

4. It's December. I'm a professional performer with a family to support, so I:
   a. Refuse to accept holiday shows (it's the holidays!)
   b. Pick and choose a few gigs and sacrifice a few presents for the family
   c. Postpone family holiday activities to get as many paying performances as possible

For each of the following questions, choose the statement that most accurately describes your attitude:

5. I prefer to:
   a. be the master of my own schedule and priorities
   b. take direction from others
   c. work as part of a team
   d. work with small groups
   e. work with larger groups
   f. work alone
   g. work with the public clientele

6. My lifestyle preference is:
   a. The good life – nice car, eating out at restaurants, owning a home
   b. Whatever works – driving a 10-year-old beater, mac 'n' cheese, renting a cheap apartment
   c. Movin' on up – starting out on a shoestring is okay, but I want the best eventually

7. I thrive in the following environment:
   a. High energy, high stress situations
   b. Laid back and safe situations
   c. A changing environment that isn't too crazy but isn't guaranteed peace and quiet, either

8. I would be happiest with:
   a. A regular pay check (both amount and frequency) and steady work
   b. A free schedule that doesn't tie me down even if it doesn't guarantee steady income
   c. A steady part-time job that doesn't pay all the bills, but it's a start

9. My attitude toward compromise is:
   a. I'm really easy-going; whatever people need is fine
   b. I'm pretty set in my ways once I've made up my mind
   c. I've got strong ideas, but I'll listen to yours
   d. I don't

10. I take rejection and:
    a. Work even harder (it challenges me)
    b. Back off to recover (rejection is hard for me)
    c. Keep on going as if nothing happened (it doesn't bother me)

11. My organisation skills are:
    a. Unbelievable – I always know where every scrap of paper is, where I need to be and when
    b. Not so hot – I can get by with a great performance, so who will notice if I'm late?
    c. I'm working on them
    d. I'm random and at peace with chaos

Now review your answers
- Is the security of regular hours and a regular pay check important to you?
- Do you enjoy lots of variety and freedom?
- Do you work best with clear structure and expectations?
- How resilient are you?
- How motivated are you?
- Can you accept the fact that performing musicians work mostly weekends, evenings and holidays, the times many other people are playing?
- What is your interpersonal style, that is, how well do you 'play with others'?

Chapter 8
Getting What you Want I

Deciding what you want

Contributed by Dawn Bennett

The answers to these questions are likely to frame future career decisions and will be fundamental to developing an emerging professional identity and clear self-image. Answer each of the questions as a self-reflection before exploring them further in groups, as a class, or online.

1. What are your most rewarding experiences inside of music?

   _____
   _____
   _____

   1.1 What was rewarding about them?

   _____
   _____
   _____

2. What are your most rewarding experiences *outside* of music?

   _____
   _____
   _____

2.1 What was rewarding about them?

2.2 How do they relate to those things you most enjoy within music?

3. What things would you like to try or to develop more fully?

4. What would you like to learn more about?

5. What are the strengths of your character?

6. What are you good at?

7. What are you passionate about?

Chapter 9
Getting what you want II

Following your passion

Contributed by Dawn Bennett

Look at the matrix below. Write what you are passionate about and then consider the other words within the matrix. Highlight what you already know or have developed, and which areas need more work. Relate all of this to your passion – the thing that drives you to do music.

CHAPTER 9: GETTING WHAT YOU WANT II

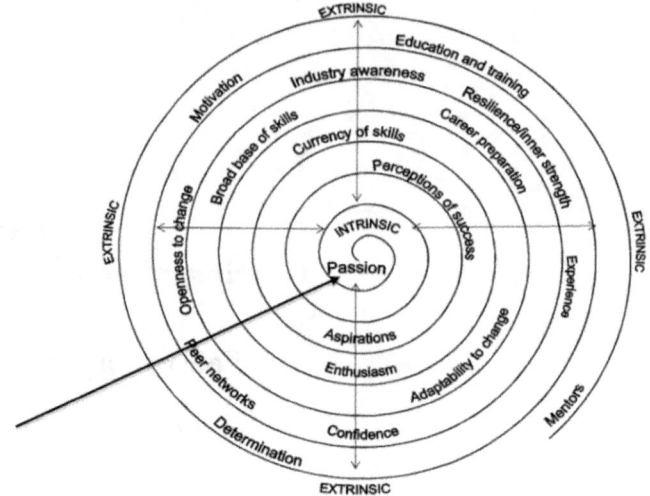

What are you passionate about? (from Bennett, 2008)

_____
_____
_____

Chapter 10
Musician Profile II

Following your passion

Contributed by Dawn Bennett

Angie is a violinist who trained and worked in Europe before returning to Australia to raise her young family. Her work in Europe and Australia spans orchestral and chamber music performance, teaching, and a quartet which combines poetry, stories and music to provide innovative concerts and workshops for children and adults. Her career has been underpinned by an overwhelming passion for music, and she has explored her interests in diverse ways.

I don't think you really discover that passion, what your strengths are, until you've been through a whole lot. Performing was what I loved doing most. I'd always seen teaching as something that would happen alongside the performing, not ever take front seat because I have too much fun performing. But you have to fix what you're doing around where you are, which you can always do as a musician because there's always work for you, wherever you are. You have to go out and make it though.

I knew at the age of twelve that this was what I was going to do. That was the first time I sat in a really big symphony orchestra and I was so in love with the feeling of being part of something so great and that has never, ever left me. And it never occurred to me for a single moment after then, what else can I do with my life? I just knew. I didn't think I was particularly madly talented. It was just what I loved and that was what I was going to do. I had a complete, single-minded passion for what I was doing. I feel very, very lucky and privileged that I had wonderful teachers right from a very young age who instilled a love of music and the need to learn to value that creativity. That to me is most important.

I came to realise, when I started working exclusively in small groups in a chamber orchestra or a string quartet in Hamburg, that I didn't have to deal with that whole orchestra hierarchy and structure and the frustrations you have with not being able to use every minute of every rehearsal constructively—because that used to drive me nuts. And so I worked just with the string quartet and we were single-minded about what we did, and the music was absolutely paramount. And I mean once that's in your blood you can't stand fluffing around.

I chose to come back to Australia and I discovered within a very short time that I wasn't going to have enough performing to keep myself happy, so I knew I was going to have to create it. So I did. I'd always made up stories with music, read stories and recorded them with suitable music, sort of illustrating them to make it really fun to listen to, colourful music, and kids used to love it! And somebody said, 'You should do this for a living' and I said 'Yeah sure', you know. But by the time I realised it was really good, there were a lot of commercial things like that on the market and so I missed the boat. But the idea was good. I always had great ideas but never really followed them through. So I thought, 'if I'm going to follow this idea through, this is my last chance. I'm gonna give it a go'.

So, I could see how wonderful it was for my kids to be read to, and to listen to poems and stories. And I saw children who were hardly ever read to. It's such a wonderful thing to be able to lose yourself in a story, or in words, poems or music. We have such a duty to give back what we can to children, especially those not in privileged places, where you can find the most creative, wonderful people. So we decided to see how we'd go with performing poetry and string quartets. Sounds pretty dorky, but it's amazing when you do it in a fun, visual way and turn it into stories. I combined my passions of words, poetry, music and working with children into the one thing. And I could have a lot of fun by dressing up, playing barefoot on hot days, which is fantastic. I mean where else can you play the Shostakovich string quartets barefoot on a hot day? And it just develops all the time.

We do workshops with children. If they want to commit to doing a project over a month or two months we do a performance, then two of us go in, our actor and myself, and while he's working with one class I'm working with another, and at the end of the project we weave a whole story together. We work like maniacs in between. The last show we did was within five weeks with eight classes and about 160 children all performing. With the next project I'm going to get the kids to get an audience, so 'you have to make posters, you have to go and talk, you have to go into the community, you have to let everybody know'. So we're teaching them the whole caboodle, which is what we had to learn the hard way!

Then, seeing how much the teachers and adults love it, we've developed programs for adults, which is the icing on the cake because it's a difficult market to break into. Putting on concerts or performances you have to go into the whole entrepreneurial thing of finding venues and getting an audience together. Grant applications, story of my life, writing a million grant applications. I found myself doing things that I never thought in a million years I would be doing. But I do get very upset when people ask when they first meet you, 'What do you do? Oh you're a musician, oh that's lovely'. Well it is lovely because you're doing what you love and it's a way that you can earn a living. But it's bloody hard work, bloody hard work. And so much of that work does go unpaid, and you just have to take that into account. But the thing is we will do it whether we get paid or not because we have to do it to exist. That's what it boils down to in the end.

And for me, well I got to the stage where I knew I didn't want to be in an orchestra. I just had to create something where I thought I could make a difference. I'd had more than 20 years working in really good orchestras with great conductors and great people, so I had a lot to draw on. I can look back and say, 'Oh wasn't that great!' But I don't have the real desire to do that sort of work any more. I don't need that any more. I'm really happy to see other people going there. Social networking and inspiring kids with crazy ideas, that seems to be what I'm best at and it's what I love doing. I've worked out a way to make it my life.

Chapter 11
Getting what you want III

Likes and dislikes, strengths and weaknesses

Contributed by Dawn Bennett

Reading and group work

Another useful lens through which to look at your career is to consider how your likes and dislikes, strengths and weaknesses can be accommodated. Work with a small group so that you can complete steps 3, 4 and 5.

1. Read Musician profile II: Following your passion (tool 10).
2. In the following chart, list the things you like and dislike doing. Then, consider your strengths and weaknesses. Include at least five things in each quadrant, and refer back to 'Plotting your preferences' (tool 4) for more ideas.
3. Discuss the results with other people in your group and add to the chart from that discussion.
4. Focus on your dislikes. Find other people who like doing some of these things, and discuss how you could work together.
5. Focus on the weaknesses. Discuss strategies to strengthen these areas, and decide when you will tackle each one. Are there any you can avoid altogether? If so, how?

CHAPTER 11: GETTING WHAT YOU WANT III

Likes	Dislikes

Strengths	Weaknesses

_____
_____
_____
_____
_____
_____
_____
_____
_____

Chapter 12
Musician Profile II

Filling in the gaps

Contributed by Dawn Bennett

Dr Jan Gwatkin is a Perth-based pianist who describes the excitement found in continually developing and combining new goals and interests to create her career. She talks of the passion that underpins her activities.

When I left school I had an audition at Auckland University and I felt that I was too young to go, so I didn't. I decided to go when I felt that I could do it justice, and I wanted to be really sure that I was going to want to be a musician. So I decided to go travelling for ten years and do all kinds of things and at the end of ten years I'd decide, which is exactly what I did. And that's when I chose to become the very best piano teacher I could be, after seeing some absolutely monstrous piano teaching.

The reality of studying is that as much as you want to play—which was all I ever really took pleasure in—you don't actually get a lot of time to play what you want to play because you have to do all the written work and then you have to do accompanying. Your practice sort of goes out with the morning fairies. I always felt from my degree that I didn't get to show the practical skills I have in performance, so I decided that I would continue to perform. And then I got interested in all these other things. I was out there teaching and it was all just a little bit ho-hum, and it wasn't creative enough for me. So I started to research different methods of teaching, which then led into classroom teaching, lecturing at university and lots of other things like travelling overseas and writing papers.

My interests have developed along the way. My core principle of being the very best piano teacher I can be has broadened during my learning because I've found that having knowledge of learning principles that you get in general classroom education (and that we didn't get as music students) has been an absolute godsend. I didn't learn this at university; I learned it a lot later. I learned most about teaching through studying Orff-Schulwerk and Suzuki with a music education lecturer at another university. So I did all my music education through that avenue rather than formal learning, and that led to my Masters degree. I feel as though I've come in the 'back door', but I've had some really good teachers and really good grounding. I think it's really important to know a lot about different methodologies because everybody learns differently and you should be teaching the learner, not the method.

And then, because I still wasn't very satisfied with the standard of piano teachers who were coming to me for lessons, I decided to do a PhD on accreditation for piano teachers. I just do so many things every day. I'm now designing courses in music for other people, I lecture, I perform, I examine piano, and I examine music education students going out to their practicum experience in primary and high schools. I've just finished my PhD. I have travelled the world extensively going to wonderful, wonderful conferences and I've made some really great friends along the way. I have such a diverse role and I can run it all from home and choose when to work and when not to work.

But in the goal of still trying to fill in the gaps, now I feel I've done 20 years on writing and research and you can't really go much higher than a PhD, so I've decided to backtrack and do more work on my performing skills. Paris is coming up this July and I hope Paris is ready for me! I was invited to an international piano workshop in Paris by the keynote speaker at one of the conferences I went to last year. I didn't think I'd ever go, and it was a dream-come-true so I accepted within about 90 seconds. And I've spent the last six months in an absolute panic because now I actually have to perform again at that level, so I've got to build up that stamina and everything again. But I'll do it and I can't wait to go.

I would definitely let young and intending musicians know that they're not going to be performing their entire lives and all their careers unless they're very, very lucky. And while a lot of the young graduates I talk to don't even want to think they're going to be teaching in any shape or form, because they feel it's the lowest of the low, I think when they realise what you can do with that now, and where you can travel, and where you can go, I think that's what I'd bring to it: the joy of, the excitement of teaching; the joy of learning in different areas than just playing the piano, and that it's all associated. To me, a musician is somebody who absolutely adores what they do and in that context wants to know as much about it as possible in all of its realms, then apply it really well in lots of different ways. The most important attribute is flexibility: having an open mind and knowing that everything counts. When you've done your training, don't just stop. Don't get stuck in a box. You should always be going to bigger boxes and don't get frightened by what people tell you. Just go with your passion and where it leads you, and you'll end up in the right spot.

Thesis search link: http://www.library.uwa.edu.au/library_services/theses

Section 2
From Career to Community

Chapter 13
Community I

Teaching artists at work

Contributed by Angela Beeching

Part I reference: Chapter 3

A partnership between Four Nations Ensemble and a grade school in New York

Our approach is to engage students in a project that involves their skills and imagination and which helps us, the musicians who are strangers in and unfamiliar with their communities. We ask a group of 9th or 8th graders to work as a marketing agency for our ensemble. (Those taking part have had some introduction to business and run a school store.) Four Nations doesn't know enough about them, their families and friends, and doubts if we can attract an audience to our programs of music. Their job is to get to know our product (classical music), get to understand the market (through surveys and interviews in their school), and develop an advertising campaign for classical chamber music that appeals to the market while remaining truthful to the product (truth in advertising).

There is never any pressure to 'appreciate' the music, only to observe and describe it. At the end of the school year, they present Four Nations in a concert. Tickets are available at the school store. Students manage the concert hall with the help of the school staff.

We have regular business meetings during the year to discuss the writing of copy and interpretation of the survey results. Here we can work on verbal, written and math skills. This is an important argument for the viability of the program. Posters, art and copy are discussed as if we were employees of a major advertising firm. You might imagine that I offer lots of input, but mostly I try and clear away the thicket of resistance to imagination. Decisions and materials must come from the students so that they can recognise themselves in each final product.

Concurrently we begin working with other students in all grades, from Kindergarten to year nine. There are regular mini-concerts (fifteen to twenty this year), at which time we introduce them to the chosen repertoire. Our sessions include performances and then the sharing of responses, from emotional to creative. All the pieces on the 'big' concert program are heard throughout the year. In this way, students enjoy the pleasure of recognition - one of the most important in the appreciation of concert music.

For discussion

- For the young students who participated in the project, what opportunities were there for learning?
- What specific kinds of learning were called for in this project (subject areas, personal growth, particular skills and personal qualities developed)?
- What specific skills are needed to be a successful teaching artist?
- What kinds of teaching artist-related work have you done? Did you like this experience? Why or why not?
- How could you gain more teaching artist experience and skills?

Chapter 14
Getting to know your Dream Job

Contributed by Dawn Bennett

Research activity

Key into the information sources for the location/s in which you would like to live and work. Over a six-month period, track opportunities that interest you. Read the local headlines and find out what the music scene is like. Look up organisations with which you would like to work and check their websites on a regular basis. The following questions relate to a performance goal, but you can tailor them for your own personal use.

- How many full-time performance jobs did you find for your instrument over the six-month period?
- Where were they?
- What were the salary ranges?
- Now consider the two best positions, factoring in locations in which you would like to live and work.
- What is the average salary in each location?
- How much would it cost to live there?
- What other expenses might there be?

CHAPTER 14: GETTING TO KNOW YOUR DREAM JOB

- Once each position is filled, look at the website to find out what experience the successful applicants possessed.
- Find out how many people applied for the position.
- Finally, map out what steps you need to take in order to reach your dream job. Consider each step as a rung on a ladder.

Chapter 15
Community II

Finding your mission

Contributed by Angela Beeching and Dawn Bennett

Whether you think about the following questions on your own, in discussion with others or even in essay form, they are important philosophical questions for all musicians. They are important because the answers have profound practical implications for the career choices you make. It is important to remember that questions such as these should be revisited regularly throughout your life in music.

1. What do you want your music to achieve?
2. How do you want to connect with others through music?
3. How can your music become a valued service to a community?
4. Have you been inspired by examples of music as a force for change? If so, describe them and reflect on the meaning they might have for your own career.
5. What is your mission? In other words, what do you most value? How do you want to contribute as a musician to making the world a better place?

Headstone activity

A fun (though macabre) way to think about this is to think about how you would like to be remembered. What would you like your obituary to say? What would you like someone to say at your funeral? What would you like written on your headstone?

Or, on a more positive note, think of a major award or honour. Why might you someday be nominated for one of these? What would colleagues say about you and your work at the acceptance event?

Suggested essay topics

- It is interesting to consider ways in which musicians throughout history have been involved in community life. Select a musician from earlier times and explore the ways in which that individual worked to better the musical life of the community or region in which they lived.

- Read the brief social history included in Chapter 1 and compare the activities of musicians in the past with those illustrated in the profiles of musicians working today. What changes have there been? What has remained the same, and how have musicians over the centuries dealt with common issues?

- Interview local musicians to explore the range of activities in which they are involved. Write up your findings, focussing on the ways in which musicians interface with the world in which they live.

- Create a flow chart or spreadsheet of the individuals and organisations with which a local musician is involved on a daily, weekly and monthly basis. In a short essay, discuss these relationships: how they work, why they are important and how people benefit from these social and professional interactions.

Chapter 16
Transitioning to Professional Life

Introduction

Contributed by Janis Weller

Part I reference: Chapter 4
Introduction and overview of transitioning activities

"Luck favors the prepared mind," said Louis Pasteur, and as music students approach the end of formal schooling and the beginning of professional life there are numerous ways soon-to-be graduates can enhance their chances for good luck and a fulfilling professional life. As we've seen in previous chapters, career success for musicians requires a wide range of integrated skills beyond the purely musical. Along with musical artistry, musicians need an entrepreneurial mindset and the personal attributes to make it work.

The 'transitioning' resources focus on ways to prepare for this exciting but often undefined transition from your virtually lifelong identity as 'student' to the emerging identity of 'profession-

al.' In combination with the other activities, they introduce reflective and practical approaches to help prepare for a move out of the familiarity of school life where structure is provided, expectations relatively clear and efforts rewarded directly, to the vastly more uncertain professional musician's world of work. Suddenly, graduates need to generate many work opportunities. Instead of a degree plan to follow, now they must create both short-range and long-term goals and the strategies to implement them on the fly, often with little outside guidance. The good news is that there are tremendous opportunities for the aspiring professional who is prepared, curious, hard working, and yes, lucky.

There is no magic formula for getting started or for sustaining a rewarding career over time. Developing musical talents and skills to the highest possible level comes first, of course. As you have seen throughout this book, there are also many practical, non-musical skills you will need to discover and hone. But the transition from student life to professional life encompasses so much more. While change is fundamental to life, however much we may sometimes wish it were not, it is our attitudes and approaches to change and growth that may help us define our perceptions of life and career success. Learning to embrace change can have a major impact on our career sustainability.

For example, the fundamental methods of communication and connection continue to transform and expand dramatically throughout global society. Opportunities for growth and innovation are 'virtually' limitless in this interconnected world, and the music industry models this vivid, profound growth. While sometimes exciting and often uncertain, the deeply rooted changes in technology taking place around us every day also provide wonderful future prospects for creative and innovative individuals.

Highlighted throughout the transitioning activities are real-world stories of young musicians who are successfully navigating the early years of their very diverse careers, along with some questions and activities for reflection and discussion.

Allan's story in Chapter Four provides opportunities for self-reflection:

1. Using the definition of 'self-authorship' in Chapter 4, consider the *composed* and *improvised* elements of your musical life at this point in time.

2. How are you balancing the core academic foundations of your musical education with your emerging, individual artistic voice?

3. Jot down an example of a time when you took an artistic risk. Was the risk worthwhile? Have you continued to take appropriate artistic risks?

4. In what ways do you combine your musical experiences with your core musical knowledge and skills as you create your original musical voice?

Chapter 17
Transitioning I

From professional student to professional musician

Contributed by Janis Weller

Graduation dilemmas and possibilities

Unlike students pursuing careers in the professions of engineering, finance, law or medicine, graduates in liberal arts fields (such as philosophy, history or English literature) rarely have a clear-cut, predetermined path into professional life. For these students, the college years may be more about getting a broad education while pursuing deep interests, talents and passions, rather than a purely vocational track. For those in music, whose education and training encompass a combination of liberal arts and professional-level skill development, the path may seem relatively clear on the surface but often proves much more elusive upon graduation. We have seen that career training and awareness have traditionally been low on the list of priorities in the education of emerging artists. Until rather recently, the broad range and extremely high level of skills and knowledge required to enter this highly competitive field has meant that not much attention was given to just how one goes about discovering what that career might encompass and how one actually makes it a reality.

Taking time to reflect on your attitudes about work, your motivations and self-awareness, and your perceptions of the 'real' world, is some of the most useful pre-graduation work you can do. Educational activist Parker Palmer represents the spirit of career reflection by saying, "Our deepest calling is to grow into our own authentic self-hood, whether or not it conforms to some image of who we set out to be" (Palmer, 2000, p. 16). He continues: "As we do so, we will not only find the joy that every human being seeks – we will also find our path of authentic service in the world" (ibid). Palmer makes a key point here: the journey to so-called success in life is not only about you and your personal accomplishments (sorry to burst that bubble). Thoughtful alignment of your career direction with the roles of artists in society means that you are likely to have a greater positive impact on the world as well (see more about musicians and community in Chapter 6).

Some students on the cusp of the 'real' world may have unrealistic expectations or perceptions of themselves and find setting meaningful goals challenging (Sharf, 2002). Whether as an idealist or a fatalist or someplace in between, it can be tempting to resist direct confrontation of the challenges to come. If you see yourself even a little bit in this description then the practical tips, skills to develop, resources, and opportunities to build professional connections throughout this book may be the most attractive to you. However, if you simply develop generic career skills without understanding *why* and *how* they apply within *your* life, you potentially miss a wonderful opportunity. Plunging into a particular career path without consideration for goodness of fit and opportunity may lead to disappointment or years spent pursuing personally inappropriate directions.

The differences between a pretty good career fit and an excellent career fit can appear slight but feel profound for an individual. Recognising and acknowledging your true strengths, and crafting a career path that builds on those strengths, can lead to deeper career satisfaction when strengths align with interests and passions.

Mentors, colleagues and authors

Finding a balance between the philosophical and the practical can help. Seek out mentors, role models and more experienced colleagues who can help smooth the transition. Taking time to read, reflect, write, and discuss your ideas and concerns with colleagues and teachers can relieve some of the 'end of student-hood' stress and help you realise that many concerns about this significant life transition are pretty universal.

Books such as *Let Your Life Speak, Art and Fear, The War of Art, The Savvy Musician, Beyond Talent* and many more can provide perspective and common ground with other musicians, along with good questions to ponder as you plan. Dante's story is similarly useful in considering how an open awareness and a willingness to tap into resources is essential when building a very eclectic career.

Dante, a 15-year-old African-American guy, was slumped in a chair with headphones on and his eyes closed. I tapped him on the shoulder and said, "What are you listening to?" He glanced up with a dreamy look and said, "Tchaikovsky." That was our first meeting, over thirteen years ago now. In high school, Dante was a talented bassoonist, conductor and composer. After graduation he headed off to a major conservatory to pursue his dreams in all those areas, eventually focusing on composition. After conservatory he spent a gruelling year scoring student films before moving home to the Midwest to pursue his evolving musical passions. He reconnected with high-school buddies, forming a live hip-hop band (Dante on keys) that would land a major-label deal and tour full-time for three years. He continues to perform and record successfully with that band today. He continues his classical music interests as well, returning to his high-school youth orchestra to become an assistant to the conductor/music director. He formed a chamber orchestra of adventurous young professionals with the twist that their performances would take place in bars and clubs, and among other projects he performs with a straight-ahead jazz trio. Today, in his late 20s, Dante's widely varied musical pursuits include a day-job as Community Liaison back at the community music school where we first met, where he helps young musicians like himself access the training they need to develop their skills and dreams. For Dante, music is not defined by genre, and concerts are not defined by venue. He moves fluidly between worlds that rarely overlapped for many musicians in previous generations. Good music is good music for Dante, and he continues to explore and develop his skills and passions.

School-to-work transitions for musicians

As a soon-to-be-graduating college senior, life as a student, while hectic and often stressful, is very comfortable on some levels, often encompassing nearly all your personal memory and experience. Ending the secure familiarity of school and embarking on the uncertainty of the so-called real world may energise some students while others find the thought daunting. But the transition may not be as neat and linear as students might hope.

One of the great challenges of transitioning into professional life is the sudden loss of both specific directions and a support structure for music making (Bayles & Orland, 1993). Graduation brings a sudden end to the highly structured life of a music student. School years, for all their stressors, are often fairly certain in their expectations. Course requirements, lessons, juries, recitals, rehearsals and concerts are spelled out explicitly, and other people do much of the behind-the-scenes work. You sign up for a course, get the syllabus, attend class, do the work, and get a grade based on your work and accomplishments. You generally know what is expected of you, when it must be completed, and the standards of excellence to which you will be held. Almost all the structural pieces are already in place and your job is to follow policies and procedures in a timely way. Professional life is rarely that straightforward. Project forward to the day after your long anticipated college graduation. What now? Where do you start? What are the first/next steps you need to take? When do they need to happen? What level of excellence must you reach to 'succeed' at whatever you most want to do? Will you be prepared to step into this unknown world and master it? Accepting personal responsibility for your life and career is another important facet of awareness as you ponder next steps after graduation.

As an independent DIY (do-it-yourself) musician your career progress depends on consistent and persistent effort, personal motivation, goal-setting (and tweaking) abilities, and the unrelenting work ethic needed to move a professional career forward. These important skills may not have been overtly taught in school, although they are often an integral expectation in educational settings. What's more, there are rarely obvious 'right answers' to situations, opportunities and challenges that arise in the professional world.

Businessman David Shakarian famously said, "I never worked a day in my life. It's not work when you love what you do" (Shakarian, n. d). Professional musicians often work long hours with little time off. Many enjoy not only creating and sharing music but also the behind-the-scenes work necessary for performances to happen. "I'm always working," a young professional singer said recently, "but I love everything I do, whether I'm performing, giving an interview, or building my audience through social media. It's all fun and rewarding for me". Others simply tolerate the necessary business side as a means to enabling more performances. John Snyder, five-time Grammy winner and professor at Loyola University, says however:

> There's no reason to expect every musician to do every job. It's redundant, inefficient, and unlikely to happen. But there are plenty of kids out there who could care as much about marketing and social networking as their roommates care about playing in a band. Impact will ensue if all of these people get together and create a community of shared values in which each member plays his or her part. It's a networked company, not a hierarchical company. (Personal communication, 2009)

Collaboration and partnerships will encompass a vital part of your career, so develop and nurture relationships and seek out people whose skills and interests complement yours. Nobody has to do everything, but the work has to be done.

Paying your dues: Talent isn't enough

Another important element of the transition to professional life is the shift from the relatively homogeneous population of campus life to the lively variety of the wide world beyond. Developing diverse colleagues and friends across several generations, vast levels of experience and a range of cultural and world views, is a wonderful and stimulating aspect of post-collegiate life and a great opportunity to expand your collaboration and partnership opportunities.

You probably know your relative place in the pecking order of the conservatory, but what will this look like once you have left campus? Avoiding arrogance but modelling appropriate self-confidence, and balancing that confidence you have in your artistry and skills with a humble willingness to learn from colleagues and mentors who have been in the field for some time, can help smooth your transition into professional life. Experienced professionals often enjoy mentoring young artists and they can provide everything from support and encouragement to gigs and other opportunities. Like Dante, reach out to professionals you admire. Ask if you can buy them coffee or lunch and talk about their work, or about performing or composing or whatever interests you. Be a good listener. Rich and mutually beneficial relationships can grow from these encounters.

References

Bayles, D., & Orland. T. (2001). *Art & fear: Observations on the perils (and rewards) of artmaking.* The Image Continuum: California.

Palmer, P. J. (1999). *Let your life speak: Listening for the voice of vocation.* Quakerbooks: Philadelphia.

Sharf, R.S., (2002). *Applying career development theory to counseling.* Third ed. Brooks/Cole: Pacific Grove, CA.

Note

The David Shakarian quote was retrieved from http://www.answers.com/topic/shakarian-david

Chapter 18
Careers Panel

How did you get here?

Contributed by Dawn Bennett

An excellent and fun way to learn about the interesting careers of musicians is to host a careers panel. Invite three to five faculty members or practising musicians to be on a panel. These sessions generally take between 60 and 90 minutes and they work best if the room is small enough not to need microphones. The sample questions below provide some examples, but challenge students to supplement these with at least three of their own. Ask students to think about what they *really* want to know!

CHAPTER 18: CAREERS PANEL

Sample questions

What do you wish you had learned when you were an undergraduate?
Where do you want to be in five years' time?
What do you want to be doing in five years' time?
What was your first paid job in music?
What was your worst ever experience in music?
If you won the lottery this week, what would you change about your work?
Who are your heroes?
What did you do in the year after you graduated?
What skills do you think all musicians need?
What attributes do you think all musicians need?
What would you change about music degrees?
What graduate study do you recommend, and why?
How many different jobs have you held at any one time?
What do you most love to do in music? Why?
What are the negatives of being employed full-time (in an orchestra, or perhaps in a university)?
What kinds of music do you listen to?
What are the pitfalls of working as a freelance musician?
What are the good things about freelance life?
If you could go back in time to when you were 20, what would you do?
What do you think a musician is?
What do you do to relax?
What do you recommend we do whilst we are studying, to get ahead?
What is your dream job?
What in music do you hate doing, and how do you avoid it?
How do you practice?
Do you have any regrets about your career so far?
How do we get people to come to our concert rather than someone else's?
If you had the keys to Dr Who's TARDIS, where would you go and why?
Who is the most useful person you ever met in music, and why?

Your questions (what do you *really* want to know?)
1.
2.
3.

Chapter 19
Getting Inspiration from Others

Contributed by Angela Beeching

Claire Chase, flautist/co-founder of the successful ensemble ICE (International Contemporary Ensemble), sums up the experience of being a musician-entrepreneur:

> *Our generation of young musicians, despite the economic challenges that we face, is experiencing an unprecedented freedom. We can do anything we want to do. We can produce our own concerts, release our own albums, create our own communities and our own movements, and we don't need a lot of money to do this. We just need great ideas, we need a spirit of adventure, and we need each other (thick skin is good to have, too).* (Orchestra Musician Forum, 2008)

Refer to Chapter 3 for the full story.

- If you could do anything you want, what would you do?
- What are your great ideas?
- What *kinds* of musician do you want to be?

Chapter 20
Reading and Reflecting on Musician Biographies and Profiles

Contributed by Rineke Smilde

This volume features many biographies and profiles, and still more will be created through activities such as holding a careers panel (tool 18). The following reflections refer to the three musician biographies featured in Chapter 7. When asked to critically reflect on biographical accounts, it is a good idea to base your response on questions such as these.

- Read Chapter 7 and describe your own lifelong learning. Discuss what you might need to do in order to keep learning.

- The biographical accounts of Isaac, Daniel and Wendy are very different, but they have issues in common. Reflect on these differences and common issues and make links to your own 'biographical account'.

- Identify and reflect on the crossroads—key decision points—in your personal and professional development. Who played a significant role at these times? To whom did you go for advice? What can you put in place now for the next time you face a major decision?

- Biographical accounts raise a number of challenges and opportunities within the musical profession: for example, creative workshops in the health sector or prisons, or innovative cross-arts collaborations. Look for examples of these and reflect on what might be of interest to you. What, specifically, interests you, and what will you need to make it a reality? What is the first step, and when will you begin?

- In Chapter 7, educational leadership is described as a niche. What is the relationship between your performing and your teaching? What might your personal educational leadership look like, now and in the future?

Section 3
Survival Skills

Chapter 21
Musician Profile IV

Orchestral life

Contributed by Dawn Bennett

This profile comes from a young brass player. The musician secured his first principal position in 2002, while he was in his third year of undergraduate study, and he later moved to a major European orchestra. At the time of the interview he had yet to commence the new position. He describes life in an orchestra, the 'sparkle' that makes orchestral work enjoyable, getting ahead, and his future career plans. His identity has been hidden at his request, as have the names of the orchestras.

I'm a trombone player. Right now I am the principal of a symphony orchestra. I got my job here in my third year at the Academy and now I am ready for a change. Now I spend half the time in the [major] orchestra. I was very close to winning the audition as second trombone last January and I've been there 10 or 15 times this season to play with them and to go on tour and to record. They never hire people they don't know, so now I've been playing with them a lot and they know me and I know them. Next year there will be a new audition and I will just have to do my best and hope I get the job. When they call I go to my boss here and say, 'Is it possible for me to take time off, or can I pay for a substitute?' 'Yes, of course', he says. He's very supportive.

The 'sparkle' is a way I describe orchestral musicians where there is the sparkle of being excited and passionate about music. Actually, yesterday I was feeling down, you know. We have seven orchestras here and we are in the same union, so when I go to work we have so many meetings about whether we need a trash can right here and, you know, do I wish to vote for that if we need a trash can right here? And that's not the point of our job. Yeah I want to do some more. People just complain about little things and I'm really fed up with it. Also if I'm in rehearsals that finish at 2pm, you know, if we have half a page left of a whole symphony and we know when we're done with that we will be off, and it maybe takes five minutes, people will finish at 2pm anyway, you know – come on!

In the major orchestra there is sparkle in all the players. Also I think it's a matter of taste – if you like the conductor or if you like the music or something. But overall you just need to sparkle, you just need to enjoy your work and be in charge of your instrument and the group and everything to make it work.

It is true that when you are in an orchestra you're not in charge. And that's why people get so, I think, they lose their creativity. But you are in charge because you are in charge of your instrument. That's a very important job and you are creative in that. We play three opera productions a year and this year the conductor is amazing. He's a very young Swedish guy and he's now in the semi-big orchestras in Germany. He makes that sparkle, but we need to get it without a conductor like him. Everything is: 'Monday morning and it's raining'. And if the management of the orchestra don't keep up the beat with life outside then the whole thing can malfunction, they're lost.

Learning languages is really important. As a youngster we don't think we will need a language like German. But now I see why I need German because I'm sitting in a section where they are speaking together in German and I can't get it. I went on tour with the orchestra this summer to France, where there is an opera festival, and we played Siegfried. It was fantastic, but I couldn't remember any French from school. I went to a store and I wanted to buy a ham sandwich, and I said, 'Je suis un jambon', and that means: 'I am a ham'!

This year I teach all of the trombone students at the Academy for one hour. I like teaching. I like to make them sparkle. Actually, it's a great feeling for me to solve their problems. I like that. It's becoming a challenge for me to be the best in the world to analyse their problems and fix them. I like that. I didn't think I would be interested in teaching when I was a student. Not at all. I went to Chicago in 2002 and I've been there once a year ever since to take lessons with Michael Mulcahy, who's from Sydney. He's brilliant. The season before last I took one year's leave from the orchestra to go to Chicago all year and take a performance certificate. To watch Michael Mulcahy teach me I was convinced that I could do it as well. I didn't have the tools before, but after Michael I have a whole toolbox.

To be in music you have to trust in yourself. And also you have to get inspired and be inspired and really do anything – if you hear a piece of music, get the music and learn it and always be inspired. In my practice rooms I always have ten or fifteen sheets with quotes that Michael said or I learned, and I just hang them on the wall. And even though I know them and I listened to them so many times, I still can sustain more.

Also you need to do some aggressive things to make your practice sessions fun: enjoy your practice. And that's very hard, especially when you are placed where there is no sparkle. Then you have to do it even more. Sometimes the orchestra zaps my energy, and when I'm done playing I can't do anything. I have a mental coach and she is not a musician so she has some other ideas of how you prepare and it's really nice just to do something else.

Ten years from now in my dreams I will be playing with the major orchestra full-time. I don't know. I don't think I want to do this for the rest of my life. Of course if I'm in the major orchestra I will be the happiest man on earth and of course I will do my best – but for the rest of my life, I don't think so, I don't know. I want to own my own café or own a hotel. I want to be a waiter actually. It's very strange!

Chapter 22
Getting a Head Start

Finding your mission

Contributed by Rosie Perkins

Challenge 1

Engage in as many musical and non-musical activities during higher education as possible.

Why?   This makes you better equipped for portfolio careers, and enables you to discover and try new possibilities.
How?   Pursue diverse activities outside, or in parallel with, your specialism.
When? Right now! Find out what is available inside and outside of your school, community and professional networks. Look online and offline.

Challenge 2

Do not be afraid to challenge your aims and plans.

Why?   Jack (Chapter 2) took the difficult decision to turn down high-profile solo work because it did not fit with his musical aspirations. This decision forced him to reconsider what he actually *wanted* from his career.
How?   Give yourself space to think through and talk over what is important to you. Enlist the support of your instrumental/vocal teacher, lecturers and peers.
When? Right now! Ask yourself what you want from your career every time you make a decision or undertake one of these challenges.

Challenge 3
Take ownership of your learning.

Why? You need not scrap your dreams if you feel that they are becoming unachievable. You do, though, need to know what your goals are and how you plan to achieve them.

How? Identify what you need to do to achieve your aims. Seek out opportunities to do this or, if existing opportunities are not there, create your own.

When? Right now! If you know what you want from your learning, you are much more likely to achieve it.

Challenge 4
Work out what 'career' success means to you.

Why? Success is so often assumed to be one thing or the other, but knowing what it is for you will help you make key career decisions.

How? Consider again the objective and subjective elements of your career and how these match up for you: what is most important to *you* in *your* career?

When? Right now! Remember, however you define success, you will still need to be diverse, flexible and open-minded in order to respond to your career as it changes over time.

Chapter 23
Challenge

Action plans

Contributed by Angela Beeching

- Search for opportunities: take auditions and apply for programs, festivals and fellowships
- Subscribe to mailing lists with organisations who provide funding or list opportunities
- Find a mentor/s with whom you can discuss plans, issues and projects. Include someone outside of your area of music or your immediate circle of activity
- Work as an intern with an arts organisation to learn about the business side of a career
- Develop teaching artist skills and get involved in audience and community engagement projects
- Explore how technology can help your career: create a MySpace musician profile, or use another social networking tool and relate these pages specifically to your professional work
- Find a project, commit to it, and get going!

CHAPTER 23: CHALLENGE

Can you achieve one of these every three months? Commit to three things now and write deadlines for each of them. Take them along to class and find people with whom you can collaborate.

Project 1:   Deadline:

Project 2:   Deadline:

Project 3:   Deadline:

Chapter 24
Musician Profile V

Finding the sparkle

Contributed by Dawn Bennett

This story comes from European pianist Dominik Falenski, who was born in Berlin and is now based in Denmark where he is finishing his Masters degree. He begins by talking about how he came to be a pianist and then describes different experiences that have shaped how he views his career both now and into the future.

I chose music because I love it. I chose music because it was more of a challenge and my teacher was very demanding. I still love it very much. Very much. I started late—quite late—and when I got into the conservatoire I wasn't the best who came in, but I developed very well. I'm doing my Masters now. I have completed my fourth year—I have one left—and right now I'm just practising and teaching.

I have not the ambition to be as great as Vladimir Ashkenazy but I want to be a very good pianist. The young ones starting always want to be at the top. I wanted it myself. I don't know what changes. I want to practice very much but I want to, you know, develop in other directions as well. I don't need to be at the top. Who knows where one is going to be. There's a lot of business in my life and I chose it. I just practised seven hours a day for the first two years. It didn't make me happy because I felt excluded. You have to participate in social life and you have to be a part of the system – to feel like you're a part of it. Now I can do something that the others won't. So I can do something that makes a difference. I enjoy it.

I'm teaching in the music school. Teaching is very important to my professor and she emphasises it very much. When you do it very well then you can enjoy it, but when you're not good at it, it's not fun. Recently I was assistant teacher to my professor. It was one weekend and there were 32 pianists and there I was, 'assistant professor'!

The Pianorama program comes from my professor. She's a wonderful professor: she's very engaged with the students and we have activities that we are all engaged in. We played all Etudes Tableaux of Rachmaninov in Copenhagen, Berlin and nine other places, and this developed a team spirit. We are always playing concerts together, so it was just logical to create a society so that people from the outside can see – I mean we know how great music is, but many people outside don't know! We write newsletters to the audience and they come to every one of our concerts and they are fans. They are people who come every time, and it's really wonderful because at some concerts at the conservatoire there are not many people. But when we play, it's full. Always. It's so wonderful. It's because a lot of people are very interested and they can follow us – our lives. It's a lot of work. Good fun though.

We thought about a study tour and we thought Berlin would be good. I come from Berlin so I said I would organise it. Then after Berlin I said maybe somebody else would like a go, but nobody did so it was my turn again with Moscow. I like it! Each time we decide where we want to go (the last tour was Holland – the Netherlands). Then I plan everything with my professor. She says we should do this and that and then I organise the trip.

We write applications for funding if we have to. Mostly we get a bit from the conservatoire and a bit from another company that we know very well, but when we went to Moscow we wrote a lot of applications and received a lot of money. We followed a plan: we played some works of Carl Nielsen, a Danish composer, in Moscow. Because of this the Carl Nielsen Foundation gave us a lot of money for the trip. You can always do these things.

My favourite tour was Moscow. We visited the Tchaikovsky Conservatoire and for me it was life-changing because I wished to study in Russia. We gave two concerts and we attended concerts. They were good concerts. We looked at the city and we watched classes at the conservatoire. But it's a sad place because it's so worn down. When I came back I decided I would stay here.

Now we are organising a new international competition and this is huge! Right now it's a bit in the way of my wish to practice, but it started with the last study trip, which was to Holland. We visited a competition and I asked my professor why we shouldn't have a competition here. She said it would be nice and she would help and her name would be on it. We have made the brochure, the program is finished and we have the conservatoire on board. The music house gave us their concert halls and we have the pianos tuned for free. But what we need now is money: prize money, money to pay participants for sleeping accommodation, things like that. I think I will spend one or two months just practising and then I'll see how we'll go and get the money.

I have no idea where I want to be in ten years' time. I have thought about it so much, but it doesn't really matter. I mean, I know that I will never have problems earning money. I'll have to see. It's easy just to work at the music school, but you *have to make something special to be happy. I wouldn't be happy being the 'normal' teacher. There are so many normal teachers—you know they walk like this—they walk very sad! I don't know. It will be many things at one time. I will always teach—this I know—and always play.*

Pianorama:http://www.pianorama.dk
Arhus European Piano Competition: www.pianocompetition.dk

Chapter 25
Transitioning II

From awareness to innovation

Contributed by Janis Weller

What's changing and how do I make it work for me?

We will start with some vital personal attributes and skills that can literally make or break your fledgling music career. While not musical *per se*, they form the foundation for developing and sustaining a meaningful life and career.

Preparing to enter professional life is ultimately less about specifics ("Should I use Twitter to promote my activities?") and much more about an open attitude and the personal attributes you bring to the table, such as perseverance, resilience and a knack for making (and keeping) friends. Later on, this resource will address a variety of specific, tangible ways you can set up and run your career, but we will start with the more *in*tangible core: some key personal characteristics that are easy to overlook when you might prefer spending time practising, polishing up your résumé or building your network.

Awareness: A window on yourself and the world

First, awareness. It is a simple concept with profound implications for your career, and provides a good starting point for talking about the actual transition from life as a student to that of a professional. Awareness—of the field and profession of music, about yourself and the larger world around you—prepares you to see the music world as it is today, your potential roles within it, and likely future directions. A heightened sense of awareness on all these levels can serve as both your internal and external radar, helping you create and modify appropriate goals and head in directions that align with your ambitions, passions, talents and resources. The emphasis here is on *you*, not the dreams or expectations of your family, friends or teachers, and not necessarily on the hierarchical career paths we have been trained to see as defining 'success' in the field. This is not to say you should lower your ambitions and dreams. Not at all. Rather, a well-developed sense of awareness coupled with an open, flexible attitude provides insights on many levels that can lead to new creative approaches.

Within the field of music, and the world in general, profound change is taking place at an unprecedented pace. A heightened sense of awareness is important at this global level too. How can you stay abreast of (or create) changes and innovations without becoming completely overwhelmed? Which resources (people, organisations, web sources) can provide information and ideas you need to spur your creativity and your career, and how do you determine their value and validity? When does information overload slow you down or pull you away from making music, and how do you manage that? How can you accept and adapt to new directions as they emerge, and at the same time anticipate and innovate for the future? How can you hone your sense of personal and world awareness?

Awareness can help put you out ahead of the curve, in front of the cutting edge, where you have a better chance to anticipate new directions and take innovative action. Developing your sense of awareness and opening your attitudes toward the music world will help you enter professional life with eyes wide open.

Activities

Discuss the questions above with teachers, mentors and colleagues; read Chapters 1-4 from *Art and Fear* (Bayles & Orland, 2001); read Chapter 1 from *Let Your Life Speak* (Palmer, 1999); explore the website artistshouse-music.org. Publication details are included at the end of chapter 4.

Chapter 26
Transitioning III

Know thyself – temperament and personality

Contributed by Janis Weller

"We must have the hide of an elephant and the heart of a butterfly."
–Metropolitan Opera baritone Thomas Hampson

Building on talent, by acquiring and developing the skills and knowledge to develop your potential, leads to artistry. These elements shape the fundamental goals of college music programs. All are centrally important, of course, but they are not sufficient by themselves. Our individual temperament and personality traits greatly influence career development, and extending awareness in these areas can be very helpful as you launch your career.

"Temperament may best be described as a general term describing the 'how' of behavior. It differs from ability, which is concerned with the 'what' and the 'how well' of behaving, and from motivation, which accounts for why a person does what he is doing" (Thomas & Chess, 1977, p. 4). This classic definition of temperament separates it from ability (talent) and motivation (the drive individuals express in pursuing musical and career goals). While certainly influenced by experiences in life, temperament is generally described as essentially innate, a predisposition to act and behave with a particular level of energy and emotional response. Awareness and acceptance of personal temperament styles can help identify and motivate work toward career paths that provide a good fit for individual abilities and temperament. The activities to follow can help you learn more about your temperament in relation to your career.

Challenge

Traditionally, attaining superior musical skills and knowledge forms the primary goals in preparing for a career in music. This is the educational centrepiece of music schools of course, and the central motivation for many students. As you have read throughout this book, music schools are discovering that entrepreneurial skills and attitudes not only provide useful means for launching the fledgling careers of their highly accomplished graduates, but may also be absolutely vital for doing so in the rapidly changing artistic marketplace. And the pace of change is staggering. For today's college seniors or recent graduates, the music industry (and after all, it is a huge and lucrative business) is already a vastly different place than when they started college. The explosion of technology innovations alone has opened exciting new opportunities for connecting music with the world along with whole new skill sets for musicians to master.

More music schools, particularly conservatories, are realising that with large numbers of highly trained and exceptionally talented young artists graduating every year from fine schools it is vital to help alumni enter the field with a competitive advantage, and that non-musical career skills are not simply intuitive, but can be learned. Over the past decade or so, more music colleges have launched entrepreneurial programs, career centres and seminars focused on the musician as an entrepreneurial small businessperson. Be sure to take advantage of career-training opportunities on campus. It may take some extra effort to attend special events or workshops or squeeze in another elective course, but the pay-off for one's career can be substantial. If your school doesn't run anything, look for activities in the business school or in the music sector.

Activity

For a simple temperament-related activity, ask someone who knew you as a very small child (age 2 or even younger) to choose three words that described you at that stage. Examples could be sensitive, active, social, stubborn, moody, and the like. Do you see yourself in those words today? Our temperament tends to be quite stable through life, even as we grow and mature and develop.

Chapter 27
Skills and Attributes I

Professionalism

Contributed by Janis Weller

Work with someone else to develop a list of professional attributes that you feel cover both artistic and non-artistic aspects of professionalism in the music workplace. Allow only two or three minutes to generate as many professional traits as you can.

As a class, transfer the lists to the board and continue to generate additional positive attributes of professionalism, discussing selected traits. Share stories that illustrate the various traits (or stories that demonstrate times when professional traits were lacking).

Individually, write a brief reflection paper on your personal views of the elements that characterise professionalism and how you approach or will approach this in your own life and career. Include examples from your own experience. Bring this reflection to the next class meeting.

Chapter 28
Skills and Attributes II

The Team Approach

Contributed by Dawn Bennett

Complete the skills and attributes challenge on professionalism (tool 27) and then consider the following list of those skills and traits (attributes) typically found in successful musicians. You might want to read one or more of the musician profiles included in Part II or within the chapters. Tools 28 and 29 will also be useful references.

- Initiative
- Resilience
- Perseverance
- Optimism
- Interpersonal skills
- Creative problem-solving
- Organisational skills
- Planning skills
- Ability to see opportunities versus obstacles

- Ability to give and receive constructive criticism
- Knowledge of individual strengths and shortcomings

Few successful musicians possess all these strengths. Most successful musicians collaborate with others who can supply the missing ingredients. Successful musicians learn both how to compensate for what they lack and how to capitalise on their strengths.

Challenge – find people in your peer group who have strengths in different areas and make up a team that encompasses all of the above. The completed chart from the activity Getting what you want III (tool 11) will give you a head start.

Chapter 29
Skills and Attributes III

Skills audit

Contributed by Dawn Bennett and Angela Beeching

How much do you know?

Very often, people have a skewed perception of their own abilities. They may take their skills and experience for granted, or they may have an exaggerated sense of other skills.

To take a closer look, list the skills you have, both musical and non-musical, and include a brief example of how you have used each skill. Be sure to include essential skills and experience such as leadership, organisation, communication, computer and research skills, as these are all extremely relevant to managing a music career. If you have the opportunity, discuss the results with other people.

Next, find ten jobs in the arts and business and look at the criteria. What are the most common selection criteria? How would you respond to these? You will find a sample list on the next page.

Think about your ensemble activities, student and community involvement, part-time work, voluntary work, concert involvement and other activities.

Do you lead rehearsals?
Do you organise events?
Do you meet performance or assessment deadlines?
Do you work independently?
Do you have to be flexible in order to balance everything?

Common selection criteria: How much do you already know?

The following dot points are among the most common selection criteria across the workforce. As such, they represent broadly transferable skills and attributes. Other than for audition-based performance positions, musicians will almost certainly need to write to each of these criteria at some point in their careers.

How do other people address these criteria? Do you have these skills? Do other people think you have these skills?

Challenge: Address three of the following criteria using no more than half an A4 page for each one. Exchange these with peers until you have a set of drafts. Ask people in your network for great examples.

- Ability to maintain confidentiality
- Ability to work as part of a team
- Ability to work independently
- Ability to work under pressure
- Ability to find creative solutions
- Attention to detail
- A flexible and adaptable approach to work
- Computer skills
- Interpersonal skills
- Organisational/planning skills
- Supervisory skills
- Good written and oral communication skills

Chapter 30
Expanding the Skill Set

Contributed by Michael Hannan

Introduction

Read Chapter 8 and reflect on the skills developed by Michael Hannan during the course of his protean career. For example, his first job was as the accompanist for a choir. This work required secure piano technique and good sightreading skills. However, he was able to develop the range of his work by developing additional, related skills. These included the ability to realise figured bass (creating an improvised accompaniment by interpreting numbers written under the bass line), sightread full scores, and transpose the parts for instruments such as French horn, clarinet and saxophone. These particular skills enabled him to accept work as a repetiteur for an early music opera company. Had he pursued this line of work, he would have needed to add European languages, vocal coaching and choral conducting to his skill set. As he points out, it is no accident that a typical career path for a conductor includes being a repetiteur. This is because the job requires intensive engagement with the details of full scores as well as directing rehearsals. The exercises in this book have so far challenged you to identify the skills you think might be relevant; however, there are many others about which you may not have thought.

Exercises

- Make a list of all the skills described in Chapter 8, in the other musician profiles, and in the musicians you most admire. Look for skills relating to performance, composition, musicianship, technology, business and teaching, as well as generic skills such as written and oral communication.
- Make a list of your own musicianship and allied skills and rate them on a scale of one to five, with five being highly developed skills. Then refer to the following skills. Rate these skills first in terms of how relevant you think they are to your career, and then in terms of how developed they are.

Performance skills

- Instrumental or vocal technique
- Playing by ear
- Memorisation (of music learnt by ear)
- Memorisation (of notated music)
- Music score reading (interpretation of notation conventions)
- Sight-reading (fully notated music)
- Sight-reading (chord charts)
- Sight-singing
- Transposition by ear
- Transposition from notated music
- Ability to keep a rigid tempo in performance
- Ability to maintain good intonation in performance
- Performance practice knowledge (of music from different periods, genres or cultures)
- Ensemble performance skills
- Improvisation skills (style-based)
- Repertoire knowledge
- Rehearsal skills
- Music direction skills
- Conducting skills

Stagecraft skills

- Stage planning
- Stage etiquette
- Stage movement and gesture
- Communication with the audience

Aural recognition skills

- Intervals
- Rhythm and metre
- Harmony
- Identification of instruments and performance techniques

- Frequencies: Cycles per second of tones
- Electronically-produced audio signal processing [effects]
- Tempo: Beats per minute [bpm]
- Textural and structural techniques

Notation skills

- Chord chart writing
- Scoring
- Transcription skills (notating performances from recordings)
- Music notation software programming skills

Theoretical understandings

- Music analysis methods
- Harmonic theory
- Acoustical theory
- Music cognition
- Historical knowledge
- Knowledge of other musical cultures

Composition skills

- Orchestration and arranging
- Electronic orchestration (programming)
- Composition techniques (of different periods and genres)
- Lyric writing
- Synthesis
- Synchronisation of music to image

Technology skills

- Live sound reinforcement
- Lighting and projection
- Sound design
- Stage management
- Sound recording, editing, signal processing, and mixing
- Music production
- Sound and lighting systems design

Other technologies

- Multimedia
- Website design
- Graphic design
- Desktop publishing

Business skills

- Knowledge of industry structures
- Career planning
- Intellectual property
- Standard contracts (for performance, recording, publishing, agency, management, merchandising)
- Negotiation
- Self-promotion
- Public relations
- Entrepreneurship
- Networking
- Audience development
- Small business management (business structures, financing, market analysis, marketing, marketing technologies, business planning, insurance, business communications, office management, office technologies, etc.)
- Project management (planning, team building, quality control, budgeting, sponsorships, grant applications, conflict management, time management, project evaluation)

Generic skills

- Written and oral communication
- Creativity
- Social interaction
- Leadership
- Computer literacy
- Information searching
- Critical analysis/evaluation
- Cultural awareness
- Professionalism/ethics
- Social justice/ethics
- Reflective practice
- Benchmarking

Questions, activities and reflections

- Are there any of these skills you don't have, and which you think might be useful for your career as a musician? Why do you think they would be useful?
- Do you consider any skills in the list to be irrelevant to your career? Why do you consider them to be irrelevant?
- Prioritise the skills you wish to develop as essentials for your career development.

- Interview musicians who have acquired musical and allied skills that you consider would be useful to you. Ask them how they developed these skills and what they need to do to maintain them.
- Conduct a review of the available literature associated with the skills you are interested in acquiring. Describe what you have learnt from reading these texts. You will find many reading sources in the further reading section following Chapter 8.
- Investigate the availability of courses of study that would help you expand your skill base. These might be local face-to-face or online offerings.

Chapter 31
Challenge

Volunteering

Contributed by Glen Carruthers

It is extremely useful to include on your résumé volunteer musical activities that range from performing and teaching to arts administration. Here are some examples of activities in which you might become involved:

- Create a list of community-based music organisations in your area (everything from community bands to summer camps for children). Are professional musicians involved in these organisations and, if so, in what ways are they involved? Is there a role for you to play in these organisations?

- Volunteer to lead musical activities at a local community centre, home for seniors, pre-school, etc. Seek professional guidance in planning these activities and keep a journal of your successes and failures.

- What community outreach activities are organised by the professional arts organisations in your area (symphony orchestra, schools, colleges, choirs, etc.)? Is there a way for you to become involved in these activities?

- Organise one or two musical activities that will benefit the community in which you live. Seek support for these activities by preparing a grant application and by soliciting local businesses for one-time funding.

Chapter 32
Transitioning IV

Practical strategies for transitioning into professional life

Contributed by Janis Weller

Start it and work it!

'Start now!' may be among the simplest and most effective suggestions for building a career. Rather than wait for an elusive 'perfect time' to begin your career, consider performing (and/or teaching, composing or producing) during your college years as skills and ambitions develop. Jump-start your musical career while still in school, because the more professional experience you can amass, the easier it is to continue and further expand your work once you graduate. Instead of starting essentially from scratch at that point, you will already be building repertoire and contacts as well as musical and business abilities. Perhaps you are already gigging with a chamber ensemble or teaching a few students. Maybe you are composing jingles or repairing instruments or conducting a choir. With some strategic thinking, deliberate 'circle building' and focused action while you are still immersed in your studies, you can prepare yourself for a smoother transition after graduation. While it can be challenging to make the time in a busy schedule, music-related work can pay much better than many traditional unskilled jobs. Bobby and David's story illustrates this approach beautifully.

As roommates at a liberal arts university in the Midwest, Bobby and David started their career dreams early and put those plans into immediate action while still college students. Bobby majored in music (classical voice and guitar) with an entrepreneurship minor, and David majored in marketing with a music minor (keyboard). The two composer-performers started out with a good balance of skills and attitudes towards making a living in music. They wasted no time getting started. As college sophomores they began composing and recording music together, compiling original CDs, which they shopped around to local music houses that licensed music for film and advertising. After a while, one of these music businesses asked them to do a couple of ad spots on spec (unpaid) for a client. That led to some paid work, which continued throughout the rest of their college years. By the time they were ready to graduate, one of the music houses was ready to 'hire' them as independent contractors. They were given the space and equipment to jump into their work full-time, along with a modest monthly stipend and percentages on any work they did that was sold or licensed. In the several years since they graduated with BA degrees they have created music for numerous ad spots and film trailers and have licensed original work for films, TV and advertising. They have figured out what they didn't already know about the music business and technology through a willingness to explore and practice. They always say "yes!" to clients' requests and then figure out how to make it work. In addition, they keep their personal artistic vision alive and well by composing and performing in their own musical projects on the side. Nimble, prolific and creative, Bobby and David have developed expertise that is built on the foundation of their formal education but which extends far beyond what they learned in the classroom.

Bobby and David are terrific examples of how a college education prepares students to continue learning over a lifetime and build on the opportunities and changes that come along.

A second, important action that will help increase the effectiveness of any career-building strategy has its roots in the thinking of pragmatist philosopher John Dewey, who suggested simply, "Just work it". It is unnecessary to solve every challenge or opportunity completely or immediately. Instead, make a start (see above) and do what you can. 'Just work it' is a terrific mantra for action, and can free you to simply begin a project rather than worry if everything is perfectly aligned or if you have enough skills or preparation.

Many of life's most exciting and unexpected opportunities happen quickly (remember the quote that led Chapter 4: "Luck favors the prepared mind"). Preparation is an important key to building a successful and sustainable career, in both musical readiness and in the 'business of you.' A little future planning also ensures readiness for those last-minute opportunities on which careers can be launched and later sustained. It is vital, therefore, to keep skills sharp at all times and to cultivate the ability to recognise, create and accept appropriate opportunities as they come along.

It was after 11pm on Friday night and Raoul had finally made it back to his apartment after an exhausting week at his day job. A bit discouraged that his musical goals hadn't moved forward much that week, he sat down with a soda to relax and think about making weekend plans. Just then, his cell rang. It was Brad, a college buddy he hadn't seen in a while, inviting Raoul over to his place. "Hey, I'm here with an old high-school friend of mine and her boyfriend, Mike," *Brad explained,* "c'mon over!" *Raoul really just wanted to fall into bed and forget his uninspiring week, but agreed to meet them at Brad's place. It was at that last-minute chance meeting that Raoul started talking with Mike, a fellow musician. By the time Raoul left Brad's apartment that night, he had an appointment to meet Mike the following Tuesday, and that meeting turned into a paid gig. A year later, Raoul and Mike had completed well over a dozen projects together, landed a long-term contract, and were planning their own production company.*

Raoul was well prepared as an artist, and getting out of his apartment that night worked out for him in a very productive way. Luck truly favoured Raoul's prepared mind, as it has for Bobby and David. These stories both illustrate another vital career-building element: *It's not just who you know, it's who knows you.* It is to this that we turn in resource 33.

Chapter 33
Networking I

Building circles

Contributed by Janis Weller

It's not just who you know, it's who knows you

A living, evolving, working network of professional contacts forms the vital core of an emerging career. The old adage 'it's not what you know, it's who you know' has a powerful ring of truth, but in practical application 'who you know' doesn't take the process far enough. For example, you can have a database or phone or Rolodex full of professional acquaintances, but if you don't actively stay in touch with those contacts they will not do you much good over time. Developing professional contacts and keeping track of them is easier than ever in today's mobile and digitally connected world, but it is also important to create workable systems for managing circles of contacts and keeping them fresh. This section will provide some ideas for starting and managing these processes.

Everyone has many circles of connected colleagues, friends, family and community, any of which may prove useful as you develop your career. Sometimes these circles overlap (the musician's world really is a surprisingly small place), and other times they are distinct from one another. Developing an intentional approach to building these circles of contacts, along with an effective contact management system that fits career aspirations and lifestyle, will prove invaluable as you launch your career and sustain it over time. The next section provides a step-by-step circle building process.

Circle-building: Getting started

Start by drawing circles on a large piece of paper, and name each circle for a group of people you are connected to. For example:

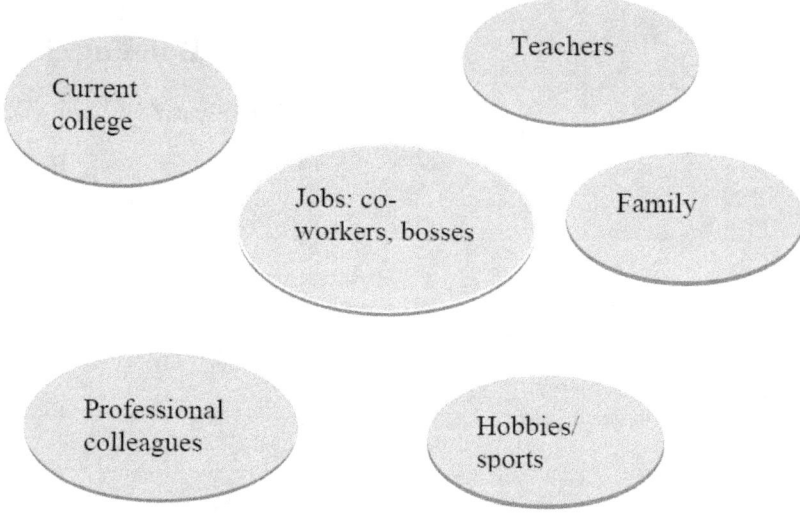

Here are a few more categories to help you get started.

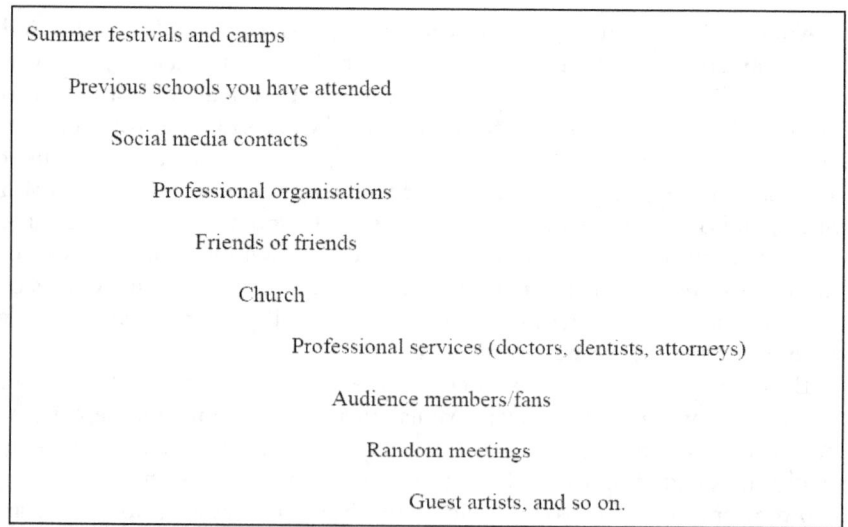

After adding as many circles as you can think of (you can always add more later), choose one circle to work with first, and begin building out the categories of people you know. For example:

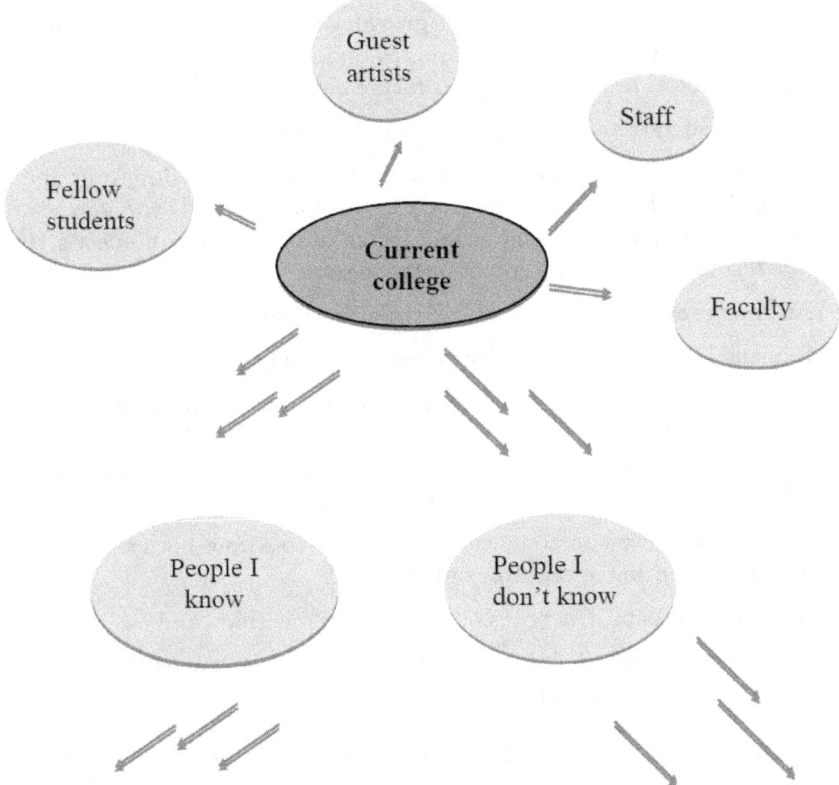

Once you have figured out the major categories of potential contacts within a circle, start identifying people that you already know within that category, along with those you do not yet know but may be interested to meet. Continue that process throughout all the layers of circles within one of your large categories before going on to another. Through this process, you will begin to realise how many contacts you have already made, and how many potential connections are virtually at your fingertips to develop. Keep adding names without judging an individual's likelihood of being helpful to your career at this time. Look for points of connection between your circles, too. For example, perhaps your high-school band director plays in an orchestra with one of your current teachers. This exercise is an easy and graphic way to realise the breadth of circles you already have and, at the same time, identify some places where you might want to develop circles more actively.

There is no greater resource in building and sustaining a career than personal relationships developed over time. To build and develop your circles, it is vitally important to be out in the world on a regular basis. Musicians spend substantial amounts of practice time tucked away in solitary practice rooms, but interacting with people provides an important career balance to practising, along with opportunities to build your circles. Here are a few quick suggestions for setting up your future circle building:

- Attend concerts and go to shows, on and off campus
- Volunteer to help with events on campus. Host a reception, staff an information table, tutor fellow students, become a peer advisor, join an advisory committee, help plan events, offer to be a driver for guest artists (see resource 31 for more volunteering ideas)
- Attend art events, whether music, visual art, dance or theatre
- Join and become active in relevant professional organisations
- When you're in a group, make a conscious effort to meet (and also reconnect) with people. If that sounds outside of your comfort zone, try reaching out to just one other person in the room. Introduce yourself, ask questions, and be a good listener. Repeat!
- When you meet someone you would like to know better, suggest a follow-up meeting over coffee or lunch
- Always send thank-you notes or emails after meetings; and
- Stay in touch with brief 'thinking of you' emails every once in a while with those you do not see regularly.

Sometimes students resist this sort of conscious connection making and complain it feels like fishing for new contacts you can 'use'. Remember that circle building is a two-way street. You are not simply tapping other professionals for their contacts and expertise, you also bring your own expertise and contacts to the conversation. As an active member of the professional community, as well as a good listener, you will inevitably have much to offer others. So in actual practice, circle building simply means building professional relationships and friendships. It is rarely clear which connections will 'pay out' over time, or if ever. Some new connections evolve quickly into working relationships; others simmer for years. Quite often, they evolve in directions you could never have predicted, and that is half the fun. Do not get too invested in any one contact or their perceived value to you. Above all, take good care of your circles – they are the heart and soul of your career.

Build your circles by building your personal reputation as a fine musician who is a dependable colleague, a hard worker, punctual, fun to spend time with, and who goes the extra mile when necessary, so others will want you as an important part of their circles. In the long run, it always pays off to be genuine, authentic, honest and personable in your personal interactions. In the highly competitive world of the professional musician, almost everyone is an accomplished musician; that is a given. There are expectations of musical quality, to be sure, but your potential colleagues are also interested in a low-maintenance, dependable colleague. One additional thought: judiciously avoid losing a contact over a dispute or disagreement. Regardless of who is 'at fault', the end result of burning a bridge with anyone can be very difficult to repair and can have long-lasting negative consequences.

Keeping track of your circles

At first, your circles may feel quite manageable in an organisational system as simple as your mobile phone. Initially you know all your colleagues pretty well, know their stories, and know their musical strengths and weaknesses. But project your career out five years into the future. Now your various circles look like a juggler's hoops in flight. Maybe you attended a conference or a summer festival and met dozens of new people in a short timeframe. Some of your new contacts are people you played with once, some others you may have met casually, still others you may work with regularly. Many of the people you have met may know other people in your various orbits, but can you keep it straight who knows whom? Figuring out workable systems to manage and safeguard your contacts simply and efficiently will pay big dividends as your career develops. The key is choosing multiple systems that you can sustain given your personality, lifestyle and professional needs. For some, that contact list may be focused on a mobile phone; others may prefer a spreadsheet or database, or a notebook of business cards. Whatever you choose, be sure you have sufficient backups.

Most contact management systems fall into one of three general categories: digital, online or hard copy. Some of these overlap and you will want to back up your lists of contacts in a couple of different formats to protect this valuable asset. What if your computer crashes? Your gig bag is stolen? You drop your phone in a puddle? Valuable information central to your career could be lost in a moment without careful backup. So consider developing multiple, flexible circle management systems.

Digital systems are computer-based word processing, database or spreadsheet methods for organising your contacts. These take some time to set up initially, but are often fairly easy to maintain and are especially handy to reorganise according to your needs (by name, instrument, city or other criteria). These files are most easily retrieved if you have easy access to a computer, carry your laptop with you most of the time, or can synchronise your smart phone with your computer. If not, you may want to consider your computer as more of a backup system and go with more portable methods. You can back up digital files with hard drives or zip drives, as well as via inexpensive Internet storage systems (such as Google Docs, iDrive and many others) for your most valuable information. These are particularly handy when travelling. You might even consider printing important files occasionally.

Business cards never go out of style and are an important circle building career tool. Ranging from virtually free versions available online to expensive custom-designed versions, they fit easily in your wallet and are an effective way to share your contact information (and collect that information from others). Find a simple, professional-looking design through the online providers, or if you're lucky enough to know a graphic designer, consider bartering for some design services to create a personalised look for your business card. In general, keep the information on your business card simple: your name, what you do, and contact information (mobile, email, website) is usually sufficient. Keep your business cards with you at all times, not just when you're officially 'on the job.' Opportunities to share them can, and often do, happen anytime. If you are interested in paperless systems, consider taking a quick phone photo of each new business card and store them virtually. The apps available for this improve in efficiency all the time.

Other old-fashioned, paper-based systems can be just as handy and reliable. An address book is easy to carry in your gig bag, and a Rolodex or notebook can organise the business cards you collect along the way if you like the hard copy route. Just as with your digital storage, be sure to have a backup for your hard copy systems.

Using the social media revolution as professional tools

The pace of change in digital communication defies description and will have moved in new directions by the time I have finished typing this sentence. So rather than discussing or critiquing a litany of social media sources useful as professional tools for musicians, let's consider the implications and importance of these changes to the lives of musicians.

The first step is often an attitude adjustment: social media are frequently seen as just that - social. Many students use these sites to stay in touch with friends, plan parties and the like. Using social media professionally does not need to preclude using it for purely social reasons, but the two should remain distinct and separate. Horror stories abound of employers following up on applicants by checking out social media sites and recanting job offers based on what is found there. So be savvy. Recognise the powerful tools available for developing your career, and keep those separate from other uses of these media.

There are dozens and dozens of entrepreneurially oriented sites offering almost endless ways for musicians to build their DIY careers via the Internet. How do you follow the expected trends without being swallowed by them? How do you maintain your social media sites and still find time to practice and perform? These are not always easy questions to answer, but social media is here to stay, and as an ambitious 21st century musician you need to both understand social media and, very importantly, decide in which ways you will engage with it. Here are a few quick tips:

- Look for aggregator sites that automatically connect your social media sites to save some time
- If social media does not intrigue you, find others who are happy and fluent with that world and barter services with them
- If you have an interest and good skills in this area, you may be able to hire out your services to others
- Find artists you admire who have a strong social media presence and get ideas from them; and
- Use blog sites related to social media as a filter for new ideas and options. www.socialmediaexaminer.com is a good example.

To summarise circle building:

- Seek out opportunities to meet new people and reconnect with long-term friends/family/colleagues
- Build relationships for the long term (and do not burn bridges, no matter how tempting it might be sometimes)
- Be a good colleague – a strong musician who is reliable, pleasant, on time, and prepared
- Keep your contact lists organised and accessible in more than one format
- Explore and make use of social media in personally and professionally appropriate ways.

Chapter 34
Networking II

Who else do you know?

Contributed by Michael Hannan

If you have completed the circle building exercise (tool 33), you will have begun the process of identifying your existing and potential professional networks. This activity prompts you to expand them even further. In Chapter 8, Michael Hannan focused on the value of professional networking in forging a career. For example, he discussed how he and his business partner drew on a network of musician friends to put together a demo tape cheaply so they could pursue work writing advertising music. He also wrote about their systematic strategy of making appointments with the creative directors of all the advertising agencies in their city, with the hope of interesting them in their music. In addition, he stressed the importance of the network he had on tap as a tertiary music student: the network of fellow students and teachers. Throughout his chapter, Michael reflected on how each new opportunity for expanding his professional music activities was dependent on previous contacts he had made.

The following exercises are designed to help with the development and maintenance of your professional network, building further 'circles' into your network.

Refer to the following list and use it to expand your current list of all the people in your professional network. Again, group the names into categories with a new circle for each.

- Your peer group
- Musicians you work with regularly
- Musicians you know who are able to deputise for you
- Contacts (musical directors, administrators) at music companies that have employed you in the past, even for just one performance or teaching session
- Producers in music/media with whom you have done recording work
- Recording engineers with whom you have worked
- Players in current and previous groups, including youth groups
- Composers/arrangers whose music you have commissioned, played or recorded
- Venue operators who have hired your services
- Corporations who have hired your services
- Venue operators of venues you have hired
- Music equipment hire companies you have contracted
- Previous teachers, conductors and guest artists
- Live sound/lighting operators you have contracted/worked with
- Critics/journalists who have reviewed your performances/compositions or written about you
- Editors (if you write for the press yourself)
- Broadcasters (who have interviewed you, championed your music)
- Designers who have done work on your promotional material, merchandise and website, etc.
- Merchandise business contacts
- Contacts at media organisations who you use to advertise your services
- Your music teachers (past and present)
- Your students (if you have a teaching practice)
- Contacts at schools
- Your fans
- Your online social network 'friends'
- Your online discussion groups (e.g. music technology forums for Sibelius, Finale, Cubase, ProTools, etc.)

If you are a composer/arranger, make an additional list (or create circles) under the following headings. If your specialism isn't covered here, create a new list for that too.

- Conductors, performers or ensembles who have played or recorded your works/arrangements
- Other composers with whom you collaborate
- Other creative workers (e.g. lyricists, librettists, designers, orchestrators, producers, audio engineers, etc.) with whom you collaborate
- Organisations, companies or individuals who have commissioned works from you

- Publishing companies to whom you have been contracted
- Contacts at copyright collection agencies
- Intellectual property lawyer

Chapter 35
Networking III

Reflections

Contributed by Michael Hannan

Having created lists (circles) of people in your professional network (see tools 33 and 34), reflect on the following questions:

- Are categories relevant to your work missing from the list?
- Are there any categories you feel are irrelevant to your career progress and development? Justify your responses.
- Where are the gaps/weaknesses in your professional network?
- Make a realistic list of network contacts you would like to have and indicate what advantage you believe you would gain from them. What can you do to develop these contacts?
- How much do you know about the professional networks of the people in your network? Would you be able to tap into these other networks, perhaps by offering to share network information?
- Having assembled your list of contacts, can you think of possible projects/partnerships that bring together members of the network?
- Are you up to date with contact information about all your network contacts? How do you keep in touch with the members of your professional network?

- What sources of information are you aware of to help expand your network: for example music industry directories, trade magazines, music industry associations?

- Do you participate in any online social networks? How does this participation support your career as a musician? Have you investigated any social networks other than the one(s) you currently participate in: for example, genre-specific music networks?

(See the end of Chapter 8 for more readings and information on networking)

Contributing Authors

Dawn Bennett is a Professorial Research Fellow with Curtin University in Perth, Australia, where her research focus is the working lives and economic circumstances of creative artists and the development of identity among students and emerging professionals. She holds postgraduate degrees in education and music performance and has worked as a classical musician, teacher, researcher and manager. Dawn has published extensively in the areas of arts education, careers and the creative workforce, including five monographs and edited collections. She serves on several editorial boards including the *International Journal of Music Education*, and she is a Councillor with the Music Council of Australia.

Glen Carruthers is Dean of the Faculty of Music at Wilfrid Laurier University (Canada). He was Dean of the School of Music at Brandon University (Canada) 1998-2008 and taught at Lakehead University (Canada) 1988-1998, where he was founding Chair of the Department of Music. His current research involves music and democracy—particularly the writings of Percy Grainger—and post-secondary music education. His articles have appeared in many sources, including the *International Journal of Music Education*, *Journal of Musicology*, *Music Review* and *Musical Times*. Carruthers has contributed to several books, is Chair of the New York State/St. Lawrence Chapter of the American Musicological Society, and is a past-president of the Canadian University Music Society.

Michael Hannan is Professor of Contemporary Music in the School of Arts and Social Sciences at Southern Cross University in Australia. He is a composer, keyboard performer and music researcher. His research interests include Australian contemporary music, film music theory and analysis, the work practices of musicians, and the education of pop musicians. He is author of *The Australian guide to careers in music* (UNSW Press, 2003), has served as Chair of the Music Council of Australia (2003-2004), and as Chair of the International Society for Music Education's Commission for the Education of the Professional Musician (2004-2006 and 2008-10).

Angela Myles Beeching is director of the New England Conservatory Career Services Centre (Boston, MA), a comprehensive music resource centre internationally recognised as a model of its kind. A Fulbright scholar, Beeching co-founded the Network of Music Career Development Officers. She has been a guest speaker for the National Association of Schools of Music, Chamber Music America, the National Conference on Keyboard Pedagogy, and the Association of Performing Arts Presenters. Angela's articles have appeared in *Inside Arts, Classical Singer*, and *Chamber Music*. Her book, *Beyond talent: Creating a successful career in music*, is published by Oxford University Press.

Rosie Perkins is a Research Associate in the Centre for Performance Science at the Royal College of Music in London. Having completed her doctorate at the Faculty of Education, University of Cambridge, Rosie works widely across music education and psychology. Her current research interests include the learning cultures of conservatoires, musicians' career development, musicians' identity, and the impact of music making on subjective wellbeing. In addition, Rosie teaches at undergraduate and postgraduate level at the RCM, with particular input into the newly devised MSc in Performance Science. Rosie sits as a commissioner to the ISME Commission for the Education of the Professional Musician and is a member of the research group Lifelong Learning in Music & the Arts in the Netherlands.

Rineke Smilde is Professor of Lifelong Learning in Music & the Arts at the Prince Claus Conservatoire in Groningen and the Royal Conservatoire in The Hague. Together with an international research group she investigates concepts of lifelong learning, aiming to make students more adaptive and responsive to change in the profession (see also www.lifelonglearninginmusic.org). For many years Smilde has been active with the European Association of Conservatoires, leading various research groups on lifelong learning. Her books, *Musicians as lifelong learners: Discovery through biography*, and *Musicians as lifelong learners: 32 biographies*, were published in 2009 by Eburon Academic Publishers in Delft.

Janis Weller chairs the Liberal Arts Division at McNally Smith College of Music, St. Paul, Minnesota, where she teaches career development and woodwinds. She has taught at the University of Minnesota, Augsburg College, and the University of St. Thomas, University of Wisconsin-River Falls and MacPhail Center for Music, where she is a former dean. She presents internationally and nationally at ISME, College Music Society, and Suzuki Association of the Americas, National Careers Conference, and National

Flute Association. Her research focuses on artist transitions, performance wellness, and new technologies. As a flautist, Janis has premiered more than 100 new works and commissions.

Acronyms

ABS	Australian Bureau of Statistics
ACMI	Australian Contemporary Music Institute
AEC	European Association of Conservatoires
AGMA	American Guild of Musical Artists
AT	Alexander Technique
BMOP	Boston Modern Orchestra Project
CBGB	Country, Blue Grass and Blues
CPD	Continuing professional development
EC	European Commission
EU	European Union
ICE	International Contemporary Ensemble
ICSOM	International Conference of Symphony and Opera Musicians
ISME	International Society of Music Education
LTP	Learning to Perform
NASM	National Association of Schools of Music
NEC	New England Conservatory (US)
NESTA	National Endowment for Science, Technology and the Arts (UK)
NMC	National Music Council
NYC	New York City
RCM	Royal College of Music (UK)
RIAA	Recording Industry Association of America
TAFE	Technical and Further Education (Australia)
UCLA	University of California, Los Angeles
UK	United Kingdom

Synopsis

How can young musicians best prepare for the real world? In a changing global marketplace and transformed music and creative sectors, in an age of information overload, what are the key issues and skills on which emerging artists need to focus? How have recent changes in the industry affected professional opportunities?

With the linking theme of exploring one's professional identity, this book is the only music career guide offering a truly international perspective, essential for creative professionals collaborating online with projects, colleagues and audiences worldwide. Leading authors from the United States, Canada, the United Kingdom, Europe and Australia explore key issues for musicians: identity formation, lifelong learning, transitions into and between work, entrepreneurship, changing workplaces, and musicians' connections with society. The authors' contributions are enhanced by discussion of work opportunities, education and training in their respective countries, especially useful for musicians interested in study and work abroad.

Practical information, perspectives and examples in Part I of the volume are complemented by the resources in Part II, written specifically for use with emerging musicians and those seeking career advice. Part II features practical exercises for career planning and exploration, for goal setting, and for developing networking and project management skills. The 35 reproducible tools are presented in an engaging format for use with individuals and groups.

For people interested in music education and training, career planning, professional survival, and helping musicians realise their dreams of success, this book is an essential resource.

Index

A

Abreu, Jose Antonio 34
academic work (see also teaching; research) 16, 66, 87, 128, 133, 138
Adams, John 135
adulthood 45-50
After Reading Shakespeare 28
Ahern, David 126
Albert Studios, J Albert and Son 131
Alexander Technique 20
Allen, Cameron 130
American Federation of Musicians 85
American Guild of Musical Artists (AGMA) 32
animateur 105
Appel, Andrew 35
apprentices/apprenticeships 4, 128
arranger 5, 85, 102, 130, 262
Art and Fear 206, 232
Arts Enterprise Club 41
Ashkenazy, Vladimir 227
Association of Teaching Artists 35
Auckland University 193
audiences 4, 7, 13, 27-31, 34-7, 57-8, 80-1, 87, 92, 103-5, 116, 120, 197, 208, 225, 228
auditions 19, 27, 31, 47, 56, 59, 86, 90, 122, 128-9, 151, 165, 176, 178, 193, 219, 225, 250
Australia Council Research Centre 69
Australian Contemporary Music Institute 136
auto-ethnography 127
avant-garde 29

B

Bach, J S 28, 128
Bachelor of Music degrees 31, 36, 50, 69, 75, 89, 106, 119, 167
Bakken Quartet 153
bandleader 102
Baroque 92, 130, 137
BBC xvii
Beatles 129, 139
Beethoven 135, 153
Berlioz 5
Beyond Talent 206
biographies (see musician profiles)
Bishop's University 82
blogs 147, 157
Bob, Sarah 29
Bologna process 99, 109, 118-9
Booth, Eric 35, 39
Borders on the Road 28
Boston Lyric Opera 32
Boston Modern Orchestra Project 43
Boston Symphony Orchestra 30
boundaryless (see also portfolios, protean) 7
Bowling Green State University 41
Brahms 5
Brandon University 92-4, 267
Brendel, Alfred 49
Bright, Colin 126
Brown University 29
business cards 171, 275-6
business skills (see also entrepreneurship, small business) 5-7, 30, 71, 111-115, 176, 244, 250, 258
Butler, Sue 132-3

C

California Institute of the Arts 37
calypso 130
Canadian Chamber Choir 90
career awareness (see also contents of Part II) 4, 6, 16, 45, 51, 59, 64, 82, 93, 110, 136, 147-8, 157-159, 161-165, 173-175, 177
career counselling (see also career development) 15, 55, 151, 173
career development 40-41, 50-2, 74, 80, 91, 113, 183, 207, 241
career goals 4, 21, 46, 64, 100, 112-3, 128, 138, 204-207, 224, 232
careers discussion panel 88, 147-8, 211-12
careers in music (see also professional life and the contents of Part II) 12-20, 92, 102, 131
Careers in music: A guide for Canadian students 92
Carnegie Hall 22
Chamber Made Opera 78
chamber music xv-xvii, 16, 27-30, 34-6, 67-8, 74, 89-90, 106, 110-2, 135, 152-3, 162, 187, 197, 207
Chamber Music America 35, 266
Chase, Claire 40, 213
children, working with 22, 29, 31, 33, 35, 74, 81, 104, 114, 169, 187-8, 247
Chopin 5
classical music 28, 31, 33-6, 66, 70, 81, 84, 90, 100, 104, 111-2, 127-9, 136-40, 152, 168, 207, 250, 267

Colburn Conservatory 37-8
Cole, Orlando 153
collaboration 4, 29, 37, 56, 105, 208, 215
College Music Society 32, 268
Collins, Geoff 130
Coltrane, John 113, 135
communication skills 8, 56-8, 72, 81, 204, 239-40, 242-44, 258
community education programs 34, 91
community music 29, 81, 105, 197-200, 201-204, 221, 247
Community Music Centre of Boston 29
Community Music Works 29
competitions 17, 121, 162
composition 26, 71, 126-139, 261
Conference Board of Canada 84-5
conservatoires 12, 15-6, 26-7, 101, 112, 115-117, 121, 228
copyright 136-138
creative industries 65
creative workshops 102
cultural industries 64, 66
cultural policies 103
Curtis Institute of Music 37-8, 151, 153

D

dance 34, 254
Danish Amateur Orchestra Association (DAO)
deputising 137, 262
Dermody, Susan 132
Dewey, John 248
Different beats 69, 71
digital arts media 92
Doctor of Musical Arts 37, 71
Doctor of Philosophy 31-3, 71, 106, 134, 266

Domus xv, xvii, 106
Dudamel, Gustavo 30-1
Dust Poets 90

E

ear (aural) training 131, 133
Eastman School of Music 37-8, 41, 168
Economic and Social Research Council 26
El Sistema 30-1
Ellis, David 126
Elmer Iseler Singers 90
emerging adulthood (see also transition to adulthood) 46, 49-50, 56
entrepreneurship 3, 5-6, 22, 41, 46, 71, 81, 111, 113, 137, 148, 177-8, 244
epistemological foundation 53
Erickson, Eric 47
ethnomusicology 71, 88, 135
European Association of Conservatoires (AEC) 39, 101-106, 119
European Erasmus Program 109
European music academies 100, 107, 120
European Union (EU) 99, 119-20
expectations 6, 11-15, 18, 46-9, 56-7, 80, 88, 179-81, 204, 206-7, 232, 256
experiential learning 51, 92, 111

F

Faber Music Ltd 128
Facebook 16, 52, 76, 77, 122, 157
Fairlight (computer) 130, 135

Falenski, Dominik 74, 227
festivals 34, 37, 225
Findlay, Wayne 130
Florestan Trio xvii
Four Nations Ensemble 35-6, 195
freelance work 2-3, 28, 30, 56, 72, 75, 114, 126, 128, 131, 138, 167-8, 212
Freud, Sigmund 47
funk 53, 126

G

gagaku 134-5
gamelan 135
Gaspar Cassado Competition 154
Gaudier Ensemble xvii
Ghanaian drumming ensemble 135
Graduate Diploma in Education 70
Graduate Diploma in Music Composition 36-7, 70, 134, 172
graduate study 70-1, 151, 210
graduates (see also careers) 13-4, 22, 46, 59, 100, 108, 119, 2324
Grammy awards 43, 2068
grant application 29, 41-2, 66, 90, 103-4
Greenhouse, Bernard 153
Gross, Eric 127
Grove Dictionary of Music and Musicians 172
Guardian, the xvii
Guildhall School of Music and Drama, London 116-7
Guitar for Beginners and Beyond 139

H

Haimovitz, Matt 28
Harawi 132
Hendrix, Jimmi 28
higher education (see also conservatoires, undergraduate study, graduate study) 8, 16, 20, 22-3, 26, 31-2, 36, 45-6, 49, 52, 55-7, 59, 70, 77, 84, 99, 101, 106, 109, 116, 138, 192, 223
Higher Education Arts Data Service 31-2
hip-hop 205
Hirst, Rob 136
Höbarth, Erich xvii
Houston Symphony 28

I

identity, (see also possible selves, professional identity) xiv, 3, 67, 11-21
improvisation 28-9, 39, 52, 102, 105, 111-5, 122, 132-4, 136, 168, 242
Independent, The xvii
Indiana University 37
innovation 102-3, 148, 177, 204, 231-32, 234
Inside Higher Ed 56
intellectual property 13, 65, 136-7, 244, 263
interactivity 87
interdisciplinary studies 93, 105
Intermezzo Chamber Opera 30
International Conference of Symphony and Opera Musicians (ICSOM) 31, 152
International Contemporary Ensemble (ICE) 40, 213

international mobility 4, 109, 120
internships (see also participatory learning) 40
interpersonal skills and style 6, 20, 39, 53-4, 152, 179, 235, 238
intrapersonal foundation 52-3
intrinsic satisfaction xv, xvi, 28, 66, 68, 85, 87, 137, 204

J

J Walter Thompson (JWT) 130
Jackson, Michael 49
Jacobs School of Music 37
Janigro, Antonio 153
jazz 29, 34, 38, 49, 51, 53, 88, 90, 104, 113, 125-6, 133, 138, 168, 207
Jewish music 113
Juilliard School 37
Jung, Carl 47

K

Kamins, Ben 18
Kauffman Foundation 41
Kelly, Jim 121
Klein, Natalie 4
Knowledge Base of the Music Council of Australia 77-8

L

La Camarata di Bariloche 153
La Scala 27
La Trinité 131
labour market xv, xvi, 4-5, 7-8, 12, 21, 28, 31-4, 36, 40, 47-8, 59, 64-9, 70, 75, 77-8, 84-7, 89, 100-2, 105, 126-8, 131, 133-9, 205-7, 249, 261
languages xvi, 132, 220, 241

Laurier Centre for Music in the Community 91
leadership 38, 102, 110-1, 114-6, 239, 244
lexicography 8, 134-5
Lexicon of Musical Invective 135
liberal arts 39, 69, 203, 250
librettists 262
life skills 107
lifelong learning xiv, 3, 7, 91, 93, 99-102, 104, 106, 108-123, 215
lifestyle 138, 148, 179-81, 254, 257
Liszt 25
Lorange, Kirk 131, 139-10, 144
Los Angeles Philharmonic 30
Loyola University 208
Lyon, Greg 131
Lyric Opera of Chicago 32
lyric writing/lyricist 136, 243, 262

M

Magolda, Baxter 46, 50-1, 53-4
Mahler, Gustav 45, 53
Manfred and Penny Conrad Centre for Music Therapy 91
Manhattan School of Music 36-7, 41
Manitoba Music 86
marketplace, global (see also labour market) xiv, 3-8, 31-3, 36, 51, 65, 89, 234
Marriner, Neville 153
Masters degree 70-1, 75, 120, 167, 194, 227
matrix of intrinsic and extrinsic influences 74, 91, 185
McCann Erikson 130

McGill University 82, 279
Memorial University of Newfoundland 92
mentor 3, 5, 40, 52, 54, 59, 72-3, 111, 114, 116, 206, 209, 225, 232
Messiaen, Olivier 131-3, 139
Metropolitan Opera 27, 233
Midnight Oil 136
military band 5, 136-7
Minnesota Orchestra 153
mission (finding your...) 29, 38, 148, 201-2, 223-4
mobility 4, 7, 99, 109, 120
money (see also salaries) xv, 4-5, 19-21, 29-31, 38, 126, 130-1, 159, 164, 172, 213, 228
moonlighting 86
Morey, Carl 83, 93
motivation 13, 19, 29, 59, 73, 116, 164, 166, 206, 208, 233, 235
Mozart xvii, 49, 53
Mulcahy, Michael 220
multi-lingual 75
multicultural 103
multimedia 70, 137, 243
music consumption 81, 83-5, 137
music copying 8, 129
music curriculum 38-9, 46, 55-6, 59, 73, 116, 133, 139
Music Entrepreneurship Center 41
music industry (see also music sector entries, labour market) 5, 8, 33-4, 36, 38, 41-2, 50-1, 55-7, 69-71, 77, 100, 101, 105, 111, 114, 126-32, 136-43, 175-6, 195-6, 208, 224, 225, 227, 234, 239, 242, 244, 247, 249-50
music industry magazines 8, 79, 132, 153, 266
music sector in Australia xiv, 64-84, 77-8
music sector in Canada xiv, 7, 66, 77, 82-92
music sector in Europe xiv, 5, 7, 17, 31, 37, 39, 64, 66, 72, 81, 99-116, 119-122
music sector in the United States xiv, 29, 31-4, 40, 46, 48, 66, 73
music therapy 38, 69, 71, 77, 88, 91
Musical America 32
musician profiles 16, 75, 89, 110-5, 138, 151-2, 167-9, 187-9, 193-4, 21, 219-20, 223, 227-9, 268
musician's lifestyle quiz 148, 179-81
musicians in society 7, 79-94
musicology 8, 71, 79, 88, 127, 132, 134
MySpace 42, 58, 139, 225

N

Napster 65
National Association of Schools of Music (NASM) 31, 36
National Endowment for Science, Technology and the Arts (NESTA) 65
National Endowment for the Arts 34
negotiation 32, 70, 137, 244
Nelsova, Zara 153
nerves/ performance anxiety xv, 72, 111, 136
networking xiv, xvi, 40, 57-9, 104, 108, 127, 132, 137, 139, 149, 187, 206, 223, 225, 231, 244, 253-4, 256, 258, 261-3, 265-6
New England Conservatory 27, 33, 39, 41

New Gallery Concert Series 29
new media (see also technology) 57, 105, 256-7
New York Philharmonic 35
New York Times 28
New Yorker 29
Nielsen, Carl 226
Nielsen, Liz 67
North Carolina School of the Arts 37

O

objective facets of career 14, 29, 157, 222
occupational health and safety 70, 136-7
Ogawa, Noriko xvii
Open University xvii
Opera Australia 66, 68, 78
Opera Roadshow 92
Orchestra Canada 86
orchestral life (see also orchestras) 27-8, 66-8, 86-9, 168-9, 187-9, 219-21
orchestras 5, 14, 30-1, 35, 38-40, 68, 115, 121, 134, 207, 213, 219
Orff-Schulwerk 194
organist 5, 66, 131
outreach (see also community work) 90-3, 247
Oxford University 24-5
Oxingale Records 43

P

Paganini 5
Palmer, Parker 206, 209, 232
participation 6, 30, 58, 106, 128
participatory learning 91, 105, 110-1

passion (see also expectations; intrinsic satisfaction) 6, 63, 71-3, 75, 128, 148, 183, 187, 189-90, 232
Pasteur, Louis 6, 201
Paul, Les 49
Peabody Institute 37
Peck, Marcia 153
pedagogy 36, 40, 57, 70, 121
peers 11, 21, 74, 83, 127, 129, 137, 158, 223, 240
performance xvii, 16-8, 21, 27-9, 34-7, 50, 52, 54, 57, 72, 104, 113, 115, 127-8, 132, 159
performance anxiety (See also occupational health and safety) xvi, 72, 111, 136
personality 147, 175, 233, 257
Philadelphia Orchestra 35
Pianorama program 228
Pinchgut Opera 67, 78
Plane Talk –The truly totally different guitar instruction book 139
policy 12, 103, 108, 137
polymusical 135
pop culture 34
portfolio careers (see also protean, boundaryless) 12, 15, 100, 223
possible selves (see also professional identity) 15
postgraduate courses (see also graduate study, masters degrees, doctoral degrees) 11-2, 71, 134, 138-9
pre- post concert talks 34
Prince Claus Conservatoire 116
professional development (see also lifelong learning) 69, 77, 86, 93, 101, 106-8, 116, 121, 133, 215
professional identity (see also identity) xiv, 3, 74, 91, 114, 116, 183

professional life (see also careers in music) 6, 14, 45-6, 48, 54, 58, 100, 106, 148-9, 151-2, 203-8, 231-2, 249-51
professionalism 55, 149, 235, 235
Promuse 106, 122
Proteus, protean, protean music career (see also boundaryless; portfolio careers) 7, 125-6, 140
Providence String Quartet 29
public relations 113, 137, 244
publishing 5, 33, 65, 89, 114, 131, 137

Q

Québec 82, 86, 88
Queensland Conservatorium 135

R

Rattle, Simon 4
record companies 28, 89, 104, 136
recording engineers 38, 262
Recording Industry Association of America (RIAA) 65
reflection, self-reflection 8, 18, 20-1, 91, 125, 137, 147, 174, 183-4, 204, 206, 235, 265
rehearsal, rehearsing xvi, 15, 30, 32, 39-40, 58, 67, 72, 86, 114, 126-8, 186, 220, 241-2
repetiteur 68, 241
Repetitive Strain Injury (RSI) (see injury)
reputation 37, 168, 256
research (see also academic work) 26, 72, 140, 193

reward (see also intrinsic satisfaction) xv, 6, 18, 21, 28, 30, 35, 39, 45, 55, 73, 159, 183-4, 204, 208
Reykjavik Academy of the Arts 116
Rice University 28, 37
rock bands, rock music 129, 131, 124
Rose, Gil 30
Ross, Alex 29
Rostropovich, Mstislav 153
Royal College of Music, London (RCM) 30, 161
Royal College of Music, Stockholm 116
Royal Conservatoire at the Hague 116
Rural Development Institute 92
Ruth, Sebastian 29
Ryrie, Kim 130, 135

S

safety 70, 136
Saint-François d' Assise 132
salaries (see also money) 4-5, 31-2, 68, 197
San Francisco Symphony 35
scholarships 28, 38, 131, 134
Schubert 5
Schumann Konservatorium 153
Sculthorpe, Peter 128
self authorship 50-4, 152
self image (see also identity; professional identity) 63, 84, 89, 183
service learning (see participatory learning)
Shakarian, David 208-9
shakuhachi music 135
Shepherd School of Music 43
Shostakovitch 153

Show business 132
Showcase: the Magazine of the Minnesota Orchestra 153
skills and attributes 15, 39, 41, 56, 71, 74, 82, 91, 103, 111, 126, 128, 147-8, 168, 171-2, 173-5, 191-2, 237-46
skills audit 149, 137
Slonimsky, Nicolas 135
small business 70-1, 102, 114, 126, 137-8, 177, 234, 244
Snyder, John 208
social constructionist theory 15
social learning 111
social media xvi, 28, 34, 58-9, 65, 84, 104, 139, 231, 258-9
solfège 39
songwriter 28, 89, 93, 130, 136, 140
St Andrews Cathedral Choral Society 127-8
Star-Spangled Banner 28
State University of New York at Stony Brook 27
Statistics Canada 84
Statman, Andy 113
student and teacher exchanges 108
subjective facets of career 12, 13-23, 157-9, 224
success, perception of/defining (see also career goals; identity) 3, 7, 12, 17, 20, 22, 26-8, 91, 206, 224
Suzuki 192
Swearer Centre for Public Service 29
Switched on Bach 130
Sydney Conservatorium 134
Sydney Opera House 126
Sydney Symphony Orchestra 68, 78

T

Tafelmusik 86
talent xvi, 37, 49, 55, 59, 65, 74, 91, 105, 112-3, 130, 138, 140, 123, 166-7, 185, 202-4, 206
Tarras, David 113
Tchaikovsky Conservatoire 228
teaching (see also academic work) xvii, 5, 8, 12, 19-23, 29, 31-7, 40, 56-7, 63, 66-8, 70, 72, 74-6, 80-3, 86-92, 103-27, 126, 133-4, 138, 140, 148, 152, 159, 163, 168, 174-5, 187-8, 193-4, 197-9, 204, 214, 220, 225, 227-8, 242, 247, 249, 262
teaching artist 32, 34-6, 98, 105, 145, 193-4, 225
teaching skills (see also pedagogy, teaching) 4, 36, 40, 57, 70, 104, 108, 111, 121,
Technical and Further Education (TAFE) 30
technology xvi, 7, 31, 33-4, 39-40, 65, 70-1, 81, 89, 103-4, 137, 139, 177, 204, 225, 234, 244-5, 250, 262
technology (uses of...) xvi, 7, 33-4, 39-40, 65, 70-1, 81, 89, 103-4, 137, 139, 204, 225
Telemann 5
temperament 50, 147, 233-5
tertiary study (see undergraduate, graduate and postgraduate degrees)
The war of art 206
The unattended moment 153
Theatre and Dance (Ann Arbor) 37
Thesaurus of scales and melodic patterns 135
Times Literary Supplement xvii

Tomes, Susan xvi-xvii
traits (see also personality, skills and attributes) 6, 39, 55, 63, 66, 71, 73, 149, 174-5, 194, 211, 235, 237-9
transition xiv, 6, 20-1, 45-50, 148-51, 176, 203-9, 231- 4, 251-2
Tribute to Orpheus 154
Twitter 58, 231

U

Uggerhoej, Jeppe 75, 167
undergraduate education (see also Bachelor of music degrees) 11, 16-9, 26, 69-70, 82, 127, 162-3, 219
United Kingdom National Music Council (NMC) 65
University of California Los Angeles 134
University of Colorado Boulder 41
University of Michigan School of Music 37, 41
University of New South Wales 134
University of South Carolina 41
University of the Arts in Philadelphia 37
University of Wisconsin Madison 41, 48
US job market 32-4, 66
US music industry see music industry in the United States
US tertiary education and training 29, 31, 40, 46

V

Vanda, Harry 131
venue operators 32, 262
versatility 15, 82, 126, 128
Vivaldi 92
vocalists, singers 31, 66-7
vocation (see also intrinsic satisfaction) 207
volunteering 29, 58, 82, 89-90, 149, 247, 256

W

Whittlesey, John 30
Wigmore Hall 13
Wilfrid Laurier University 91
Winnipeg Folk Festival 90
Woolf, Luna Pearl 28
Wurlitzer electric piano 134

Y

York University 91
young audiences 29, 35, 87, 92, 114
Young, George 121
Youtube 16, 46, 52, 157

Z

Zappa, Frank 135

www.ingramcontent.com/pod-product-compliance
Lightning Source LLC
Chambersburg PA
CBHW072109010526
44111CB00038B/2468